T0350955

Praise for *Demographics Unravelled*

"This book is a fascinating marshalling of evidence about how demographic forces shape many of the pressing economic, social, and political problems that we confront today."

—**Tom Sargent**, Nobel Prize Winner (2011); and
Professor of Economics, New York University

"In this deep but highly accessible book, Amlan Roy draws upon his many years of experience to explain the many ways in which demography shapes the macroeconomy and financial markets. Students and market professionals will find Roy's analysis to be at once enlightening and engaging."

—**Narayana Kocherlakota**, Former Minneapolis Fed President;
and Professor, University of Rochester

"With the benefit of two decades of research into the many aspects of an aging global economy, Amlan Roy explains to us the profound implications of demography on virtually every aspect of our welfare. In clear, practical language, he analyzes and informs - we should all read it and thank him."

—**Zvi Bodie**, Author of *Worry-Free Investing*;
and Professor Emeritus, Boston University

"This book is a must-read for anyone working on the intersection of demographics, finance, and economics. There is a wealth of data, insight, and research presented in a concise package."

—**Tobias Adrian**, Financial Counselor and Director,
International Monetary Fund

"Roy's brilliant new book unifies the vast demographics literature across debt, gender, growth, inflation, asset prices, and beyond, gauging research on its ability to look below broad population aggregates to the finer groupings that really matter."

—**Giles Keating**, Former Global Head, Credit Suisse Research;
and Board Member, Bitcoin Suisse

"Amlan's holistic, systematic, and rational framework takes out the popular misconceptions about demographics and explains how it affects, inter alia, macroeconomic policy, asset prices, pensions and retirement decisions, and the overall quality of life. Highly recommended reading for academics, practitioners, and regulators."

—**Narayan Naik**, Finance Professor, London Business School

"Amlan Roy has written a tour-de-force on the impact of demographics on economic growth and policy, pension design, and portfolio management. This book, from the global expert on demographics, is a must-read for investors, financial professionals, and policy makers.

—**Arun Muralidhar**, Co-founder,
Mcube Investment Technologies, Pension Expert (3 books)

"Amlan has been pioneering the link between demographics and financial markets at least since our days together at Credit Suisse in London 20 years ago. The accumulated knowledge that Amlan has gathered throughout his career is collated for the first time in this ground-breaking book, along with all the painstaking data-driven evidence, charts, and trend analyses that built up his reputation as a top-notch applied financial economist over the years, crossing over geographies: a must-read for all professional investors, and a source of inspiration for academics."

—**Olivier Ledoit**, Senior Research Associate,
Department of Economics, University of Zurich

"Demographics remains one of the most important and under-appreciated areas of inquiry. This well-researched book provides a clear understanding of precisely how demographic data can serve as a crystal ball into the future. Carefully researched and very accessible, it is a must-read for anybody looking to understand what lies ahead for economy and society."

—**Ranjay Gulati**, Harvard Business School,
Paul Lawrence MBA, and Class of 1942 Professor

"Renowned pensions expert Amlan Roy treats us with his state-of-the-art insights on demographics. This wonderful book is a must-read for anyone keen on truly understanding the deep impact of demographics on finance, economics, and our lives."

—**Dirk Broeders**, Professor of Pension Finance, Maastricht University, Netherlands

"As you step away from the noise of daily market fluctuations it is of paramount importance to consider how demographic changes will affect the long run macroenvironment and influence the risk/return prospects of financial assets. Amlan's book is a must-read for asset allocators and long-term investors."

—**Mirko Cardinale**, Head of Investment Strategy,
USS Investment Management, London

"This book is a must-read for economists and finance analysts, both academics and practitioners. The book is very well written by an expert on the subject of demographics (a mega trend) and dispels certain misconceptions."

—**Tom A. Fearnley**, Investment Director,
Norwegian Ministry of Finance, Asset Management

"Roy is uniquely equipped with the knowledge and insight required to understand the complex aspects of demographic dynamics. If this book will be widely read, there is hope we will cope better with demographic changes than we do today."

—**Theo Kocken**, Founder, Cardano Group;
and Professor of Risk Management, VU University, Netherlands

"Often overlooked, demographic factors are the hidden hand behind economics and asset prices. Dr. Roy provides valuable insights on how demographic factors should be incorporated into investment decisions by asset owners, particularly those in the life and pensions space."

—**Hemal Popat**, Investment Actuary, Mercer Investments

"Understanding the far-reaching effects of demographics on economic activity and financial markets is vital, and there is no better guide than Amlan Roy; this book is an important resource for those who wish to understand the interactions in all their complexity."

—**Richard Lacaille**, Global Head of ESG, State Street Corp;
and Former Global CIO, SSGA

"Demography affects many facets of economic life, yet its influence is widely under-appreciated. Written by an acknowledged expert and based on a lifetime of study, Roy's book masterfully explains just why demography is so important to our future prospects."

—**Professor Sir Charles Bean**, LSE; and Former Deputy Governor, Bank of England

"A very thorough and detailed account of many challenges facing both researchers and market practitioners in addressing difficult macroeconomic developments of modern times. The book challenges many cliches and stylised facts that surround demographics research and offers a fresh and comprehensive perspective on the subject. A must-read for students, policy makers and investment professionals interested in the intersection of demographics, macroeconomics and asset management."

—**Oksana Hrynchak**, Analytics & Product Specialist, Bloomberg;
and Formerly Credit Suisse, Goldman Sachs, & Bluecrest

Demographics Unravelled

How Demographics Affect and Influence Every Aspect of Economics, Finance and Policy

Amlan Roy

WILEY

Library of Congress Cataloging-in-Publication Data is Available

ISBN 978-1-119-79913-9 (hardback)
ISBN 978-1-119-79914-6 (ePDF)
ISBN 978-1-119-79915-3 (ePub)
ISBN 978-1-119-79916-0 (Obook)

Cover Design: Wiley
Cover Images: © wildpixel/Getty Images, Floortje/Getty Images

SKY0394203A-3228-4CA4-A58F-D1E3B92E5649_032822

To Anju, Shonai, Lilu, and Ranga

About the Author

Dr Amlan Roy is an experienced global macro-finance researcher and thought leader specialising in global macroeconomics and demographics. He presents to institutional clients in the private and public sectors across 30+ countries and is the founder of Global Macro Demographics. He is a research associate at London School of Economics' Systemic Risk Centre and an elected Honorary Fellow of the Institute and Faculty of Actuaries.

Until June 2021, Amlan was head of Global Macro Research and senior managing director with State Street Global Advisors, having joined them in 2017 as chief retirement strategist. He was managing director and head of global demographics and pensions research with Credit Suisse Investment Bank from 1998 to 2016. In a prior role as global EM strategist, he developed global risk and allocation models as an expert on financial architecture during the Asian crisis.

Amlan spent 12 years in academia, with a distinguished teaching career in the US and UK. He was UK ESRC Research Fellow, Ponders Fellow, a Boston University Doctoral Scholar and a

Government of India National Scholar. He has a PhD and MA in financial economics from the University of Iowa, an MBA from the Indian Institute of Management, Ahmedabad and an undergraduate honours degree in economics from St. Stephen's College, University of Delhi.

Jodi tor daak shoone keu na aashe, tobe ekla cholo re.
—Nobel Laureate Rabindranath Tagore (1905; in Bengali).
Translation: "If no one responds to your call,
then walk the distance yourself".

Contents

Acknowledgements

This book is the fruit of research efforts in the area of demographics over more than two decades. My initiation into demographics research owes a huge debt to Giles Keating, head of research at Credit Suisse Investment Bank, where I started the Global Demographics Project with him. Dick Hokenson, a collaborator, friend, and partner who joined Credit Suisse from DLJ in 2000, taught me a lot by sharing his knowledge as one of the experienced researchers in this area. Stefano Natella, former global head of equity research at Credit Suisse, was a strong supporter and believer, as was Lara Warner, business leaders (Gael de Boissard, Bob Jain, Tim O'Hara, Eraj Shirvani, and Stephen Dainton) provided management support at Credit Suisse, as did Rick Lacaille at State Street Global Advisors

Thanks to all my co-authors in demographics research (over the last two decades) for their collaboration, ideas, and support. Special thanks to Amy Le, my latest co-author and valuable research partner over the last four years. My growth as a researcher in this area owes a great deal to engagement and dialogue with global clients (pension funds, insurance companies, sovereign wealth funds, asset managers, endowments, private banks, foundations, central banks, regulators, hedge funds, private equity, and governments). Close partnership with several global sales teams helped me engage with global clients, and the sales partners have been a source of friendship and support.

Several influencers deserve a mention of gratitude: Andy Abel, Mukul Asher, Zvi Bodie, David Bloom, John Campbell, Jim Poterba, Steve Haberman, Andy Abel, Larry Kotlikoff, Andrew Ang, Angela Maddaloni, Orazio Attanasio, Carlo Favero, David Miles, Jim Bullard, Dirk Broeders, Theo Kocken, Luis Viceira, Tom Steenkamp, Elroy Dimson, Pablo Antolin, Arun Muralidhar, Mirko Cardinale, and David Blake.

Close friends Bala Venkatesh, Narayan Naik, Olivier Ledoit, David Webb, and Charles Bean have been there to debate, discuss, and teach me many things. Tom Frost and Tahir Wahid have been very special friends and colleagues in my career journey—my salute to them, too.

A big thank you to the Systemic Risk Centre and Financial Markets Group of the London School of Economics (LSE), which I have been affiliated with. Thank you to the CFA Institute and the Institute and Faculty of Actuaries for multiple conference speaking opportunities My thanks to the researchers and policymakers at the World Bank, International Monetary Fund, Asian Development Bank (ADB), and Inter American Development Bank (IADB).

My most important debt is to my lovely family, who have always supported me: my wife Anjana and daughters Antara and Anusha. My late aunt Subhanjali Sarkar and cousin Chitralekha were pillars of strength through many troubled times in the past, so I also owe a lot to them. And thanks to all those who have been pressuring me over the last eight years to write a book on demographics.

Finally, I would like to thank Gemma Valler and Purvi Patel of Wiley for their guidance. A very special thanks to Tiffany Taylor for excellent editorial work in improving the book's readability. Gladys Ganaden created the nice cover design. Daughter Antara chose the final cover image. Thanks to Ashok Ravi who provided tips for efficient edits at final stage.

I hope that this book contributes to inspiring readers to broaden their views and perspectives in more fields than just demographics. Viewing data and events from multiple angles provides additional richness to our insights.

Selected Abbreviations

ADB	Asian Development Bank
ALM	Asset Liability Management
BEA	Bureau of Economic Analysis
BIS	Bank for International Settlements
BLS	Bureau of Labor Statistics, US
CCPI	Climate Change Performance Index
CDR	Child Dependency Ratio
COLA	Cost of living adjustment
CPI	Consumer Price Index
CPI	Corruption Perceptions Index
CRR	Center for Retirement Research< Boston
DALY	Disability adjusted life years
DB	Defined Benefit (pensions)
DC	Defined Contribution (pensions)
EC	European Commission
ECB	European Central Bank
EMG6	Emerging 6 countries: Brazil, China, India, Mexico, Russia, Turkey
EU	European Union

Fed	US Federal Reserve
FSR	Fiscal Sustainability Report
G6	Developed 6 countries: France Germany Italy Japan, UK, US
GBD	Global Burden of disease
GDP	Gross Domestic Product
GGDC	Groningen Growth and Development Centre
GHS index	Global Health Security index
GII	Gender Inequality Index
GRFC	Global Report on Food Crisis
HALE	Healthy Life Expectancy
HDI	Human Development Index
HMD	Human Mortality Database
ILO	International Labour Organisation
IMF	International Monetary Fund
LE	Life Expectancy
LFPG	Labour Force Productivity Growth
LFUG	Labour Force Utilization Growth
MO ratio	Middle aged population to old population
MY Ratio	Middle aged population to young population
NETSPAR	Network for study of Pensions and Retirement, Tilburg
NGFS	Network for Greening the Financial System
OADR	Old Age Dependency Ratio
OECD	Organisation for Economic Cooperation & Development
ONS	Office for National Statistics
PAYG	Pay as you go (pensions)
PPP	Purchasing power parity
SDGs	Sustainable Development Goals
TDR	Total Dependency Ratio
TIPS	Treasury inflation protected securities (US)
UN	United Nations
WAPG	Working Age Population Growth
WHO	World Health Organisation
YLD	Years of life lost due to disability
YLL	Years of life lost due to premature mortality

Preface

This book is about my interpretation of demographics and its manifest implications for investments, macroeconomics, and policy. It represents more than two decades of research and synthesizes the connectivity of demographics with several subfields of economics: history, macroeconomics, international economics, labour economics, monetary policy, financial economics, development economics, etc. Repeated requests from clients, friends, and family, especially over the last eight years, have been the motivation for this book. My perspective is largely uniquely mine and like that of Peter F. Drucker[1].

I draw on my teaching and reading across various subdisciplines of economics and finance to make demographics relevant for investment practitioners, policymakers, and applied researchers. My research notes have made this discipline relevant across different asset classes (equities, fixed income, real estate, commodities, alternatives) and geographies. This allowed for creation of investment products and funds based on the applied research. I challenge many conventional perceptions as being narrow and at best partially correct, offering multiple examples.

I believe that demographics pertains to each individual on the planet and not just the young or the old. I also highlight differences across old countries and old individuals, cautioning against blanket generalizations as the only defining criterion. The idea in the book is to explain relationships between demographic variables and economic as well as financial variables in an intuitive and consistent fashion. Wherever possible data, models, and frameworks are used to embellish the ideas.

In the spirit of a "Brave New World"[2], this book challenges convention, expanding the boundaries of thought for understanding the real world of economics, investments, and policy options across multiple generations. It brings together macro and investment insights holistically with implications for individuals, companies, and countries. It discusses the important area of intergenerational fairness in a world where up to four or five generations co-exist for the first time in human history. Social responsibility and gender equality are at the core of important policy issues I discuss for a braver, better world. I hope the ideas in this book inspire discussion, debate, and understanding of issues that are critical for a better future society.

The structure of the book is as follows:

1. **Introduction.** This chapter introduces and amplifies a broader, more insightful perspective of demographics. It presents the layout and chapter sequence with a few sentences to highlight the key issues, major take-aways, and challenges to a traditionalist perspective. It should encourage readers to go to specific chapters on a deeper dive to unravel various strands of demographics.
2. **Global demographic trends**. This chapter summarises key trends with links to major public data sources. The purpose of highlighting these trends is to shed new light on several issues that readers broadly know of but often misinterpret or miss the point of. Age distributions (population pyramids), fertility, life expectancy, old-age dependency ratios, migration rates, gender

ratios, etc. are presented and discussed. The focus is on the more important differences that are typically glossed over in order to aggregate countries, regions, and cities on some common feature. For example, what are the key differences across similar-looking Nordic countries; or open economies like Singapore, Taiwan, etc.; or smaller countries in the Middle East; or the US vs. Canada or the EU4? This chapter shows why certain commonly used and aggregated metrics or indicators may be misleading. Why are the largest advanced countries different from each other in important ways? The pace of urbanisation and growth of megacities have implications for sustainability, human development, health, and education. The concept of demographic transition, which interacts with economic cycles and affects all aspects of human life worldwide, is also discussed. Data differences and interpretation provide motivation for further discussions in later chapters.

3. **Macroeconomics:** This chapter shows how characteristics and behaviour of consumers and workers affect economic growth, living standards (GDP per capita growth), inflation, and unemployment. Demographic effects are not just long-term, as these factors are also short-term variables. Consumers and workers make decisions throughout their lives, not just for the long-term. Understanding the implications for public debt, savings, and capital flows is vital to develop better policies and make optimal decisions. Economic growth is related to growth in worker numbers, worker productivity, and hours worked. I discuss why labour productivity growth is key to reviving global GDP growth in the developed world as well as major fast-growing emerging markets. Gender equality and youth empowerment are potential solutions to greater economic output. It is argued that long-term ageing-related promises are unsustainable in a lower-growth world and need renegotiation for fairer intergenerational equity. The chapter discusses the potential realisation of the demographic dividend across emerging and developed economies.

4. **Asset prices:** This chapter discusses how demographics affects equity, bonds, real estate, and commodities in terms of asset

prices and returns. The chapter presents insights from the academic literature on allocating accumulated resources over the human lifetime. Workers and retirees are faced with longer retirement periods, lower average growth, "lower for longer" interest rates, lower investment returns (equity, corporate bonds, high yield, etc.), and lower inflation than in the past. Investment returns and asset prices are influenced by consumption, savings, and investment decisions of households. Governments are faced with the responsibility of ensuring lower poverty rates for retirees in the future. The chapter presents the links between demographics and equity premia, sovereign bond yields, and sovereign ratings and also highlights equity sectors that are demographically advantaged and likely to emerge as winners.

5. **Longevity and health:** This chapter provides insights into and discusses the reasons for uncertainty regarding longer horizon resource planning for individuals and institutions. The emphasis on good health and importance of public health investments has been continuous throughout the ongoing COVID pandemic. The need to focus on healthy life expectancy and disability-adjusted life years rather than life expectancy at birth is emphasised. It is also important to know how longevity uncertainty and longevity risk management can be improved to enjoy a healthy and adequate retirement life. The models of longevity and instruments to defray longevity risk (the risk of outliving accumulated savings) need to be better understood by institutions (pension funds, reinsurers, insurance companies) to manage assets to meet longevity-related obligations (liabilities).

6. **Retirement and pensions:** This chapter highlights the importance of pension institutions amongst global financial institutions and investors. It presents a history of retirement and pensions, pension investment trends, issues facing pension funds, and design of pension systems. Issues underlying strategic and dynamic asset allocation for pensions are discussed, as are the implications of funding for corporate pension funds. The behaviour of the "new giants" (pension funds) is considered important by policymakers such as central banks and treasury

departments for the well-being of citizens as well as potential contributors to global systemic risks. The rise of defined contribution plans where participants bear the risk is not without its own issues and has led to the origin of hybrid pension systems. The chapter highlights issues for the collective world of pensions in dealing with the changing new world by adopting changes to mindsets, tools, and asset allocation. It is noted that the governance and management of pension funds is as important as the investment returns from an efficiency and comprehensiveness perspective.

7. **Gender, human capital, governance, and quality of life**: This chapter extends the focus and objective of individuals and households as well as collectively of institutions beyond monetary and pecuniary values. The extension beyond individual utility to social welfare functions and the human development index and happiness scores is essential for a world where income equality, gender equality, climate change, and corruption are serious concerns. The chapter discusses United Nations sustainable development goals (SDGs), transparency, national governance indicators, and gender scores to assess progress on a sustainable quality of life in a world where Millennials and younger generations care about the environment, equality, sustainability, fairness, and the "means more than just the ends". We note that quality of life, climate change, and happiness are considered important for a better world and should be monitored.

8. **Summary and conclusions:** A broader and deeper understanding of demographics is core to creating a better economic and investment environment for multiple generations in an ageing world. Healthy life expectancy with adequate retirement savings is essential for a responsible, sustainable future. Globalization, technology, geopolitics, and politics will interact to influence future consumer and worker behaviour.

Throughout the chapters, all the notes and references have been collected and presented at the end of the book, separated by each chapter. The References are an essential part of this book as I connect references from various different disciplines in the Notes section.

Chapter 1
Introduction

This chapter introduces and amplifies my broader and deeper perspective of demographics. It presents the layout and chapter sequence with a few sentences on the highlights, including key issues discussed, major take-aways, and challenges to the conventional perspective. It should encourage some readers to go to specific chapters for a deeper dive if they wished to read outside of the sequenced layout of the book.

This book summarises my views and research from a new angle on the subject area of demographics. When I first embarked on the initial stages of my research in this area in the millennium year 2000, I often heard interpretations of demographics related to age, youth, numbers of old, and numbers of very old. My inquisitiveness led me to delve deeper into the subject area to the etymology (word origin) of the term *demographics*. Its Greek origins stem from *demos*, which means "people", and *graphos*, which means "characteristics". My mind questioned the fact that if demographics pertained to people characteristics, how are the people characteristics within the subjects of economics and geography largely restricted to age only or the number of people only? As a macroeconomist, my view of "people characteristics" was, importantly, "people as consumers consuming goods and services" and also "people as workers producing goods and services".

This broader definition is not dependent only on age or numbers of young people.

1.1 Recasting Demographics

Broadening this definition of demographics then naturally extends to all the people in the world who are consumers, ranging from the newborn baby to the oldest centenarian, consuming the entire universe of goods and services. The aggregate consumption by individuals in an economy, which is referred to as *private consumption expenditures*, accounts for the largest share of GDP by expenditures. People's consumption of goods and services is a dominant component of national and global economic activity. A large segment of people in the population possess another characteristic: that of a worker contributing labour toward the production of goods and services, which in aggregate also leads to GDP. Thus, people are the core of any economy, and their salient features are those as consumers and workers—a far more important economic classification than that based on age or numbers of young or numbers of old. This paradigm encompasses the fact that consumer and worker behaviours are more relevant than their mere numbers or their age.

One of the world's greatest management gurus, Peter F. Drucker, had the following to say on the subject "Demographics is the single most important factor that nobody pays attention to, and when they do pay attention, they miss the point"[1,2]. This important insight by Drucker resonates with the broader interpretation of demographics that I have adopted and have been popularising for the last couple of decades in my reports, speeches, and discussions.

My first criticism was that conventional approaches to demographics by historians, market commentators, and popular writers were narrowly based on "age and numbers". There was another popular misconception of demographics (related to the former narrow view) that it was "predictable". This was based on counting people of certain age: say, if the number of 35-year-olds in a country in 2000 was X million people, then it could be said that the number of 45-year-olds in 2010 would be close to X million adjusted for certain mortality factors. The likelihood that most 35-year-olds would live to be 45-year-olds is close to 1 in most countries of the world. This notion of forward extrapolating the number of people of a given age few years ahead with near certainty or predictability[3] to evaluate their demands is incomplete. However, being Druckerian in spirit, I believe that this popular conception also misses the point by focusing on numbers of people and how many of them are expected to live T-periods ahead in the future (10, 15, 20, etc.). The more important point is not just counting the mere numbers of 45-year-olds 10 years later but rather how different they are as consumers and also as workers than the current 45-year-olds. It is therefore the behaviour of *consumers* and *workers* 10 years later that is more unpredictable, interesting, and relevant from an economic and business perspective.

The behaviour of consumers depends on preferences towards consuming today vs. saving for later, also called the *discount factor* by economists (related to the degree of impatience that an individual consumer displays), and the preference towards risk, called the *degree of risk aversion*. Dynamic models of consumption and asset pricing in the microeconomics as well as macroeconomics literature build on these two preference parameters. Consumption by people as individuals and in the aggregate also depends on the universe of goods and services they could potentially consume. Consumers in the 1980s didn't have access to the same smartphones (iPhones, Samsung, etc.), web and internet services, and online ordering as consumers of the 2000s or consumers in 2010 and 2020. Technological advances and product innovations have dramatically altered the consumption opportunity set available to individual consumers across all countries in the world, not just in the advanced, rich countries. Globalisation has extended access and availability to consumers in the poorest countries, too[4].

Both the consumer opportunity set and the preferences of consumers have changed as the world has globalised, information and education have increased awareness, and companies have innovated over time. The affordability of technological and consumer products has undergone radical changes on many fronts, which would have been hard to forecast 10 or 20 years ago even by visionaries, futurists, or pioneering innovators.

People (consumers and workers) were at the core of modern economics, as elaborated by Adam Smith's *The Wealth of Nations* (1776) and *The Theory of Moral Sentiments*. People's behaviour was also central in John Maynard Keynes' *The General Theory of Employment, Interest and Money* (1936). Keynes coined the term *animal spirits* to capture the emotions, impulses, and tendencies that influence human behaviour and used it to explain investor decisions of buying and selling assets during times of uncertainty and stress. Psychology and deviations from perfect rationality have also been highlighted by Daniel Kahnemann and Amos Tversky[5], who highlighted cognitive biases in decision-making, and Richard Thaler[6,7], who highlighted deviations from rationality in economics and the importance of behavioural economics. One of the pioneers of decision-making in organisations as well as artificial intelligence was Herbert Simon, who took an interdisciplinary approach to organisational decision-making and developed the concepts of *bounded rationality* and *satisficing*. My perspective fundamentally includes the behaviour of consumers and workers as a reflection of their characteristics.

I have another criticism of the conventional popular perception of demographics being long-term in its effects. Consumers and workers make direct contributions to the economic output of a country, a region, or the world, as mentioned earlier. Additionally, they influence inflation through effects on both the demand and supply sides. The wages consumer demands and labour costs of workers have short-term as well as medium-term and long-term effects on inflation and profitability. A flagship study by Deutsche Bank's Jim Reid[8] on long-term inflation over centuries found that demographics was one of the most important factors influencing inflation. My direct negation of this populism that demographics is long-term only stems from the fact that consumers and workers are not just long-term in terms of their economic behaviour but also immediate-term, short-term, and medium-term.

To summarise, I assert that demographics is not about age or population numbers only, nor is it only long-term in its effects, nor is it largely predictable, as it is hard to predict worker and consumer psychology in the future in the face of changing consumer opportunity sets—many of which have not even been visualised—like the current versions of the iPhone, web-based education, and online ordering

My perspective of demographics extends to a conclusion that I have been stressing over the last two decades that *demographics affects the income statement and balance sheet of every household, every company, every industry, and every country*. This is because consumers and workers are the core of revenues and costs of every producing unit, be it at the household level or company level or industry level or national level. Demographics has accounting implications on enterprise profitability if one views labour as contributing to the costs and consumers as contributing to the revenues.

By taking a broader view of demographics, I reveal and unravel the rich and deep influences of demographics on macroeconomics, investments, and policy. I paraphrase Drucker to urge readers of this book "not to miss the point when they pay attention to demographics". A better understanding of demographics is essential to facilitate their entry into a Braver (and Better) New World[9]. I strongly believe that a proper understanding of demographics will facilitate a better understanding of the dynamics of the real economy (Main Street) and the financial markets (Wall Street), as well as the divergences that have become very apparent during the 2020-COVID era.

1.2 Effects and Implications of Demographics

The focus in understanding demographics should be on understanding the effects of people behaviour at the micro (individual basis) as well as at the macro (the aggregate) level. These encompass individual interactions and dynamics within families, groups, and societies, which are a reflection of their characteristics. The failure of modern macroeconomics in warning about the global financial crisis (GFC) was highlighted by George Akerlof and Robert Shiller in *Animal Spirits* (2010)[10], another warning about not ignoring people's behaviour. While modelling the behaviour of people at the individual and aggregate levels yields many insights, the complexity of the human psyche and resultant behaviour highlights the heterogeneity across people in families, groups, and countries. We need to better understand economics and finance in conjunction with psychology, philosophy, and politics, as Akerlof and Shiller emphasise.

Trends at both the micro and macro levels testify to the impact of changing behaviour that results in observable changing core demographic characteristics such as increased life expectancy, lower population increases and growth, lower fertility rates (children born per woman), increased ratios of old to young people, and lower ratios of working-age people in the total population. These in turn also influence behaviour in terms of productivity of workers, movements of people from rural to urban areas, movements across countries (migration), and access to education, technology, and capital. Focus on age alone misses out on the fact that similar-aged people across different areas and countries exhibit different behaviour, as human behaviour is endogenous: it is different within different systems and institutional setups.

How we live, how we consume, and how we work have changed dramatically over the last few decades, with rapid acceleration due to the adoption of technology, changed awareness and knowledge, and adapting to changing work and home environments. These behavioural trends are nicely documented by Mark Penn[11] in *MicroTrends* (2000) as well as in *MicroTrends Squared* (2018). Microtrends reflect the changing behaviour of people at the micro level, which over time gets incorporated into aggregate changes displaying growing levels of heterogeneity. This is akin to a focus in the academic macroeconomics literature on micro-foundations of macroeconomics to reconcile or explain certain major macro puzzles.

The changing trends of globalisation over the last few decades, followed by a recent slowdown in the pace of globalisation, even called *deglobalisation*, are affected by changes in people's movement, trade, and government policies. I believe and argue that globalisation is a multifaceted phenomenon with a slowdown in some features such as global trade but rampant acceleration in the flow of information, IT, and capital. This is another example of the narrow interpretation of globalisation related to the movement of goods and services as well as the movement of people across national boundaries.

A correlation exists between the recent slowdown of real GDP growth in advanced countries and the acceptance of immigrants into their labour force and/or citizen population. There are many countries that rely on pools of immigrant labour—some skilled and some unskilled—to meet their workforce requirements. Even within the same region, neighbouring countries have differing immigration policies and immigrant worker shares. Population change decomposes into natural population change (deaths minus births) and net immigration (immigration less emigration). Demographics affects and is affected by both internal and external migration policies. Internal migration from villages to towns to cities reflects the growing trend of urbanisation within countries. Urbanisation growth has been much more rapid in many of the emerging market countries, leading to a larger number of megacities in the developing world such as Sao Paolo, Rio de Janeiro, Shanghai, Mexico City, Lagos, Mumbai, Delhi, Beijing, Kolkata, Dhaka, and Lahore. We shall discuss urbanisation, immigration, and globalisation in later sections of the book.

The later chapters as outlined in the preface, present data on the ongoing demographic changes, including a historical look back. The focus then is on the implications of those demographic changes on macroeconomic variables such as labour productivity, GDP growth, GDP per capita, inflation, interest rates, and public debt. Further discussion revolves around the effects of demographic changes on asset prices and asset allocation. Individual preferences toward risk and expected return influence the prices of assets. The rise of behavioural finance as a research area helps provide alternate explanations for many observed financial events and data.

A very important applied area of demographics is pensions and insurance. Increased life expectancy has resulted in uncertainties associated with living longer, given limited resources. Individuals want insurance for longer lives and also want to plan better over their lifetimes, which involves decisions on how much to save and which assets to invest those savings in. Pension funds and insurance companies invest in assets that help defray their liabilities. Strategic asset allocation and asset liability management are growing areas of emphasis for institutions that help manage liability risk for individuals. Later chapters of this book also focus on the importance of health from an individual and aggregate perspective, underscoring the importance of healthy life expectancy for society. Demographic changes have effects on inequality across generations, gender, age groups, regions, and countries. We discuss implications for inequality, human development, human capital, sustainability and public governance in later chapters, too.

People influence social change and social policies. Their behaviour is conditioned by the environment that they live in and their past experiences. The environment is determined by the interaction of various systems (health, education, labour, social welfare, legal, political, etc.) and the institutional framework. Policies have a role to play, and the role of government thereby influences the environment within which consumers and workers reside. The potentially negative implications of ageing populations have been characterised by the popular rhetoric of "the demographics time bomb", posing a threat to ageing developed countries, and several experts, including Peter Peterson, have warned of this[12,13].

In my first research foray into the area of demographics, "The Demographic Manifesto"[14], we advocated radical policy measures as part of a policy agenda for ageing countries to adopt in order to mitigate the demographic time bomb. In later policy research, I emphasised the need for coordinated and holistic policy across individuals, companies, governments, and international policy institutions to solve this complex issue of ageing, as it has manifold direct and indirect implications.

Changes in consumers and workers pertain to their changing preferences and behaviour as the environment around them changes. Endogenous changes in behaviour reflect the psychology of individuals, which differs across people irrespective of age, gender, or race; it is conditioned on a complex of experiences, environment, and background. Drucker highlights the role of the knowledge worker in a modern, evolving society and the role of information. The role of heterogeneity and diversity in decision-making in response to the changing opportunity set is reflected in the resultant outcomes and outputs.

The focus of demographics is people; and as people "live longer and live differently" than ever before, for the first time in humanity, four to five generations of a family co-exist with hardly one or one-and-a-half generations working to support them. The pressures of supporting multiple generations of members are apparent not just to families but also to governments. Many experts have characterised this ongoing phenomenon as a *generational storm*[15] or source of potential generational conflict, with the smaller, younger population group having to support a growing old-aged group. The basic question facing societies and countries as they age is one related to finances to support the ageing, as articulated very provocatively and directly by Peter Heller (2003), highlighting the urgency of planning[16] for such a future. Unprecedented demographic changes are heralding challenges and opportunities for society, industry, and governments on the path toward ensuring a profitable, sustainable, and equitable future for the population, which includes all consumers and workers. Therefore, demographics has international, intertemporal, and intergenerational effects across countries and the world.

In the next chapter of this book, I present data on core demographics, looking back and placing the current period in a historical context. I then use the data on population projections from the United Nations (UN), one of the best and most reliable sources of data both across time and countries. The UN population projections are used globally by public and private sector researchers to analyse and understand future data on populations. I refer to these as *core demographics data*, which are the lifeblood of any demographics-based analysis. The UN databases cover all the consumers in the world, as any individual in the population, whether a baby or a centenarian, is a consumer. For data on workers, I rely primarily on

International Labour Organization (ILO) data. In addition to the ILO and UN, data and research reports from the World Bank, International Monetary Fund (IMF), European Commission (EC), Organisation for Economic Cooperation and Development (OECD), Bank for International Settlements (BIS), Groningen Growth and Development Centre (GGDC), US Federal Reserve, European Central Bank (ECB), and other sources are used as and where appropriate.

Chapter 2
Core Data: Past, Present, and Future

This chapter summarises global demographic trends based on major public data sources. These trends highlight some patterns and variables that readers broadly know, but I focus on the more important differences that are glossed over in order to categorise countries, regions, and cities. For example, what are the key differences across similar-looking Nordic countries or open economies like Singapore, Oman, etc.? Or smaller countries in the Middle East? Or in the US vs. Canada or EU4? Certain aggregated metrics and common indicators may be misleading. We discuss the core demographic indicators: age distributions (population pyramids), fertility rates, life expectancy, old-age dependency ratios, migration rates, gender ratios, etc., in detail. Why and how are the oldest and youngest countries changing? We highlight the phenomenon of urbanisation and growing megacities with implications for sustainability. The framework of demographic transition is presented to show that the phases are different now than 30 years ago.

Population sizes, population age distributions, and population growth rates are the core demographic variables of interest to leaders, policymakers, demographers, geographers, and evolutionary scientists. The second half of the twentieth century evidenced the highest rates of population growth due to advances in public health and sanitation. Fewer conflicts and wars with longer periods of peace also contributed to population growth. Declining infant and maternal mortality rates combined with higher longevity were associated with the period of highest population growth between 1950 and 2000.

One of the most popular economists on the subject of population growth, Thomas Malthus[1], highlighted the dismal scenario of economic crises based on population growing exponentially—much faster than growth in land and resources. He contended that humans had a greater propensity to grow populations than maintain a high living standard, forecasting periods of economic deprivation leading to famine and disease. This controversial idea, called the *Malthusian trap*, has been widely discussed over the last two centuries.

I want to acknowledge and highlight the excellent data publicly made available by the UN Population Division to all researchers worldwide. I have been one of the biggest users and advocates of the UN Population Division[2]. This has been my first port of call for all data. There are few other data sources that provide better visualisation and draw on the basic UN data; one is Gapminder (developed by a Swedish scientist, Hans Rosling, who was interested in different types of appealing data visualisation for international comparisons and analytics).

Economic historians, historians, sociologists, and anthropologists have been interested in the evolution of the human population, which has grown most rapidly since 1950. History is of interest, but given changing regimes of economics, politics, and financial markets, I caution against falling into the temptation of extrapolating and comparing periods that are decades or centuries apart. The reason is apparent and reflected in my core thesis on demographics being about people's characteristics and behaviour, not just age or numbers of people. And people do change and adapt to their macro-environment.

The generally referred to core demographics data that we discuss in this chapter includes population size, population growth, life expectancy, median age, fertility rate, migration rates, and dependency ratios, all of which are available from the UN Population Division. The data on labour and workers is sourced from the International Labour Organisation (ILO). The behaviour of individuals as consumers and workers can be inferred based on consumption and workforce data observed ex-post from other national and international sources such as Eurostat for the EU, the Office for National Statistics (ONS) for the UK, and the Bureau of Economic Analysis (BEA), Groningen Growth and Development Centre (GGDC), and Bureau of Labor Statistics (BLS) for the US.

2.1   Economic History and the History of Global Population Trends

Studies of population numbers have been of interest to researchers and leaders, as large areas and large population sizes were considered symbols of the power and importance of empires. These have been documented in histories of ancient civilisations like the Chinese, Indian, and Egyptian followed by the Greek and Roman. Populations have been considered critical determinants of the growth of as well as the potential clash of civilisations. International relations expert and Harvard Professor Emeritus, the late Sam Huntington, in an influential book, *The Clash of Civilisations and the Remaking of World Order*[3], traced the interaction of economics, demographics, and challenger civilisations, pointing out the rise of Asia and the demographic challenge of Islam, Russia, etc. as a potential precursor to the new world order. Population dynamics also has had critical effects on the leaders of the world, influencing their ambitions to conquer other lands, as evident in the two major global wars in the twentieth century.

Carlo M Cipolla[4] and Massimo Livi-Bacci[5] are recognised as authoritative references regarding the history of world populations. Cipolla presents estimates of world population evolution between 1750 and 1950 as ranging from 750 million (+/− 100 million) to

2.426 billion (bn) (+/− 5%) as the world transitioned through the two revolutions: the Agricultural Revolution and the Industrial Revolution. The changes in energy consumption, production structures, and consumption structures are illustrated as part of the changes.

Nobel laureate Michael Kremer[6], in a historical paper, looked at long histories of population growth alongside technological change and progress in an endogenous growth framework. Economic output (as measured by gross domestic product [GDP]) is the result of a combination of factors of production that include land, labour, capital, and enterprise. These factors of production, along with technology, explain patterns of aggregate economic activity (GDP or industrial production [IP]). Kremer validates the endogenous growth models of many researchers who posited that population increases spur technological change. He finds that the growth rate of technology is directly proportional to population, all else being equal. Figure 2.1 documents the recent explosive increase in global population levels since 1950 as part of a million-year history of population.

Similarly, economic historian Angus Maddison[7] explains the historical economic performance of countries and documents the evolution of population. In earlier periods leading until the twentieth century, people entered the labour force at a much younger age and continued working until much closer to the end of life in the absence of pensions and social welfare systems. The

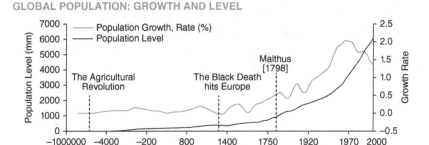

Figure 2.1 World population level.

SOURCE: Abridged from Keating, G., Hokenson, R.J. and Roy, A. (2000). The demographic manifesto: new jobs, new people. Credit Suisse Research.

normal working age was much longer, and the hours of work were also longer, due to the absence of savings institutions and investment vehicles. Maddison traces the history of the last millennium, detailing that the world population rose 22-fold, per capita income 13-fold, and world GDP nearly 300-fold. This contrasted sharply with the previous millennium, when world population grew by only a sixth, and there was no advance in per capita income. From the year 1000 to 1820, the world average income rose about 50% but was dominated by a fourfold increase in population. Since 1820, per capita income has risen more than eightfold, while population has grown more than fivefold. Maddison states that life expectancy grew dramatically alongside per capita income growth. There was a dramatic increase in life expectancy after the year 1000, when the average infant could expect to live about 24 years. A third died in the first year of life, and hunger and epidemic disease ravaged the survivors. There was a very small increase up to 1820, mainly in Western Europe. Most of the improvement has occurred since then, with life expectancy of 66 years at the start of the current millennium.

Maddison attributes the advances in population and income to three interactive processes that explain the economic performance of nations: (i) technological innovation, (ii) international trade and capital movements, and (iii) settlement and conquest of areas that had resources and land or potential to accommodate transfers of people, livestock, and crops. Adam Smith and John Maynard Keynes, too, discussed the contribution of consumers and workers in determining equilibrium prices and quantities. Other studies of historical demography are cited by Maddison as providing insights into Chinese economic performance dynamics from a long-term perspective.

From a core demographic perspective, one of the most important advances for humankind has been the dramatic increase in life expectancy since the second half of the twentieth century. Economic historian and Nobel laureate Robert Fogel[8,9] related the escape from death to the escape from the nutritional trap. Populations earlier were too weak to work to produce food, and the lack of food made them too weak to work. The synergistic improvement of health and living standards was referred to by Fogel as "techno-physio evolution"; he wrote that "it is likely that past public health reform, improvements in nutrition and other living standards, and the democratization of education, have done much more to increase longevity than has clinical medicine".

Fogel attributed the increase in life expectancy to thermodynamic factors that capture better and more nutrition, and advances in income leading to leisure and a decrease in morbidity over time. He was critical of economic researchers and scholars who ignored the contribution of nutrition and physiological factors to growth. He classified them as labour-enhancing technological factors that benefited from advances in public health, agriculture, medical services, and the household sector. Fogel related increases in life expectancy and income to the demand for leisure and pensions.

2.2   Core Demographic Variables: Data, Analysis, and Some Observations

I refer to core demographic variables as *standard variables* that capture the quantitative and qualitative aspects of an aggregate group of people, also referred to as *population*, of a given enterprise or pertaining to a given reference area. I draw on the UN Population Division database, a reference source that is authoritative and popular for its reliability and comparability across countries and regions as well as over time. In this chapter and throughout the book where the source may not be mentioned, it is by default the UN Population Division.

2.2.1   Population Size and Population Growth

The world population continues to grow, although a growth slow-down has been apparent since the turn of the millennium. The last half-century saw historically unprecedented population increases due to advances in health, public hygiene, and sanitation. Education and literacy had important roles to play alongside medicine in reducing infant mortality rates and maternal mortality rates and controlling infectious diseases that resulted in high fatality rates in the past. The world population size increased from 2.54 bn (1950) to 3.7 bn (1970) to 5.3 bn (1990) to 6.96 bn (2010) and is expected to grow from current levels of 8 bn (2021) to 8.5 bn (2025). Figure 2.2 presents the evolution of population growth rates for three UN-defined aggregate regions: the world, developed regions, and less developed regions.

As shown in Figure 2.2, the decrease in population growth from higher levels is most pronounced in advanced regions of the world, but it is worth emphasising the sharp decrease in population growth rates across the developing world and the whole world since 1990. Probably the single most important cause of this population growth slowdown is the global decline in fertility rates, which doesn't offset as many old-age deaths as in the earlier period 1950–1990. Note that developing world population growth rates that were in excess of 2% annually are now close to 1.15% p.a. (per annum), while the world population is growing at 0.98% p.a. The developed regions are projected to grow only 0.07% from 2025 to 2030. The developed world population is projected to stop growing after 2035, whereas the world population is projected to grow marginally positively until

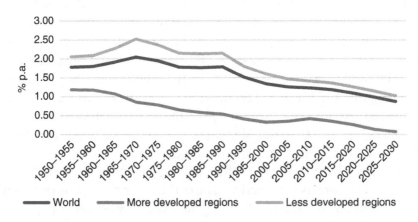

Figure 2.2   Annual population growth.
SOURCE: UN Population Division.

the end of the century as per the UN. Population decreases have already occurred in some developed countries like Japan, Germany, and Italy. Migration has played an important role in bolstering the population growth of many developed countries; we discuss this later in Section 2.3.

Although the Malthusian projections are unlikely to be realised, the world population now faces the larger, more pressing challenge of climate change. This may be the biggest challenge faced by humanity in the last hundred years and threatens survival due to the impact of human practices on land, water, and air. Global warming is a warning sign that individuals, companies, and governments across the world are growing aware of and now paying serious attention to.

2.2.2   Ageing Populations

Not only is the population of the developed world projected to shrink, with some countries already experiencing population declines, but the world population is also ageing. To live until the age of 100 would have been the wish of many people in the early twentieth century, according to economic historian Robert Fogel. However, rapid ageing has posed challenges to individuals, families, and governments in the developed world over the last few decades.

The median ages of developed regions, the world, less developed regions, and the least developed regions all display a secular increase that reflects increases in life expectancy, a topic discussed later in great detail. The gap between the median ages of the developed regions and the world reflects the catch-up potential of the less advanced regions. The median age of the most advanced countries (42 years) is more than double that of the least developed regions of the world (20.2 years), as shown in Figure 2.3a.

Figure 2.3b presents the differential age evolutions of six large, advanced countries (referred to as the G6) over the last seven decades. Particularly noteworthy is Japan—which was lower than the US in 1950—overtaking and leading the rest of the advanced countries in terms of median age. As of 2020, the US median age (38.3)

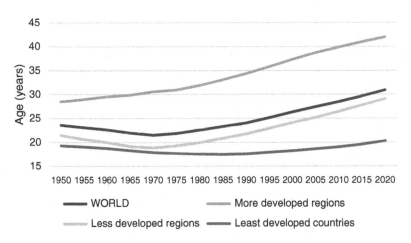

Figure 2.3a Median age (regions): 1950–2020.

lags behind that of Japan (48.4) by more than a decade. This is tantamount to roughly a generation's worth of median age increase in order for the US to catch up with Japan. It also has implications for US policy in terms of health provision, diet, and inequality across population segments as well as states. Italy has the second-highest median age, and this was evident in its vulnerability to the first phase of COVID-19 infections and deaths in Q2 of 2020.

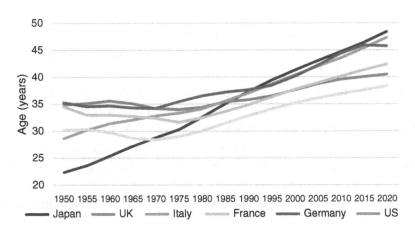

Figure 2.3b Median age (G6): 1950–2020.
SOURCE: UN Population Division.

2.2.3   Life Expectancy Increases

One of the most significant changes in human life is that life spans (longevity) have increased dramatically since the 1950s, firstly in the developed countries, followed by less developed countries and then the least developed countries. While the focus of many is on aggregates of regions as mentioned previously, one of the most important points that I make is that of wide divergences in current levels of life expectancies within a region, even in the group of most developed countries. It is very flippant and broad in generalisation terms to talk about trends within geographic regions or regions based on income or development measures. Heterogeneity challenges the broad generalisations of demographics across regions aggregated as rich or advanced countries versus groups of poorer or developing countries. I strongly caution against these broad generalisations, as the data reveals wide divergences within Europe, Asia, and North America as geographic regions. The implications of these wide divergences for other economic facets are quite stark, as discussed later. In earlier research[10], we documented and provided a firm rebuttal to the then-popular emerging thesis that the US was going to follow the Japanese demographic example of lost decades. In "From the Demographic Lens: US Is definitely Not Japan and Neither Is Germany", we dismissed the thesis based on empirical evidence.

Figure 2.4a illustrates the dominant longer life expectancy at birth increases in the more developed regions relative to the overall world and the less developed regions. The gap in life expectancies of the more developed regions vs. the less developed regions is also consistent with the differences in the median ages. Figure 2.4b illustrates the life expectancy trends across the G6 advanced countries, with Japan at the highest point and the US at the lowest. In 1950, only France had a higher life expectancy at birth than the US. On this development metric, the US has lagged behind its peers, and this is reflected in the indicators of overall human development that we present and discuss in Chapter 7.

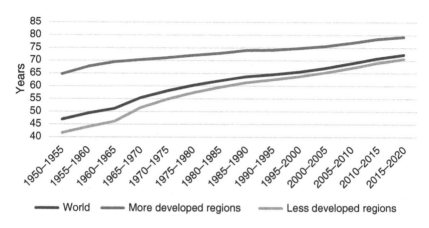

Figure 2.4a   Life expectancy at birth (region).

2.2.4   Total Fertility Rates

The trend of declining fertility rates is a global phenomenon, with women choosing to have fewer babies in both advanced and developing countries, although the rates of decline differ, as can be seen in Figure 2.5. The emancipation and education of women and the

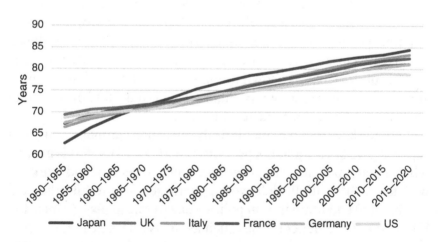

Figure 2.4b   Life expectancy at birth (G6).
SOURCE: UN Population Division.

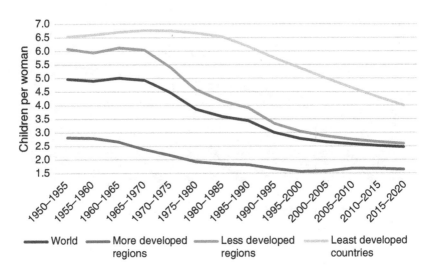

Figure 2.5a Total fertility rates (region).

costs of child-rearing explain the widespread fertility rate decline over the last few decades.

Current fertility rates in the developed world are below the replacement fertility rate (the rate at which populations replace themselves: 2.1 children per woman) at 1.64 children per woman, whereas those in the least developed parts of the world are at 4 children per woman and those for the world and less developed regions are close to 2.5 children per woman. The globally declining trend is undeniable, as shown in Figure 2.5a. The trend in the more advanced countries, shown in Figure 2.5b, is a decline over 1950 to 2020, with differences in the fertility rates after 1980: the US, the UK, and France have much higher fertility rates than Germany, Italy, and Japan. As we have argued in previous reports and fora, this is an area where gender policies (empowering women to better blend work life with family life with flexible work patterns, child-care subsidies, tax breaks, etc.) and immigration policies have a role to play. France, the UK, and a few other countries such as the Netherlands and Nordic countries have managed to offset the declines from the mid-1990s with women, work and child-friendly policies alongside practical immigration policies. This was advocated by us in 2000 in the Demographic Manifesto, referred to earlier in Chapter 2.

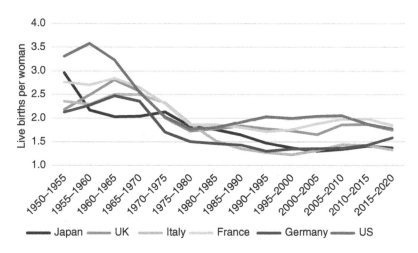

Figure 2.5b   Total fertility rates (G6).
SOURCE: UN Population Division.

2.2.5   Dependency Ratios

The non-working population of children (below age 15 in traditional definitions but now below age 20) and retirees (typically aged above 65 years) are considered dependents on the working-age population aged between 15 and 64 years. Declines in fertility rates combined with increased life expectancy have led to an increase in old-age dependency ratios.

Figure 2.6a shows the impact of ageing in the more developed, affluent regions due to higher life expectancies as a result of medical and health advances—their old-age dependency ratios (OADRs) are more than double that of the world, showing the ageing burden of older people on the working-age group. Within six advanced developed countries that we refer to as the G6 (Figure 2.6b), the OADRs display divergences in terms of their increases, with Japan leading the G6 by a huge distance. Japan is referred to as the oldest country in the world mainly because of its very high OADR relative to all the others. It is important to note that another type of dependency ratio is the *child or youth dependency ratio* (CDR) constructed by dividing the number of young non-working people (below 15 years conventionally,

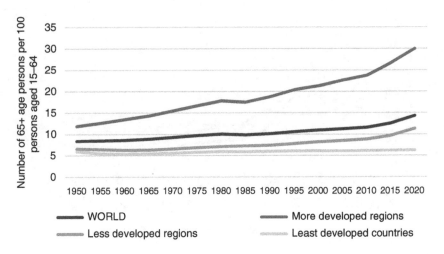

Figure 2.6a   Old-age dependency ratios (regions).

and now below 20 years or even 25 in some countries) by the number of working-age people in the corresponding 15–64, 20–64, or 25–69 age group.

In previous research, we showed that using different ranges for dependents (old or young) relative to the appropriately adapted change in working-age group numbers yields alternative dependency ratios with different implications for policymakers. Table 2.1 presents the effects of different ranges of working age (G6) on OADRs and CDRs.

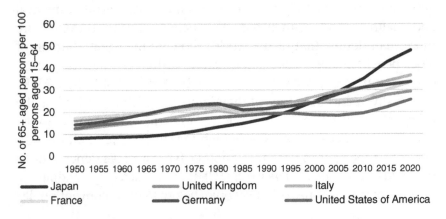

Figure 2.6b   Old-age dependency ratios (G6).

SOURCE: UN Population Division.

Table 2.1   Changing age ranges and dependency ratios.

Changes in working-age range on child dependency ratio (CDR)

	Ratio of population aged 0–14 per 100 population 15–64	Ratio of population aged 0–19 per 100 population 20–64	Ratio of population aged 0–19 per 100 population 20–69
Location	2020	2020	2020
Japan	21.0	31.0	27.7
UK	27.8	39.7	36.5
Italy	20.4	30.1	27.4
France	28.7	42.4	38.4
Germany	21.7	31.7	28.9
US	28.3	42.3	38.8

Changes in working-age range on old-age dependency ratio (OADR)

	Ratio of population aged 65+ per 100 population 15–64	Ratio of population aged 65+ per 100 population 20–64	Ratio of population aged 65+ per 100 population 25–64
	2020	2020	2020
Japan	48.0	52.0	56.9
UK	29.3	32.0	35.7
Italy	36.6	39.5	43.1
France	33.7	37.3	41.5
Germany	33.7	36.5	40.2
US	25.6	28.4	32.1

SOURCE: UN Population Division.

The first half of the table shows the effect of changing the young dependents' age range from 14 to 19 as we move from the first column to the second column: the ratio increases, as the number of working-age people in the 20–64 range is smaller than the 15–64 age group. Similarly, comparing the second and third columns in the top part of the table shows a decrease as the working-age range expands from 20–64 to 20–69. It is important to check and clarify what age ranges are used for computing the CDR, which reflects the burden of young people who are yet to join the production line.

Similarly, the second half of the table illustrates the effect of changing the working-age ranges on the OADRs. Narrowing the age range of workers by changing the entry age into the workforce leads to higher OADRs. In modern-day society, college and university education has led many young people to join the labour force later, after completing their first or second post–high school degree. Due to this trend, unless retirement age or the upper bound of the working age changes beyond 65, we are likely to see growing pressure on governments supporting individuals whose life spans are increasing but whose active working years are decreasing compared to earlier.

The pressure on governments to support not just the youth but also the elderly can be captured by adding the OADR to its analogous CDR. For example, the total dependency ratio (TDR) in Japan was 69 per 100 (48 for OADR plus 21 for CDR) in 2020. In contrast, Germany has a TDR of 55.4 and the US a TDR of 53.9. Since the government or public sector typically has an obligation to support both classes of dependents—the young and the old—beyond whatever resources the family or savings can cover, higher TDRs imply the need for more public revenues.

2.2.6   Gender Ratios

Gender equality assumes importance as a social imperative in the modern world as women face multiple barriers with regard to work, education, financing, etc. Despite increased access to resources and opportunities given to women and the higher levels of educational attainment relative to men in the most advanced countries, women still are not at parity with men in all walks of life. The focus on gender equality has been galvanised recently as part of the UN's Sustainable Development Goals (SDGs) as well as the growing corporate emphasis on environmental, social, and governance (ESG) factors, wherein gender representation on boards and senior management has assumed an urgent focus. The role and status of women need much more emphasis to level the playing field and shatter the glass ceiling. While enormous strides have been made in some countries, regions, and sectors of the world, there are many more miles to walk on this road to equality.

Figure 2.7 shows that gender ratios in the more developed regions are below 100, with females outnumbering males; this is because, given normal conditions and equality, women tend to out-live men by 2–6 years, depending on the country. While 100 represents equal numbers of males and females, it is important to note that the world had more females than males in 1950, but currently, males outnumber females by 1.7% and in the less developed regions by 3% partially explained by WW2 effects and gender preferences too. Both the less developed regions and the more developed regions are tending toward parity but are still significantly off parity.

The UN, International Monetary Fund (IMF), World Bank, Organisation for Economic Cooperation and Development (OECD), and other regional development banks have done an enormous amount of research highlighting existing gender inequality as well as advocating policy measures to ameliorate the prevalent inequities. In "The Demographic Manifesto"[11], we argued for greater female participation, opportunities, and access to mitigate the ageing time bomb. In a recent report, "Why Gender Equality Matters? Better for Growth, Debt, Equality and Sustainability"[12] using data from more than 140 countries, we showed that gender equality is an imperative

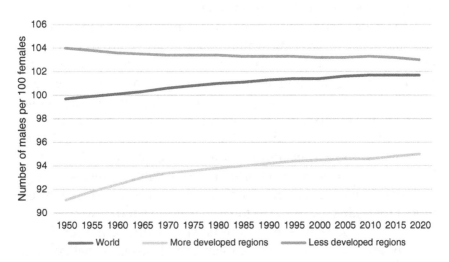

Figure 2.7   Gender ratios (regions): 1950–2020.
SOURCE: UN Population Division.

Table 2.2 Gender distribution changes by broad age group.

Percentage of female population by broad age group (per 100 female total population)

		0–14	15–24	25–49	50+	80+
World	1980	34.7	18.6	29.3	17.4	1.1
World	2020	24.8	15.1	34.6	25.5	2.3
More developed regions	1980	21.2	15.7	33.0	30.0	2.7
More developed regions	2020	15.6	10.5	32.4	41.6	6.5
Less developed regions	1980	39.2	19.6	28.0	13.1	0.5
Less developed regions	2020	26.7	16.1	35.0	22.2	1.5

SOURCE: UN Population Division.

as it leads to higher economic growth, lower debt, better sustainability, and greater overall equality.

As the age distribution changes for the whole population, so does the gender distribution by age, i.e. the number of females in different age groups as a proportion of the total. Table 2.2 shows that the percentage of women in different broad age groups has changed over the last four decades. The table displays the changes by region and the world between 1980 and 2020.

One noteworthy observation is the more than doubling of the age 80+ share of women in the total population of women in all three regions: the world, more developed regions, and less developed regions. The argument in favour of equality for women in the workplace is even stronger now, given their very high numbers graduating from universities, in excess of male numbers in most of the very advanced countries. In addition, the fact that women are living longer rails against the earlier norm of lower retirement ages for women. Women ought to have the choice to work flexibly using technology, and part-time work as well as job-sharing as this would lead to very productive gains for the workforce. The criticism that women have children and take career breaks could also be turned in their favour as a productivity-enhancing career gap. I strongly believe that it is much easier to accommodate and assimilate native women into the workforce than immigrants in each country and suggest that they should be the first source of productive labour in any economy facing labour shortages. This is a policy advisory brief I have passionately adopted since 2000, and it remains relevant today.

2.2.7 Age Structure and Population Pyramids

When the age distributions for populations are plotted from youngest to oldest on a vertical line with males and females on opposite sides of the Y-axis, the shape resembled a Christmas tree or a population pyramid with far fewer females and males at older ages relative to younger ages. However, with rapid ageing, the typically younger age structures have evolved to have an expanding middle and then taper off at older ages—this is referred to as *flattening* of the age pyramid or *rectangularisation* of the Christmas tree.

Lower fertility rates further have decreased the very large proportion of children relative to the younger age groups in their 20s through their 40s, while increased longevity has increased the share of the very old. This translates to age distributions that are no longer shaped like pyramids. We mentioned that lower fertility rates have effects 20 or 25 years later when the babies born enter the labour force. The fastest-growing age group in the world is the 80+ age group, and therefore we advocate breaking the 65+ age group into the old (65–79 years) and the very old (80+ years). This phenomenon of growing 80+ populations is occurring across all regions of the world and across all countries, from the poorest to the richest, due to the transfer of good health and medical practices from richer regions to poorer regions.

There is currently a hype in the popular press regarding the impact of lower fertility rates during the COVID period, failing to appreciate that those effects are smaller and more distant than the impact of closed borders, which inhibit migratory movements. These having an immediate impact on GDP as reported by the government of Australia.

OADRs are a very important indicator as they closely correlate with the public spending or resource requirements of governments in supporting the aged or retired in terms of public pensions,

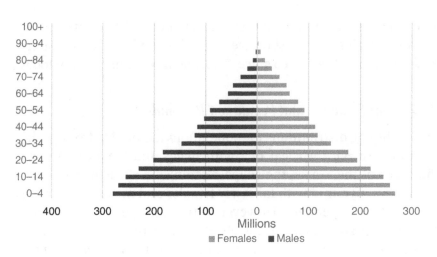

Figure 2.8a   World 1980 (age structure).

healthcare, and long-term care. As countries age, the age structure of the entire distribution across all age groups also evolves. This evolving age structure can be seen in Figure 2.8a. The rectangularisation of the population pyramid is evident by viewing the contrast between the lower and top parts of the figure.

This trend can be observed in many mature advanced economies as a consequence of increasing life expectancies along with decreasing fertility rates. We note that at older ages, the right bars (the numbers of females) are slightly longer than the left bars (numbers of males). There is, however, an important factor that we have not discussed but that has a bearing on population sizes and population growth of countries in addition to birth rates, death rates, longevity, and fertility rates: immigration. In a globalised post-war modern world, ease of travel and the sharing of information and knowledge has allowed for greater economic migration between countries and regions. A more detailed discussion of migration follows in section 2.3 of this chapter.

Figure 2.8b illustrates the progression of the age structure over four decades, representing the fact that an individual aged, say, x years in 1980 (male or female) is typically expected to be $x+40$ years in 2020, barring death due to old age or any misfortune at a younger

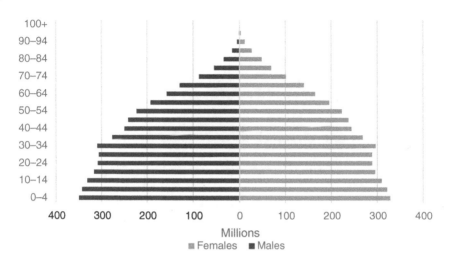

Figure 2.8b   World 2020 (age structure).
SOURCE: UN Population Division.

age. We also illustrate the evolution of the population pyramids in the US and Japan in Figure 2.9 and Figure 2.10, respectively.

Even for the US, a relatively young country amongst the advanced countries, it can be noted that the age structure flattens out or the pyramid rectangularises at the lower age groups. In contrast, Japan grew from low post–World War II economic activity levels to great heights, emerging as an economic power by 1990. Its population also grew and aged as Japan progressed over the decades.

As can be observed in Figure 2.10, Japan's population pyramid is nearly inverted in contrast with being rectangularised, as evident in the case of the population pyramids for the world and the US. It is also worth highlighting the fact that in all three cases presented previously, females at higher ages tend to outnumber males. I also stress the important point that given the very few people above the age of 100 as a share of the population, a focus by policymakers on the 100+ population would miss the point of ensuring a better quality of life first for those already straining in terms of resources post-retirement in their late 70s, 80s, and 90s. Prioritised focus should be first on those age groups and only then on centenarians.

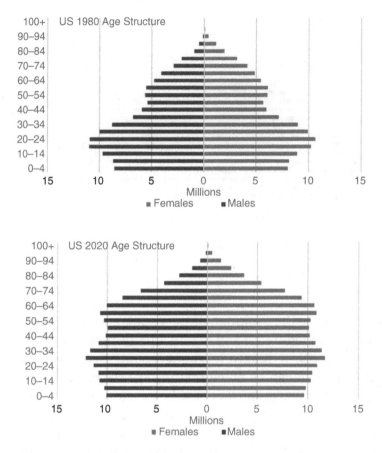

Figure 2.9 Evolution of the US age structure: 1980–2020.
SOURCE: UN Population Division.

2.2.8   The Demographic Transition Model

The *Demographic Transition model* is a model of population change attributed to Warren Thompson. It represents the transition from high birth and death rates to low birth and death rates as a country develops from being pre-industrial to having an industrialised economy. The stages of the demographic transition theory are illustrated in the following schematic.

Stage 1	Stage 2	Stage 3	Stage 4	Stage 5
High & Fluctuating Death Rates	Falling Death Rates	Falling Death Rates	Low Death Rates	Very Low Birth Rates
High & Fluctuating Birth Rates	High Birth Rates	Falling Birth Rates	Low Birth Rates	Death Rates Higher Than Birth Rates
Stationary Population Numbers	Large Increase In Population	Stable Population Growth	Stable Population	Declining Population/Ageing
	India, Indonesia, Malaysia, Vietnam, Venezuela, Mexico	Brazil, China, Thailand, US, UK, France, Chile	Italy, Russia, South Korea	Japan, Germany

Asian countries[13] are in different stages of demographic transition. They have different patterns of population growth, age structures, and life expectancy. The different demographic stages are associated with different numbers of consumers and workers and thereby have differing implications for economic growth and other factors influencing asset prices. Using Asia as an example, younger countries like India, Malaysia, Indonesia, and Vietnam are in stage 2. China is in stage 3, South Korea in stage 4, and Japan in stage 5. The stages of demographic transition are also akin to the stages of economic development (which is much broader in scope than economic growth).

Attanasio et al.[14] analyse the demographic transition for developing countries, finding that the impact of demographic changes on emerging economies may depend on the degree of international capital mobility and the extent of pension reform in developed countries.

While studying the demographic transition, Galor[15] found that the rise in demand for human capital in the process of development was the main trigger for the decline in fertility and the transition to

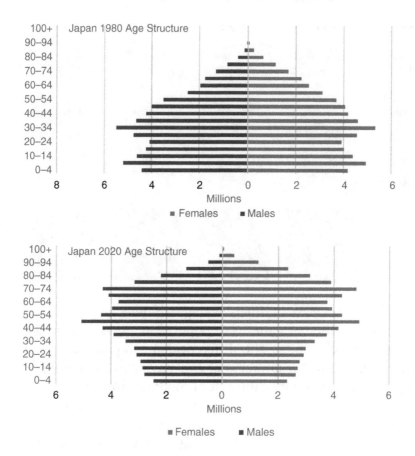

Figure 2.10   Evolution of Japan's age structure: 1980–2020.
SOURCE: UN Population Division.

modern growth. This substantiates earlier evidence based on views
that desire for human capital and costs of childbearing influence
fertility rates, which influence the dividends from the demographic
transition, discussed in Chapter 3.

2.3   The Role of Migration

Thus far, the analysis and discussion have focused on core demographic indicators restricted to people native or domestic to a region—the natives or citizens. In a modern globalised world, one of the critical factors of production (labour) has become very mobile. Since the end of World War 2 (WW2), due to advances in transportation, including sea, land, and air travel, people have moved across borders not just as explorers or in pursuit of conquests but rather to further their economic gain or well-being. The search for better human capital opportunities as a means to higher lifetime income has been an explanatory factor for migration.

In many advanced countries, with the notable exception of Japan, immigration has played an important part in shaping the composition of the population and the labour force. As we shall show using data, immigrants have contributed significantly to the economic progress of many nations, including the US, the UK, Canada, France, the Netherlands, and Germany. Immigrants have been welcome in many countries during the good times of the 1980s to the 2000s but have faced less than welcome times over the decade since the global financial crisis (GFC) due to lower growth and higher debt conditions in host countries. While immigration has had benefits for host countries, it has also led to associated economic and social costs, making it necessary for countries to estimate and focus on the net benefits of immigration.

From a conceptual point of view, the population change of a country between two dates includes two components: (i) natural population change, i.e. the number of births minus deaths; and (ii) net immigration, i.e. immigrants (incoming people) minus emigrants (outgoing people). In many important economies, immigration has made a sizeable contribution to population changes and also contributed (based on immigrants' skills) to the aggregate output (GDP) of a country.

Figure 2.11a depicts the net number of migrants coming in to the country for the G6. The contrast between Germany and Japan (two ageing leaders) is noteworthy. The US is charted on the right-hand scale due to the large number of net migrants and its higher population size relative to the other countries.

Figure 2.11b illustrates the net rates of migration normalised per thousand people. The difference between Germany and Japan is noticeable, and the increase in the UK post-1980 for three decades is also important to note. The significant role of net migration in Germany also shows up in the last 15 years. While both Germany and Japan are experiencing shrinking populations, Germany has offset that over the last few decades with immigration, which has not been a policy option used much by Japan.

It is also interesting to note the share of net immigration in population changes over five-year periods. Figure 2.12 presents the share of net migrants in the population change of advanced countries. Negative numbers can be due to either population change being negative while net migrants are positive or population change being positive and net migrant numbers negative. In some perverse cases, positive numbers could be due to negative population change as well as negative migration, i.e. where emigration is dominant.

Figure 2.12 shows the importance of migration relative to population change in advanced economies. It is important to note that

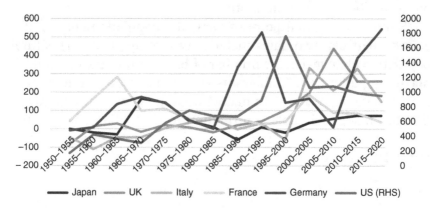

Figure 2.11a   Net number of migrants (thousands).

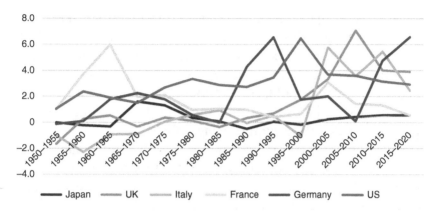

Figure 2.11b Net migration rate per thousand.
SOURCE: UN Population Division.

the downturn in Italy or exodus over the last few years is captured by the negative share of net immigration in population change.

There is vigorous debate amongst economists regarding the net contribution of migrants to any economy and when net benefits accrue to an economy from immigrants. This has often shaped the politics and policy of immigration, even in the most affluent of countries. The US, Australia, Canada, France, and the UK have had significant, sizeable immigration flows over the last few decades.

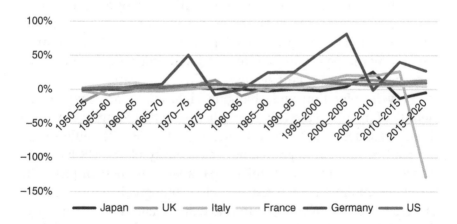

Figure 2.12 Net migrants (share of population change).
SOURCE: UN Population Division.

However, the importance and impact of immigration have come under greater scrutiny in a low-economic-growth world. When the aggregate output is bountiful, sharing with immigrants is more welcome amongst native residents or citizens across the world. The OECD's regular publication "International Migration Outlook 2020" discusses the flows of migrants and the changing nature of the countries that the migrants come from.

Paul Collier, former chief economist of the World Bank, in his book *Exodus*[16], details the various ways in which migration is changing our world. In discussing one of the most controversial questions on this topic—who should be allowed to immigrate—he considers the perspectives of the migrants, the people they leave behind, and the host societies where they relocate.

In the last decade or so, immigration has assumed greater importance, with barriers or restrictions on immigrants enforced by advanced countries during the European asylum-seeker crisis of 2014–15. Migrants from countries in the Middle East and Africa ravaged by politics and civil war attempted to swarm through cracks in European borders, forcing the EU to take a coordinated response to allowing in asylum seekers and rehabilitating them.

The sensitivity of immigration has been discussed by Sam Huntington who in his classic *The Clash of Civilisations* highlighted the issues of ideological crashes and saw well ahead of others the possibilities of Crimea, the Muslim youth bulge, and the Arab Spring: the seeds of 9/11. He argued that clashes between civilisations are a threat to world peace, but an international order based on civilisations is the best safeguard against conflicts and wars.

How immigration and changing civilisations are shaping the identity of people in the US[17] is another issue that Huntington wrote about. He stated that the values and language of British settlers were accepted by later immigrants, but the identity of the US has been eroded by challenges of assimilating massive numbers of primarily Hispanic immigrants with issues such as bilingualism, multiculturalism, devaluation of citizenship, and denationalisation of American elites. This influences behaviour and is part of the growing behavioural economics perspective on how consumers, workers, savers, and investors behave differently from the perfectly rational individual decision makers assumed in economics. Biases, limitations, heuristics, background, and institutions all matter in decision making.

Stephen Castles and Mark Miller[18] provide a global perspective, discussing and analysing the nature of people's movements and why they take place. Their analysis highlights the formation of ethnic minorities and how growing ethnic diversity affects economies, cultures, and political institutions while posing challenges to existing forms of citizenship and national identity.

Different countries within the same region and the same political unions exhibit different patterns of migration as well as different reasons for immigration. In a study of European migration[19] during the asylum seeker crisis, We illustrated that there existed differences across Germany, France, Italy, and the Netherlands in their temporal patterns of immigration, their attitudes toward immigrants, and resources devoted to the integration of the immigrants.

The OECD's latest *International Migration Outlook 2020*[20] highlights the following:

- The COVID-19 pandemic had a major impact on migration flows in the first half of 2020. Estimates suggest an unprecedented 46% reduction in the number of new visas and resident permits granted, on average, in the OECD. Part of the effect might be offset in the second half of the year, notably for international students, but the current economic downturn will also most likely aggravate the impact on labour migration.
- Overall, 2020 will appear as an historical low for international migration in the OECD area. In 2018 and 2019, the number of new immigrants who were granted permanent-type permits remained stable (about 5.3 million).
- Flows to the top two receiving countries (the US and Germany) continued decreasing, while they tended to increase in a majority of OECD countries, notably Spain and Japan.
- In 2019, partial data on humanitarian flows to OECD countries displayed a 25% overall drop, with the US accounting for most of it. Permanent labour migration rose sharply (+13%), with half

of the countries registering double-digit increases, including the UK (+42%), Finland (+29%), Luxembourg (+29%), Japan (+17%), and France (+12%). Family migration also increased in 2019 by about 2% and accounts for about a third of overall permanent flows.

There are a variety of reasons for immigration, and these differ based on both host country and country of emigration. The top two reasons are family and free movement, followed by work, humanitarian, and others. Another perspective that governs migration trends is the change in the composition of immigrants in host countries and how that influences the culture within the country. In Table 2.3, we show how the top five countries from which immigrants originate have changed over the last three decades in France, Germany, and the UK. Immigration is a dynamic and evolving process, with changing source country rankings. The last column shows the percentage of women from the source countries. Men have been the major source of immigrants in host nations, and a large share of initial migrants were low-skilled and low-cost, substituting for natives in host countries and thereby allowing them free time to do higher-skilled or higher-paid jobs. Immigration has a gender dimension that is often ignored but should not be.

Historically and even currently, population size has been an indicator of influence and power amongst advanced countries. Population sizes have changed by different magnitudes across the advanced countries in the post-WW2 era. Population change has two components that have varied in their relative importance across countries. The patterns of immigration into advanced countries have varied over time and also across countries. Figure 2.13 shows the contrasts in net migration and its relative importance across Japan, Germany, the UK, and the US over seven decades of post-WW2 history.

We note the importance of net migration as a contributor to population change in the contrast between Germany and Japan. While most people know that Japan has been largely closed to immigration, very few know of the important role played

Table 2.3 Stock of foreign population by nationality (thousands).

	2009	2010	2011	2012	2013	2014	2015	2016	2017	2018	2019	2015 (%)
Portugal	493.87868	497.642	501.81	509.254	519.5	530.557	541.569	546.1	548.7			46.6
Algeria	468.97471	466.405	466.626	469.595	476.47	483.782	495.737	505.6	518.1			47.8
Morocco	440.74116	435.188	433.445	436.429	443.379	448.534	458.237	464.9	472.6			49.4
Turkey	220.70843	221.153	219.789	217.806	216.423	215.705	215.471	212.5	211.8			47.5
Italy	173.5273	172.719	172.566	174.856	177.171	181.292	187.893	194.6	202.6			45.3

Germany

												women
	2009	2010	2011	2012	2013	2014	2015	2016	2017	2018	2019	2019 (%)
Turkey	1688.37	1658.083	1629.48	1607.161	1575.717	1549.808	1527.118	1506.113	1492.58	1483.515	1476.41	48.4
Poland	393.848	398.513	419.435	468.481	532.375	609.855	674.152	740.962	783.085	866.855	860.145	45.8
Syria	28.459	28.921	30.133	32.878	40.444	56.901	118.196	366.556	637.845	698.95	745.645	39.9
Romania	94.326	104.98	126.536	159.222	205.026	267.398	355.343	452.718	533.66	622.78	696.275	42.5
Italy	523.162	517.474	517.546	520.159	529.417	552.943	574.53	596.127	611.45	643.065	643.53	41.8

United Kingdom

												women
	2009	2010	2011	2012	2013	2014	2015	2016	2017	2018	2019	2018 (%)
Poland	549	550	658	713	679	826	855	1006	994	829		52.2
Romania	52	72	79	117	148	165	219	324	382	478		45.4
India	293	354	332	359.819	336	354	379	347	317	370		53.8
Ireland	344	344	386	356	345	309	329	330	343	350		56.3
Italy	107	117	153	125	138	182	212	262	296	311		42.1

SOURCE: OECD Migration Database.

by immigration in Germany's population. Were it not for immigration, Germany's population would have been decreasing since the early to middle 1970s.

It is also worth noting that the distinction of decreasing population goes first to Germany and not Japan. Figure 2.13a documents the negligible or minor contribution of immigration to population change in Japan: the contrast between Figure 2.13a and 2.13b is evident.

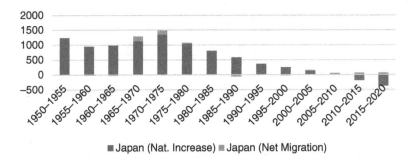

Figure 2.13a   Japan: net migration and natural increase (thousands).

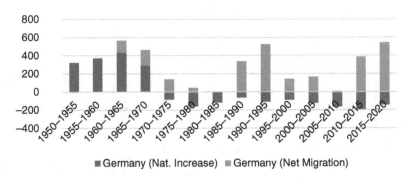

Figure 2.13b   Germany: net migration and natural increase (thousands).
SOURCE: UN Population Division.

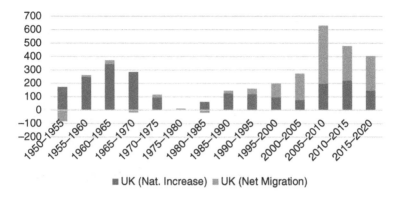

Figure 2.13c UK: net migration and natural increase (thousands).
SOURCE: UN Population Division.

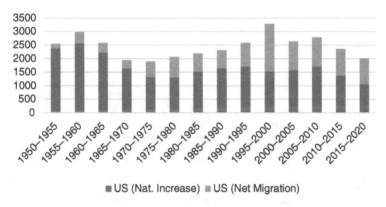

Figure 2.13d US: net migration and natural increase (thousands).
SOURCE: UN Population Division.

Figures 2.13c and 2.13d illustrate the similar patterns and importance of immigration to population change in France and Canada.

Figure 2.14 presents the permanent migration flows into OECD countries from 2001 to 2019, where the average of 2010–2018 is represented by a diamond next to the bar for 2019. 2020 is an abnormal year, and data on full-year flows have not yet been formally released.

To understand the impact of foreign-born populations in OECD countries and the Euro area, Figure 2.15 shows the evolution over

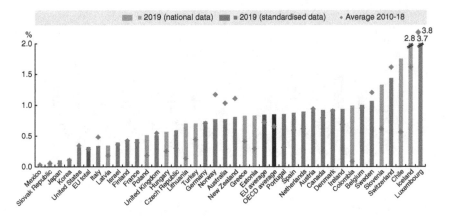

Figure 2.14   Permanent migration flows into OECD countries: 2019 (percentage of population).

SOURCE: OECD *International Migration Outlook 2020.*

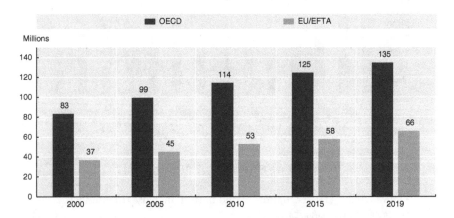

Figure 2.15   Foreign-born population in OECD and Europe: 2000–2019.

SOURCE: OECD *Migration Outlook Database.*

time. Despite recent discussions of deglobalisation, the integration and admission of foreign-born nationals into the area shows a significant uptrend. There are many forces within Italy, France, the UK, and the US that determine their political stances and decisions regarding limits on immigration and restrictions on immigrants.

A growing number of international students are coming to OECD countries to pursue tertiary education and beyond, especially a noticeable share of foreign students in masters and PhD programmes. The flow of human capital and knowledge gains, as well as skills acquired, contributes to boosting endogenous growth in many emigrant countries when the foreign-trained students return or sponsor students as well as higher learning institutions in their countries of origin.

Although immigration into many OECD countries has been the norm and widely prevalent since the 1970s, there are still differences between the native-born and foreign-born populations in their employment rates and participation rates, as shown in Table 2.4.

Further, it is important to note that as with other demographic trends, it is neither uniform nor consistent across the advanced countries—while directionally, France and Germany look similar in terms of employment rates and participation rates, they are different from Italy, where participation rates for foreign-born workers are higher than those of the native-born. This is also true of the US, where foreign-born participation rates exceed those of the native-born.

Immigration is a complex, sensitive issue and a function of attitudes, political party views, skills gaps, extent of openness, and the degree of globalisation or regionalisation. The movement of people and potential workers has implications for the GDP produced by both source nations and host nations. As discussed earlier, the causes of immigration vary.

Table 2.4 Native-born and foreign-born (employment and participation).

Year	2019			
Unit	Percentage			
Rate	Employment rate		Participation rate	
Gender	Total		Total	
Place of birth	Foreign-born	Native-born	Foreign-born	Native-born
France	58.9	66.6	67.8	72.3
Germany	70.8	78.2	75	80.3
Italy	61.4	58.7	70.7	64.9
UK	74.7	75.3	78	78.2
US	72.2	69.8	74.6	72.7

Notes: Employment rate is defined as the ratio of the employed to the working-age population. Labour participation rates are defined as the labour force divided by the total working-age population. SOURCE: OECD Migration Database.

2.4   Urbanisation

Similar to *migration*, which refers to the movement of people from one country (source) to another country (host) as part of different categories—work, family, accompanying family members, or free movement—*urbanisation* refers to the growth of urban areas accompanied by movement of people and resources from rural to urban areas.

Urbanisation has implications for health, education, security, fertility, family size, and nature of employment. It is related to industrialisation or the move away from agriculture towards manufacturing. Urbanisation has gathered pace and rapid momentum in both advanced and emerging economies: the pace of urbanisation and growth of cities in developing countries has indeed been faster than in advanced countries.

Urbanisation has implications for density, quality of life, crime, and environment as well as climate. Planning for the growth and development of urban areas and modern cities is a challenge for policymakers, architects, and urban planners as citizens' or residents' needs for work, consumption, technology, and leisure undergo changes. Lifestyle changes and regulation of design, as well as sprawl of cities and urban areas, tend to define the limits of urbanisation as well as its quality. For most of human history, people across the world primarily lived in small rural communities. Over the last few centuries, and especially in recent decades, there has been a dramatic shift of people from rural to urban areas.

According to the UN, since 2007/2008, more people have lived in urban areas than rural areas. While it is true that there are more urban residents than rural; there are some disagreements regarding the definition of *urban areas*. In the future, the trend of urbanisation is expected to continue as resources and people move away from agriculture towards manufacturing and services. A better understanding of urbanisation necessitates a proper understanding of the growth and development of cities, urbanisation rates, and the distribution and density of people.

The allocation of national resources from housing and transport access to healthcare, education, and employment opportunities is largely dependent on where people live. The UN defines *urbanisation* in the 2018 World Urbanization Prospects as follows: "a complex socio-economic process that transforms the built environment, converting formerly rural into urban settlements, while also shifting the spatial distribution of a population from rural to urban areas. It includes changes in dominant occupations, lifestyle, culture and behaviour, and thus alters the demographic and social structure of both urban and rural areas." The consequences of urbanisation are an increase in the share of urban areas and a relative decline in rural areas, accompanied by the movement of people.

The rapid and unprecedented pace of urbanisation in emerging and frontier economies has resulted in new and different population movements within domestic borders. The associated implications of population movements, temporary or permanent, have a bearing on labour markets, economic growth, and sectoral shifts from agriculture to manufacturing and services. Figure 2.16a illustrates the trends in urbanisation in the world and developed and developing regions.

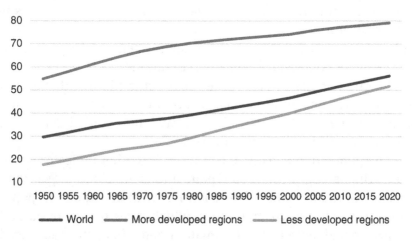

Figure 2.16a   Share of urban population (%).

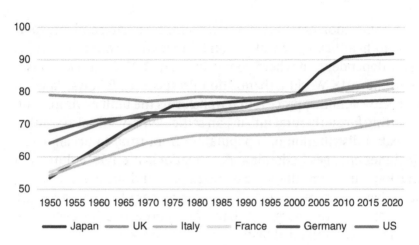

Figure 2.16b   Share of urban population (G6).
SOURCE: UN Population Division.

Even less developed regions of the world are experiencing rapid urbanisation, with more than half their population residing in urban areas. While urbanisation comes with the benefits of scale applied to good quality infrastructure, health, education, and public and social services beyond a certain limit, it can lead to diseconomies of various kinds, such as noise, air, and water pollution combined with crime and antisocial activities. Population density is an indicator that correlates positively with some of the ill effects of rapid urbanisation. Shortages of land, water, and air per person become very noticeable under such conditions.

Figure 2.16b is the analogous representation of urbanisation across the regions in the advanced countries of the world (the G6); it depicts the fact that urbanisation rates have varied across the countries, with Japan leading the rest.

The population density of countries is another indicator worth comparing along with urban populations in cities larger than 500,000. Germany is one of the countries with the bulk of its population in smaller towns and cities, which gives it a more natural ecosystem and makes it more climate-friendly than other advanced countries. Looking at the share of the population in megacities and large cities provides an indicator of unsustainable pressures on those cities.

The contrast in population densities is evident across the developed countries in Figure 2.17, and this has implications for land per person and also space to build residences, industries, parks, warehousing, airports, train stations, car parks, etc. Japan is the densest, as shown in the figure. Further, Japan's urban population[21] resides in 2 cities of more than 10 million people, 2 cities of 5–10 million, 4 cities of 1–5 million, 6 cities of 0.5–1 million, and 19 cities of 0.3–0.5 million. We shall return to this issue in the context of the comparative analysis of the UN's Sustainable Development Goals.

High-density populations can also fall victim to natural disasters such as earthquakes, floods, cyclones, and tsunamis as well as human-made ones such as the 2011 Fukushima reactor disaster or Chernobyl in 1986. They also have the proclivity for faster spread of infectious diseases.

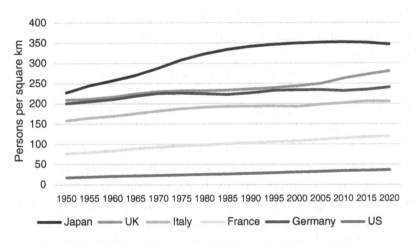

Figure 2.17   Population density.
SOURCE: UN Population Division.

2.5   Small Nation-States: Demographics

Thus far, the focus has been on large, advanced, ageing countries. What about smaller, affluent and well-educated countries like the Nordics countries, vs. smaller city-states in Asia like Hong Kong, Singapore, and New Zealand or the smaller nations within the UAE or Middle East?

Countries and regions like Denmark, Hong Kong, New Zealand, Norway, Oman, Singapore, and Switzerland share certain common demographic features: smaller size, increasing life expectancies, high education levels, good social welfare, and a good mix of natives and foreigners. Despite these shared features, there exist significant differences due to the education, health, welfare, labour, technology, and financial markets in these countries. As I asserted at the beginning of this book, it all boils down to people's characteristics (consumers and workers): they behave very differently in different settings and environments. The political systems and institutional structures also condition and influence the behaviour of consumers and workers.

The identities of these small, advanced nation-states are as different as those of the states in the US, as highlighted by Huntington in his book *Who are We?*

He explores the identity of people which is based on common values, histories, and experiences. Trust, confidence, politics, and institutions influence macroeconomics, but they also fundamentally affect people's behaviour.

As shown in Table 2.5, the small nation-states (which are smaller in size and area than large cities) have very diverse demographics in terms of their fertility rates, population growth rates (most of them are growing more slowly than the world average), life expectancies, and old-age burdens. The point that we made at the beginning of this chapter is worth reiterating: countries should not just be grouped based on a single characteristic; their underlying heterogeneity must be understood due to the nature of institutions, culture, politics, and policies that exist within those countries.

Table 2.5   Small countries' demographic differences.

	Total Popu-lation (thou-sands)	Annual avg. popula-tion growth rate (%)	Median age (years)	Total fertility (chil-dren per woman)	Old-age depend-ency ratio (popula-tion aged 65+ per 100 of age 20–64)	Net migra-tion rate (per 1,000)	Life expec-tancy at birth (years)
	2020	2015–2020	2020	2015–2020	2020	2015–2020	2015–2020
Oman	5107	3.59	30.6	2.93	3.5	18.6	77.53
Hong Kong SAR	7497	0.85	44.8	1.33	27.8	4.0	84.64
Singapore	5850	0.90	42.2	1.21	19.1	4.7	83.39
New Zealand	4822	0.88	38.0	1.90	28.3	3.2	82.07
Denmark	5792	0.36	42.3	1.76	34.9	2.6	80.68
Norway	5421	0.83	39.8	1.68	29.6	5.3	82.18
Switzerland	8655	0.84	43.1	1.54	31.3	6.1	83.56

SOURCE: UN Population Division.

2.6   Changing Longevity—Metrics Need Changing

One of the most uncontroversial demographic changes over the last seven decades has been the increase in life expectancy. Although life expectancies have increased in all regions and countries of the world, the rate of increase has differed. In order to properly address the ageing issue in the developed world, it is more important to focus on conditional life expectancy at older ages: for example, the life expectancy in years of an average Italian, Japanese, or Swede at age 65 or 80 (Figure 2.18).

The importance is underscored by the fact that in advanced countries, many people are working for half or less than half of their lives, with non-working retirement spans increasing as a share of life spans. Old retirees cost the government or the state much more than they once did due to morbidity and healthcare costs as well as long-term costs.

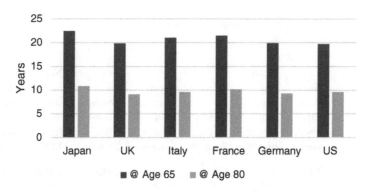

Figure 2.18 Life expectancy at ages 65 and 80.
SOURCE: UN Population Division.

As I argued earlier, the focus of individuals, firms, and governments should be on ageing well first for the 65–79 year age group followed by the 80–89 and 90–99 age groups and only then for centenarians. Focusing on the hype of people living beyond 100 years is like focusing policy on people with a net worth of more than USD $750 million. Those people are fortunate in terms of longevity and resources but are a minuscule fraction of the world's population; therefore, attention towards them ought to be proportionate in a world facing ageing problems.

There has been extensive debate regarding extensions of longevity in the future—will human life expectancy in advanced countries extend to 120 years by 2070, or will it taper off? There are two camps of longevity experts: those who use extrapolations and project that the recent history of life expectancy increases can be extended linearly into the future, and others who believe that most of the mortality improvements driving longevity increases have already been fully exploited and that therefore longevity increases have plateaued and may decrease in the future. In a Watson Wyatt[22] series of longevity lectures, James Vaupel argued in favour of rapid and further projections of longevity, whereas Jay Olshansky argued that most biomedical advances had already occurred, so life expectancy would taper. A survey of realistic projections of longevity by Carnes and Olshansky (2007)[23] tries to moderate the discussion away from fanciful longevity optimists.

2.7   Changing Social and Individual Behaviour

There are forces at the individual, family, and societal levels that have modified consumer and worker behaviour through changes in the mean age at first marriage and mean age at childbirth. These have profound implications for female labour force availability and participation rates. The UN mean age for women at first marriage has different periods and methods for observations for marriage data, and therefore I present data using national sources from the UK and the US to illustrate the fact that age at first marriage is increasing. I complement that data with data from Eurostat for European countries from 2007 to 2018. France reported male mean age at first marriage at 35.2 years (2018), up from 32.2 years (2007); Germany reported male mean age at first marriage at 34 years (2017), up from 32 years (2007); and Italy reported 35.2 years (2018) vs. 34.6 years (2007).

Figure 2.19 records the secular uptrend in mean age at marriage for England and Wales using ONS data.

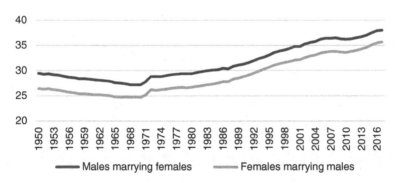

Figure 2.19   Mean age at first marriage (years): England and Wales.
SOURCE: ONS.

A similar uptrend is discernible in the data for median age at first marriage in the US using US Census data, as displayed in Figure 2.20.

Both men and women are getting married later, their marriage rates are lower over the last few decades. Figure 2.21 shows the increasing age at first childbirth for women across the G6 countries. This has major implications for family structure, the number of children per woman, as discussed earlier, and the demographic dividend. One of the consequences of higher female education and employment rates is that women have realised the opportunities and choices available to them and also the costs of child-rearing in terms of both money and time. The decision to have fewer children has more to do with education, child-rearing costs, and the desire to provide a better quality of life for their children. This is a common trend across all countries, rich or poor, and transcends religious beliefs and social norms. Declining fertility rates are one of the main features of stages in the demographic transition model discussed earlier. Getting married later and having children later is a contributing factor to lower fertility rates in the context of the typical age range of childbearing. We discuss this in Chapter 3 in the context of the demographic dividend, one of the important theories

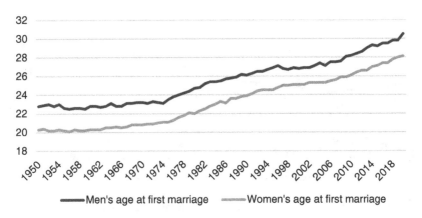

Figure 2.20   US median age at first marriage (years): 1950–2020.
SOURCE: US Census Bureau.

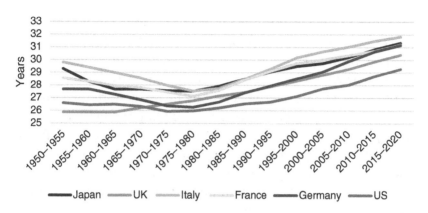

Figure 2.21 Mean age of childbearing (G6).
SOURCE: UN Population Division.

explaining the economic progress of countries through the influence of demographics.

This is another factor pertinent to women that affects family life and, in particular, life cycles of work and consumption. Women are having children later in life, and that explains part of the lower fertility rates globally—women having children later partly due to higher education and starting careers but also correlated with later first marriage rates and lower marriage rates.

2.8 Multiple Generations

One of the key features of modern societies and countries since the 1970s, in particular—but most evident in the 1990s and 2000s—is the co-existence of multiple generations. The existence of a toddler with a parent in their 20s, grandparents in their 40s or early 50s, great-grandparents in their early 70s, and sometimes great-great-grandparents in their 90s has been historically unprecedented. The traditional focus of demographers, economists, and sociologists has largely been constrained to three generations, but the existence of four or five generations of a family with only one prime earning generation is a novelty. The need to focus on looking at two generations of co-existing retirees from the same family is important, as the health, consumption, income, and wealth of two generations of retirees (those in their 60s with parents in their 80s, or those in their 70s with parents in their 90s) are very different.

Robert Fogel[24] studied generations of US cohorts in terms of their living standards, health, and consumption in the Early Indicators project going back to the days of slavery in the US. He found that the federal pension system records constituted a very promising data source that might be used to answer a wide range of questions regarding health, migration, and labour force participation for a large population segment from the mid-nineteenth century through the first quarter of the twentieth century. Larry Wimmer described the records used in the project as follows: "These records provide us with an important benchmark on infectious and chronic diseases before our modern understanding of germ theory, before widespread public health programs, and before the introduction of modern intervention into disease treatment—a benchmark against which to judge the enormous improvements in medicine and life expectancy taken for granted in the twentieth century." The data reveals much about labour force participation among an ageing population a generation before the introduction of Social Security and other pension programmes.

The classification of various generations within the US and understanding differences in attitudes has also been done by the Pew Research Center[25]. Using age-cohort analysis of generations gives researchers a tool to analyse changes in views over time and provides a way to understand how experiences interact with the life cycle process to shape people's views of the world. Age cohorts allow researchers to go further and examine how today's older adults felt about a given issue when they themselves were young. The typical US population generations have been classified based on their birth years as follows: the Greatest Generation (before 1928), the Silent Generation (1928–45), the Baby Boomer generation (1946–64), Generation X (1965–80), the Millennial generation (1981–96), and Generation Z (1997–2012). The Baby Boomer generation is classified differently in Europe and Japan than in the US, as they had baby booms at different times. We discuss these generations in later chapters, highlighting once again that while age is a determinant of attitudes and behaviour, it is not the only determinant.

A recent *Harvard Business Review* article[26] documents that generational differences at work are not as significant as conjectured by many commentators and the press. They found that most of the evidence for generational differences in preferences and values suggests that differences between these groups are quite small. Actually, there exists a considerable variety of preferences and values within these groups. They found that, although individual people may experience changes in their needs, interests, preferences, and strengths over the course of their careers, sweeping group differences depending on age or generation alone don't seem to be supported.

So what might really matter at work are not actual differences between generations, but people's beliefs that these differences exist. These beliefs can get in the way of how people collaborate with their colleagues and have troubling implications for how people are managed and trained. They state that their research suggests that workplaces are brimming with age-related stereotypes and meta-stereotypes and that these beliefs are not always accurate or aligned.

2.9   Conclusion

This chapter highlighted demographic trends and presented core demographic indicators, using the UN Population Division as the primary critical standardised source. A historical perspective of the trends from 1950 onwards was used to provide context for the world, selected regions, and advanced countries. The important topics pertinent to the movement of people within a country and across a country—immigration and urbanisation—were discussed. The point regarding heterogeneous demographics of countries both small and large was made. The importance of conditional life expectancy and the theory of demographic transition was high-lighted to place countries in different stages on a combination of certain key demographic variables.

In addition to stressing the point that similar-sized or similar-looking countries have different underlying demographic features, it is important to mention that countries are in different stages of demographic transition. The stages of demographic transition are also somewhat related to stages of economic development, which is broader than just economic growth. Very young African countries are in stage 1 or 2, with Japan and Germany in stage 5 and experiencing shrinking and very old populations.

Longer, healthier lives should be the focus for individuals, families, and society. We are living in historically unprecedented times of greater longevity combined with a feature that may not be repeated in the future: the existence of four to five generations of a family. Behaviour is very important to understand as consumers and workers evolve and adapt to changes in the macro-environment.

Chapter 3
Demographics and Macroeconomics

As an applied economist with training in macroeconomics and asset pricing, my endeavour in the real world has been to connect theories, models, and subjects and, wherever possible, put them to the test with data. As I had illustrated with a lot of data in the previous chapter, my focus has been to test stories, anecdotes, and hype, putting them to the test of data and consistency. In a world of quick propagation of news, trends, and views, I believe that it is very important for us to focus on testing whatever we can against data and provide evidence for our views and priors. This chapter is about explicit linkages between demographics and economic growth, inflation, and unemployment and, more particularly, the role of fiscal and monetary policy in an ageing world.

When I started my research on demographics in the early 2000s, I was advised to read many popular books on ageing by well-known authors who were followed by investors and analysts. I read many such books with very well-argued near convincing theories based on past trends using casual extrapolations and portending to be more like futurists. Catchy phrases like "Demographics Is Destiny", "Age Quake", "Population Time-Bomb", "Demographics Time-Bomb",

"Looming Disaster", etc. dominated a lot of the mainstream demographic discussions. I tried to stay strong to my training, my bias toward data and testing of theories and Peter Drucker's warning of "people missing the point". This chapter presents a macroeconomist's perspective of demographics.

3.1   Demographics and Economic Growth

I discuss the impact of demographics and economic growth, first focusing on the contribution of demographic-based factors to GDP growth trends. *Gross domestic product* (GDP) is the summary measure of aggregate economic activity, and its nominal version presents the value (over a specified period) of all goods and services produced domestically. Real *GDP* is the inflation-adjusted counterpart used to understand the physical aggregate of economic activity by taking away the value change due to price effects.

In this chapter, I discuss a GDP framework that I have been using[1,2] and presenting for nearly 15 years to global institutional investors. It uses a national accounting framework of GDP set out by the European Central Bank. Essentially, the three components that add up to give GDP growth are working-age population growth, labour force productivity growth, and labour force utilisation growth. This is an *identity*, meaning that these three components must add up exactly to give GDP growth as per an accounting decomposition of real GDP:

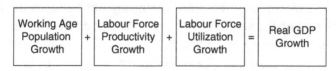

The technical details are presented in the papers listed. This framework accounts for worker numbers, their productivity, and their annual hours worked in contributing to real GDP growth. Intuitively, real GDP growth depends on growth in the number of workers in the labour force, their growth in labour productivity, and their growth in hours worked. The role of technology, capital-labour ratio, human capital, skills, and labour intensity in terms of hours worked are all relevant and incorporated in this approach. This is part of a growth accounting framework that allows for an explicit understanding of the relative contribution of the factors to growth.

The figures that follow provide a rich decomposition analysis based on decades of how and which factors contributed to the GDP growth of the G6 countries (France, Germany, Italy, Japan, the UK, and the US). This allows me to again demonstrate the heterogeneity of demographics and its contribution to the different growth patterns across the advanced countries. One of the major lessons I wish to share is that it is misleading to lump advanced, rich countries into generalised groups while ignoring or disregarding their structural and institutional differences. That is also why former Japanese Prime Minister Abe stressed the role of structural reforms in helping Japan come out of its "lost decades"[3]. Figure 3.1a and Figure 3.1b provide valuable insights into the relative dynamics of factors underlying Franco-German economic growth.

These figures present seven decades of GDP decomposition for France and Germany. Of the G6 countries, I choose to compare and contrast France and Germany, then Italy and Japan, and finally the

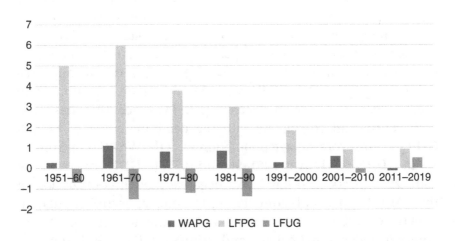

Figure 3.1a France GDP growth decomposition: 1951–2019. Annual percentages.

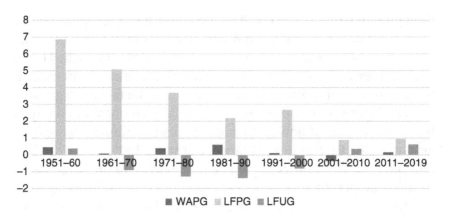

Figure 3.1b   Germany GDP growth decomposition: 1951–2019. Annual percentages.
SOURCE: UN, GGDC.

UK and the US. The reasons are mainly demographic and follow Chapter 2, where we saw that Japan and Italy are the oldest countries based on old-age dependency ratios (OADRs). The US and the UK are open economies with common features of immigration and economic structure as well as open capital markets. France and Germany are the largest European economies, with features and policies that set the stage for the rest of the EU's 25 countries to follow.

Examining the French economic growth pattern, average annual growth rate patterns over seven decades exhibited a decline from 1951–2019 as follows: 4.6, 5.6, 3.39, 2.49, 2.11, 1.26, and 1.32%, respectively. From Figure 3.1a it can be inferred that labour force productivity growth (LFPG) was the dominant contributor to French economic growth. Declining LFPG since 1961 has been both causal and coincident with the declining trend of French GDP growth. Working-age population growth (WAPG) contributed 1% to GDP growth over 1961–90 and 0.5% to GDP growth in the 2001–2010 period and has had a negative growth contribution in the latest decade. As highlighted in Chapter 2, overall population growth depends on natural growth and net migration, covering both domestic and external policies and attitudes. LFPG is influenced by advances in higher education rates, skills training, technology, and the structure of the economy: i.e. the share of sectors (agriculture, manufacturing, and services) in the GDP and labour force.

On examining the growth pattern of Germany in Figure 3.2b it can be noted that, similar to France, its labour productivity growth declined sharply. The German decade-wise GDP growth annualized averages over seven decades from 1951 onwards are 7.74, 4.22, 2.76, 1.37, 1.93, 0.89, and 1.72% respectively. However, the decline in LFPG started in the 1950s, whereas in France, LFPG began to decline in the 1960s. In terms of WAPG, the contribution to economic growth has been much lower than in France (comparing the two figures) but slightly positive. Labour force utilisation growth (LFUG) was a negative contributor to growth over 1961–2000, implying that the average hours of work did not grow. The relative contribution of LFPG is more dominant in the German case and reflects technology, human capital, education, and the larger share of manufacturing within the economy.

Figure 3.2a presents the Italian decomposition of growth over 1951–2019. Italian decade-wise annual average growth over the seven decades since 1951 has been 6.01, 5.89, 3.62, 2.22, 1.69, 0.32,

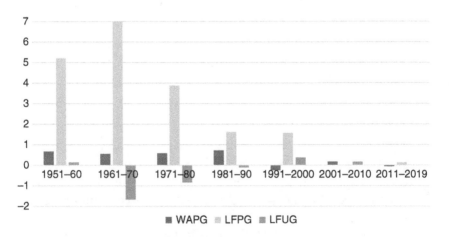

Figure 3.2a   Italy GDP growth decomposition: 1951–2019. Annual percentages.
SOURCE: UN, GGDC.

and 0.07% per annum (p.a.) respectively. Its LFPG exhibits a decline similar to that of France, but with a difference: it has been nearly missing in its contribution to economic growth—almost negligible, to be precise. Over 1951–1980, the LFPG was above 5.5% on average; but since the 1980s, it was near 1.5% over two decades and then nearly zero in this millennium. As in the German case, Italy's WAPG was close to 0.5% p.a. over 1951–1990. Its LFUG has been very low and also negative over the latest two decades. An important conclusion regarding Italy's growth experience over the last two decades could be the near non-contribution of all the factors of growth: WAPG, LFPG, and LFUG. This is similar to the Japanese experience of decades of negative growth.

The first comparison of Japan with Italy in Figure 3.2b is that the last two decades have seen low growth following the much higher growth period of 1951–1980. The Japanese annual average growth numbers over seven decades since 1951 are 8.67, 10.34, 4.61, 5, 2.15, 1.24, and 1.19% p.a. The Japanese growth numbers on average are higher than Italy's over the last three decades, which have been classified by several experts as its "lost decades". Figure 3.3 demonstrates the high but declining contribution of LFPG to real GDP growth in Japan. WAPG in Japan has trended downward from 2% p.a. in the 1950s and 1960s to −1% p.a. over 2011–2019. LFUG,

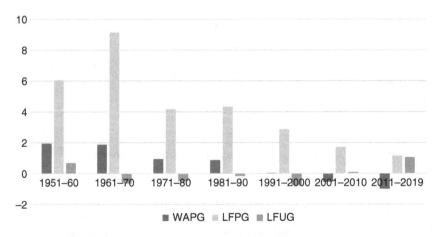

Figure 3.2b   Japan GDP growth decomposition (1951–2019). Annual percentages.
SOURCE: UN, GGDC.

which reflects growth in average hours worked, has been almost a non-factor in terms of contributing to growth.

Figure 3.3a illustrates the growth decomposition for the UK over 1951–2019. The annualized average growth rates over the last seven decades were 2.68, 2.87, 2.21, 2.92, 2.5, 1.66, and 1.84% p.a. respectively. The importance of LFPG and its declining trend over 1951–2019 is noticeable. WAPG has made a small and declining contribution to economic growth, but it has turned negative over the last two decades; it is at levels close to one-fourth or one-fifth of some prior decades. LFUG has made a very small contribution to GDP growth, trending close to zero and negative over six decades but making the highest contribution to GDP growth between 2011 and 2019. This is an exceptional feature of the recent UK GDP growth contributors relative to the other countries. In common with Germany and France, the UK has all three contributors positively growing and adding up to the last decade's average annual GDP growth of 1.84%.

Figure 3.3b presents the contributing factors and their evolution over 1951–2019 for the US. The most distinguishing feature of the US growth contributors is that all three factors have been mostly positive over the last seven decades. Both LFPG and WAPG have declined from their levels in the 1960s and 1970s. LFUG, however, has been the dominant contributing factor to GDP growth in the

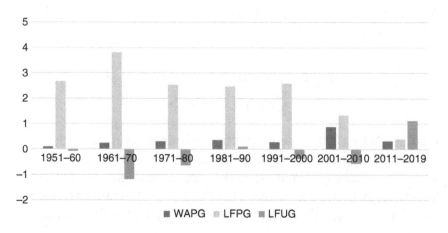

Figure 3.3a UK GDP growth decomposition: 1951–2019. Annual percentages.

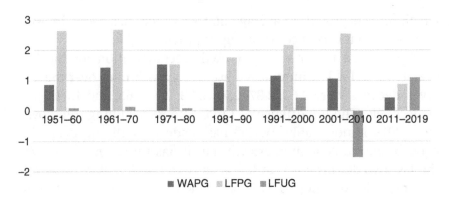

Figure 3.3b   US GDP growth decomposition: 1951–2019. Annual percentages.
SOURCE: UN, GGDC.

US for the last decade, similar to the UK experience. It is a feature of the country's dynamic labour markets that hours worked growth could make a positive and dominant contribution to growth in the past decade. Relative to the other countries, the US has experienced the most stable growth, on an annualised basis, of all the G6 countries. In terms of growth over seven decades starting from 1951, the annualized growth rates were 3.57, 4.22, 3.13, 3.49, 3.74, 2.07, and 2.41% p.a. respectively.

This section has focused on the underlying dynamics of growth over seven decades for the G6 advanced countries. Detailing how demographics affect GDP growth was relevant before discussing GDP per capita growth.

3.2   The "Demographic Dividend" and GDP per Capita Growth

GDP measures aggregate production within a country, while GDP per capita measures living standards. GDP growth indicates how fast the economy expands, GDP per capita growth indicates advances in living standards. People's living standards are calculated by dividing GDP by population size. GDP growth is related to underlying factors; population growth, which is needed to deflate or adjust GDP growth to arrive at GDP per capita growth, is one of the most important core demographic indicators discussed in Chapters 1 and 2.

Many of the most populous countries are also large economies. For example, China and India, with population sizes of 1.4 bn+ and 1.3 bn+, have the second and sixth largest economies, respectively, by GDP. When their GDP levels are divided by their huge population sizes, their GDP per capita is much lower than that of smaller, advanced economies and city-states. It is misleading to infer the affluence of a nation's citizens by the level of its GDP. Instead, it is important to focus on living standards: GDP per capita.

The *demographic dividend*[4,5] theory was articulated by David Bloom and his co-authors in reports on the importance of the population age structure for economic growth. They concluded that the age structure, more than population size or population growth, affects economic development. They stated that reducing high fertility can create opportunities for economic growth if the right kinds of educational, health, and labour-market policies are in place. In research on ageing, Jay Olshansky highlighted characteristics of fertility, mortality, and migration and how these components of population change influence, and are influenced by, the physical and social environments in which people live[6]. This focus on age structure is related to the ageing indicators discussed in Chapter 2: median age, dependency ratios, and (visually) the population pyramids. The United Nations Family Planning Agency (UNFPA) classifies countries with demographic opportunity as those entering a period in which the working-age population has good health, quality education, decent employment, and a lower proportion of young dependents. Smaller numbers of children per household lead to more significant investments per child, more freedom for women to enter the formal workforce, and more household savings for old age. The national economic payoff is a *demographic dividend*.

Ronald Lee and Andrew Mason[7] extend the discussion to per capita income, stating that the first dividend phase could last five decades. They suggest that in this first dividend phase, the labour

force temporarily grows more rapidly than the dependent population, freeing up resources for investment in economic development
and family welfare. Other things being equal, per capita income
also grows more rapidly.

If a country's population has a greater share who are of working age, the productivity of the working-age population can yield
a demographic dividend of economic growth if policies to exploit
this opportunity are in place. A combination of the working-age
population alongside health, labour, human capital, savings, and
investment policies can help create the potential for wealth or the
demographic dividend. The existence of policies to help capture
the demographic dividend is essential. I have argued that Asia captured more of the demographic dividend than Latin America due to
a good confluence of such policies. Further, I believe Africa could
do similarly or even better if health advances at younger ages and
political stability improved. The window of opportunity for the
demographic dividend has passed some countries by, according to
Mason et al.[8], who assess the potential for a second demographic dividend for ageing developed countries. They infer that age-specific economic outcomes vary across countries, reflecting culture, behaviour,
and public policy, among other factors. Thus, the economic effects of
changing age structure vary across countries and are influenced by
public policies in response to the opportunities and challenges.

Changes in population age structure lead to changes between the
number of people who are producing and the number who are consuming. Countries with very young or very old populations have *few
producers relative to the number of consumers*. However, during the
transition between a young and an old population, countries enjoy
age structures with heavy concentrations in the high-producing
ages. This is the underlying basis of the first demographic dividend.
Mason[9] provides estimates and periods of demographic dividends
for different regions of the world as follows (start year, period in
years): industrial countries (1970, 29.7 years). Eastern and South-
east Asia (1977, 46.6 years), South Asia (1983, 60.7 years), Latin
America (1974, 47.9 years), Sub-Saharan Africa (1995, 49.7 years),

the Middle East and North Africa (1978, 52.3 years), and the Pacific Islands (1975, 48.6 years).

Mason et al.[8] create a framework based on the effective number of consumers and workers to connect their life cycles to income growth and the demographic dividend. They found that the first dividend is realised when the support ratio (the number of effective workers per effective consumer) increases and is quantified by the percentage increase in the support ratio. Other things being equal, a one-percentage-point increase in the support ratio produces a one-percentage-point increase in income per equivalent consumer. The size and duration of the first dividend depend on various factors, including those that influence age structure and those that influence the life-cycle profiles of labour income and consumption. Based on the analysis by Mason et al., the first dividend phase began for the world in 1973 and will end in 2025. During this period, the increase in the support ratio adds about 0.3 to 0.5 percentage points per year to growth in income per equivalent consumer.

This framework is parallel to that in Section 3.1, where demographic components contribute to GDP growth. This section extends it to the demographic transition, as also shown in Figure 3.1. The demographic transition directly explains that GDP growth coincides with lower population (low fertility rates) and also explains the growth in GDP per capita growth or living standards. The realisation of the dividend requires holistic policies in education, human capital, and investments.

Galor[10] studies the demographic transitions of countries, focusing on the effect of lower fertility rates on lower population growth and higher income per capita growth. The study finds that historical evidence does not support that the decline in mortality accounts for the reversal of the positive historical trend between income and fertility or the decline in population growth (i.e. fertility net of mortality). He asserts that increases in the rate of technological progress induced a reduction in fertility, generating a decline in population growth and an increase in the average level of education. Further, increases in the rate of technological progress induced a reduction in fertility, generating a decline in population growth and an increase in the average level of education.

Developing a unified theory of growth[10] consistent with endogenous growth theory, Galor argues that the rise in demand for human capital and impact on process of formation of human capital triggered reductions in fertility rates and population growth and fostered technological advances. He stresses that the demographic transition allowed economies to divert a larger share of factor accumulation and technological progress from increasing population growth toward human capital formation and income per capita. Dekle[11] studied the link between Japanese demographic change and the savings-investments balance, highlighting the impact on living standards (GDP per capita). He projected an increase in GDP per capita until 2010, despite ageing, and mostly declines thereafter.

3.3   Inflation

Consumers and workers dominate my perspective of demographics, and they contribute to the demand and supply sides of inflation. Pressures of excess consumer demand lead to demand-side inflation. Likewise, supply-side shortages and increasing worker costs or input costs such as oil lead to supply-side or cost-push inflation. Inflation has been a significant issue in macroeconomics and refers to the increase in aggregate prices captured by indices such as the Consumer Price Index (CPI), core CPI, Personal Consumption Expenditures (PCE) price index, GDP deflator, etc. As Adam Smith and Keynes—founding fathers of economics—highlighted, both the output or level of economic activity and the level of corresponding prices matter.

A long-term study of centuries of inflation by Deutsche Bank[12] concluded that demographics and population growth were the most dominant forces to influence inflation, especially its acceleratory trends over the last three centuries. The rapid explosion of inflation post-1950 coincided with that of population. Why since 1950? The report by Jim Reid and his team suggests that it was due to a confluence of forces, ultimately underpinned by a unique explosion in the global population.

Understanding consumers and their decisions resulting in final consumer expenditures is at the heart of microeconomics and macroeconomics. Preferences toward consumption and risk-taking are closely related to demographic characteristics. In Chapter 7, we discuss utility, social welfare, and happiness in the context of consumption, income, and wealth. Nobel laureate Angus Deaton[13], in his classic *Understanding Consumption* (1992), develops a great introduction to individual preferences over goods and over time to explain consumption and risk in an individual's decision-making context. He then relates them to savings, interest rates, consumption volatility, and precautionary savings in the context of households in aggregate within the economy and across generations.

As consumers' and workers' behaviours evolve, their longer lives and changing life cycles have profound implications for individual and aggregate demand for consumption and, ultimately, GDP. Over a decade ago, I explored this from the angle of both a consumer and a worker in "Longer Lives, Changing Life Cycles: Exploring Consumer and Worker Implications"[14], highlighting that economic and financial research has paid little attention to changing consumer and worker psychology in aggregate macro models. Life-cycle changes have accompanied unprecedented life-expectancy increases. An average individual's life cycle includes earlier socialisation/learning as a toddler, more years of education through school and college, delayed marriage and parenthood, school breaks, college breaks, career breaks, multiple jobs, phased retirement, caring for children and older parents, and extended retirement periods.

We further highlight that the implications for financial markets of these changes are vast, from financial education to developing new products for savings, insurance, and investments to risk management and active asset allocation. These life-cycle changes create opportunities for new financial services products across banking, insurance, reinsurance, derivatives, and multi-strategy asset allocation. Real estate, infrastructure, hedge funds, and private equity will also have rich and varied roles to play against the background of changing consumers and workers.

Rapid inflation in parts of the world in the 1970s and 1980s led central banks toward inflation targeting and central bank independence mainly since the start of the 1990s. Given the types of inflation, demographic effects on aggregate demand shifts (due to population size, population growth, or age structure) or aggregate supply shifts (due to labour force, hours worked, or productivity) would influence inflation.

Bullard et al.[15] analysed the interaction among population demographics, the desire for intergenerational redistribution of resources in the economy, and the optimal inflation rate. They contrasted populations dominated by young cohorts versus those dominated by older cohorts. They stated that young cohorts have no assets, with wages as their primary income source, and prefer low real interest rates, relatively high wages, and relatively high rates of inflation. In contrast, they opine that older cohorts work less and prefer higher rates of return from their savings, relatively low wages, and relatively low inflation. Their model allowed the social planner to use inflation/deflation to try to achieve the optimal distortions; and changes in population structure are interpreted as the ability of a particular cohort to influence the redistributive policy. When older cohorts have more influence, the economy in a steady state has a low level of capital and a low rate of inflation. When young cohorts have more control of policy, the opposite happens. Their results suggest that ageing population structures, such as those in Japan, may contribute to observed low rates of inflation or even deflation.

In a study on ageing Japan, Yihan Liu and Niklas Westelius[16] found differential effects of ageing on productivity and inflation across prefectures (like states) in Japan. Further, looking at Eurozone ageing and numbers, Bielecki et al.[17] argued that low fertility rates and increasing life expectancy substantially lower the natural interest rate. Central banks are likely to face long periods of low inflation as they hit the lower bound on nominal interest rates if they ignore the impact of demographics on rates.

In stark contrast, Goodhart and Pradhan[18] argued that ageing will lower saving rates, increase real wages, and result in high inflation, and they thereby criticise mainstream central bankers and economists. Their thesis of a "demographic reversal" is driven by (i) increased dependency ratios leading to a larger number of effective consumers than workers driving inflation; (ii) ageing leading to lower productive labour, which will increase workers' bargaining power and real wages' share of income; and (iii) rising long-term yields on maturities of 10 years or longer, as savings are likely to decline more than investments due to young households' demand for new housing and corporates' greater investment in capital. They criticise the implicit assumption that investment will decline more than savings for the future. Few central bankers and others remain sceptical of these conclusions by them based on the slack within the economy caused by COVID unemployment (especially in emerging markets with informal labour forces); the lack of dynamism in ageing countries, which curbs investment; and the role of technology in compensating for lack of productive labour.

The above analysis ignores labour that is available but unutilised due to gender bias and the potentials of outsourcing. In "The Demographic Manifesto"[19], we argued for a policy mix of flexible working beyond fixed retirement ages; empowering women, allowing them through technology and flexible labour practices to better blend work life with home life; and selective migration based on the skills gap. We advocated the abolition of the mandatory retirement age and its replacement with a recommended retirement age. Many of these practices are being adopted by governments, the public sector, and the private sector in ageing countries like Japan, Switzerland, Sweden, Denmark, Finland, etc. The impact of potential gender equality, selective immigration, outsourcing, and technology cannot be captured by pure mechanistic exercises. This is a case of endogenous policies affecting retirement, work, consumption, savings, and education.

To fully appreciate consumer and worker impact on inflation, it is essential to understand the differences in consumer expenditure patterns and wealth across different age groups. The age structure is important as consumption and savings patterns differ across the 25–34 and 65–74 age groups, as does wealth. In "Changing Global Consumers"[20], we concluded by showing the following: (i) G6 countries' consumers accounted for 50.3% of world consumption and thus had the world's largest consumer markets. Consumers in the six major emerging countries that I focus on which are collectively called EMG6 (Brazil, China, India, Mexico, Russia, and Turkey) account for 19.6% of world consumption, and their consumption share was growing. (ii) Old people were the largest consumer group, as they were the richest age group. Consumption shares for the 50+ age group accounted for 58.1, 54.2, and 59.7% of total consumption in Japan, the US, and Germany, respectively. (iii) Young adults consumed relatively less than their corresponding cohorts born a generation or two earlier, start accumulating assets later due to more years in education, and experience high youth unemployment and high student debt levels, which put additional pressure on them. (iv) Working women are a new group of consumers, and increasing numbers were being educated, working, and becoming richer. *Understanding the age cohorts' spending, saving, wealth, and work patterns is critical relative to understanding aggregate and average consumption expenditure patterns.*

The *micro-aspects of empirical macro data* are very important for understanding disaggregated underlying behaviour. Internet usage, debt patterns, age at marriage, and age at childbirth have also changed over the last few decades. The patterns of consumption differ among Baby Boomers, Millennials, Gen X, and Gen Y. In his books *MicroTrends* and *MicroTrends Squared*[21,22], Mark Penn documents small changes across consumer patterns and behaviours across age groups, families, and society and highlights these small changes that affect markets and economies in the aggregate.

Penn builds an insightful and compelling narrative toward understanding present and future consumer trends in *MicroTrends*. He highlights emergent changes in behaviour based on changing individual relationships ("internet marrieds", "commuter couples", "cougars", "sex-ratio singles", etc.), work life (retired workers, extreme commuters, stay-at-home workers, "wordy women", and "ardent Amazons"), religion ("moderate Muslims", Protestant Hispanics, interracial families, pro-Semites, and "stained-glass-ceiling breakers"), health and wellness ("sun-haters", "30-winkers", "southpaws unbound", "DIY doctors", "hard-of-hearers"), and other topics that are a must not only for marketing and advertising companies to understand but also for central banks, economists, and investors, due to their deeper implications. He updates and expands those trends by including technology ("new addicts", "digital tailors", "techno-advanced people", "droning on and No-PCers"), health and diet ("pro-proteiners", "nonagenarians", "kids on meds", "speed eaters", "wellness freaks", cancer survivors), lifestyle ("single with pet", "roomies for life", "footloose and fancy-free", "nerds with money", "intelligent TV", "uptown stoners", "armchair preppers"), and politics ("happy pessimists", "old economy voters", "closet conservatives", "militant dreamers", "couch potato voters") as trends shaping consumer behaviour. These are the micro-foundational forces underlying the "animal spirits" discussions of Akerlof and Shiller referred to and discussed in Chapter 1.

Inflation expectations are considered an important determinant of future inflation. The current major debate influencing central bank policies and their attitudes involves factoring in inflation expectations. While there are several methods to infer inflation expectations, it is important to understand and note that inflation and other consumer attitude or risk surveys are influenced by the demographic characteristics of the survey respondents. Bryan and Venkatu of the Cleveland Fed[23] documented that people report very different perceptions and predictions of inflation depending upon their income, education, age, race, and gender—a strange finding that may provide an important clue to understanding how to interpret survey data about inflation expectations.

Juselius and Takáts[24] find a stable and significant correlation between age structure and low-frequency inflation. In particular, a larger share of dependents (i.e. young and old) is correlated with higher inflation, while a larger share of working-age cohorts is correlated with lower inflation. The results are robust to different country samples, time periods, control variables, and estimation techniques. Mojon and Ragot[25] find that an ageing workforce with higher participation rates of older workers can explain lower inflation rates. They find that the Phillips curve (the curve depicting the inverse relationship between inflation and unemployment rates) is still relevant after accounting for cross-country variation as wage inflation responds to changes in the unemployment rate.

Table 3.1 depicts consumer expenditures on different items by age group. It is worth noting that as people transition through

Table 3.1   US consumer expenditures by age: 2019 (expenditure shares).

Item	Under 25	25–34	35–44	45–54	55–64	65 and older	65–74	75 and older
Food	14.9	12.9	13.0	13.0	12.3	13.1	13.3	12.8
Alcoholic beverages	.8	.9	.7	.9	1.0	1.0	1.1	.8
Housing	32.4	35.9	33.0	30.9	30.5	34.8	34.0	36.2
Apparel and services	3.6	3.3	3.3	3.1	2.6	2.6	2.7	2.4
Transportation	21.1	18.0	18.3	17.3	16.4	14.9	15.7	13.7
Healthcare	3.8	5.5	6.4	6.9	8.6	13.6	12.3	15.8
Entertainment	3.5	4.2	4.9	5.0	5.7	4.7	4.9	4.5
Personal care products and services	1.2	1.1	1.2	1.3	1.2	1.4	1.3	1.6
Reading	.1	.1	.1	.1	.1	.3	.2	.4
Education	7.6	2.1	1.6	3.5	2.6	.7	.8	.5
Tobacco products and smoking supplies	.5	.6	.5	.5	.6	.4	.5	.3
Miscellaneous	.8	1.2	1.3	1.4	1.7	1.6	1.6	1.7
Cash contributions	1.1	1.5	2.9	2.7	3.4	5.1	4.7	5.8
Personal insurance and pensions	8.5	12.7	12.8	13.4	13.2	5.7	6.9	3.5

SOURCE: US Bureau of Labor Statistics.

different age groups, the share of expenditures on items varies considerably.

Table 3.2 provides the UK analogue showing that consumer expenditures vary by the age of the head of household.

Therefore, focusing on the aggregate or average consumer may not be representative or accurate, as age shares change based on age, and so does behaviour. Consumer expenditures influence demand-side inflation, and the age structure matters. Similar data differences exist across the Euro region and Japan. It is important to understand that changing behaviour across age groups also reflects

Table 3.2 UK household expenditures by age of household reference person. Financial year ending 2018

	Less than 30	30–49	50–64	65–74	75 or over
	Average weekly household expenditure (£)				
Food and non-alcoholic drinks	48.50	67.40	66.90	57.60	46.40
Alcoholic drinks, tobacco, and narcotics	11.10	12.30	15.30	14.50	7.10
Clothing and footwear	21.70	31.80	27.70	18.60	10.60
Housing (net, fuel, and power	135.50	91.60	65.50	52.00	46.60
Household goods and services	35.10	43.10	46.30	44.30	25.60
Health	3.60	6.20	8.00	8.30	7.50
Transport	65.40	97.20	99.30	69.20	31.00
Communication	17.60	21.50	19.20	14.40	10.50
Recreation and culture	49.80	77.80	91.00	81.30	47.60
Education	14.10	10.20	12.50	[1.30]	
Restaurants and hotels	49.30	60.30	56.50	43.30	22.70
Miscellaneous goods and services	42.60	51.20	43.00	37.10	35.40
All expenditure groups	494.50	570.60	551.10	442.20	292.70
Other expenditure items	60.50	95.70	82.00	64.70	43.40
Total expenditure	**554.90**	**666.30**	**633.10**	**506.90**	**336.10**

SOURCE: Office of National Statistics.

attitudes, psychology, and a complex of available opportunities and past experiences.

An important point to note is that in addition to age, household size has an influence on consumer expenditures. A consequence of industrialisation and urbanisation is lower fertility rates and smaller household sizes: women have fewer children, and the economics of families leads to smaller households. *Gender, education, income, and household size are a few other determinants influencing changing consumer expenditure patterns.* Mark Penn[21,22] highlights the impact of small changes in counterintuitive trends and consumer choice that build up to influence consumption, work, education, relationships, leisure, technology, and politics. He says that business and policymakers cannot ignore these sociological trends as they will soon lead to significant changes.

The supply side of inflation is affected by wage and productivity increases. Human capital, technology, and age structure all play a role in influencing the productivity of workers. Younger workers typically start with lower productivity levels but have greater labour productivity growth, whereas older workers have higher productivity levels and much lower productivity growth. In "The Demographic Manifesto"[19] and "Demographics, Productivity and Technology"[26], I advocate that higher productivity growth can be achieved by hiring younger workers and women. In addition, a better blend of younger and older workers sharing experiences and youthful dynamism could lead to higher growth rates, as the US experienced in the 1980s and 1990s compared to Europe and Japan, which had similar capital and technology. This underlies the recommendation for extended working life flexibly with the use of technology, as seen in many ageing countries. Labour force participation rates by age groups have also been increasing, with older ages as individuals and households face longer retirement periods. If the labour supply increases relative to demand, then wage pressures and the impact on inflation are likely to be lower.

Figures 3.4a and 3.4b highlight the differences in female economic activity rates across developed countries, which are a reflection of both institutional labour market features and attitudes toward working.

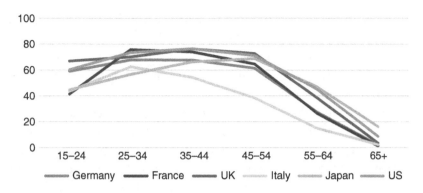

Figure 3.4a Female economic activity rates by age: 1990.

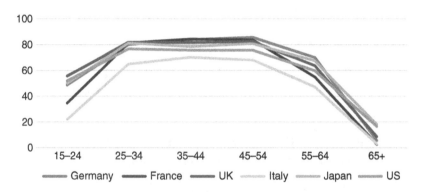

Figure 3.4b Female economic activity rates by age: 2019.
SOURCE: International Labour Organization.

Female economic activity rates tapered off between 45 and 54 years of age in 1990, but in recent times the economic activity rate drops off at age 65+. Japan sets the example with late-stage working amongst females above 65 years. The policy implication is very evident in the Sustainable Development Goals on gender equality and full utilisation of the labour force, as highlighted by the Organisation for Economic Cooperation and Development (OECD) in a series of policy publications in the 2000s: "Live Longer, Work Longer". As females outlive males and, in advanced countries, are more educated than males in terms of numbers of university graduates, empowering women to work would help fiscal sustainability, as we argue in the next section. Female labour force participation rates have increased over the last three decades alongside advances in education, greater labour market access, and fewer children they need to rear.

Similar to female economic activity rates, male economic activity rates have been extended beyond 65 years with a sharp drop off after 65 but the relative economic activity rates are lower in each age group (Figures 3.5a and 3.5b). Japan, the oldest country, leads in terms of extended male participation rates beyond 65, with more

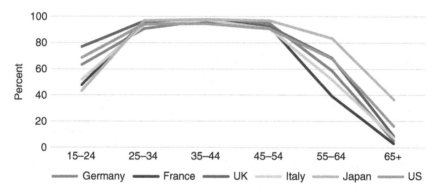

Figure 3.5a Male economic activity rates by age: 1990.

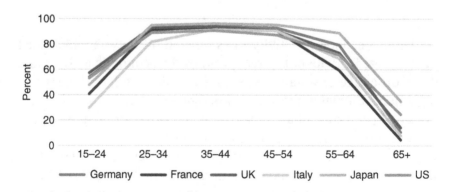

Figure 3.5b Male economic activity rates by age: 2019.

SOURCE: International Labour Organization.

than a third of the males economically active in the labour force. In contrast, Italian male economic activity rates decline very sharply, with France a close second. The policy lesson for all advanced countries is that 65 as a retirement age is not sustainable due to the enormous burden of ageing on a smaller, younger workforce that must support the retirees for 20+ years or so. Extended male working lived beyond 65 years and increases in activity rates at younger ages are essential to increase future WAPG and GDP growth. Mandatory retirement ages and long-dated retirement promises are antiquated today as they create sustainability strains and governance challenges that were not anticipated in the past.

On the supply side, wages and input costs like oil prices contribute to wage increases. But as Figure 3.6 shows, average wage increases have not been very significant over the last two decades across the major advanced countries. The smallest increases over the last five years can be observed for Japan, Italy, and France.

Wages of workers should ideally change and move in line with productivity changes. However, it is essential to note that nominal wages exhibit downward rigidity and are asymmetric in their relative moves upward relative to downward. While Figure 3.6 displays range-bound positive increases in wages ranging between 0 and 2% mainly for the advanced countries, Figure 3.7 displays declining labour

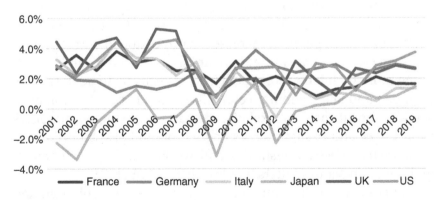

Figure 3.6 Average wage year-on-year changes (local currency basis): 2001–2019.

SOURCE: Organisation for Economic Cooperation and Development.

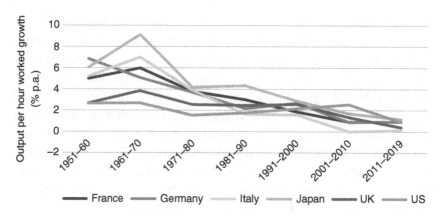

Figure 3.7   Labour productivity growth: 1951–2019.
SOURCE: Groningen Growth and Development Centre.

productivity growth per hour—as we discussed earlier, a significant contributor to declining GDP growth. This is one of the biggest challenges for advanced ageing countries. I have been advocating for more than two decades and have also discussed earlier, increasing labour participation rates of women and youth, who have higher labour productivity growth rates, is a potential policy solution that requires holistic labour market reforms.

The higher growth rates over 1970–2000 contributed to greater economic growth during that period. When labour productivity growth increases due to technology or human capital advances, all else being equal, it pushes the supply curve to the right, which is disinflationary in general. Increases in wages due to market conditions, excess demand, or wage bargaining power can result in wages rising more than labour productivity. This is likely to be in specific high-demand and trending sectors like technology, select financial services, healthcare, etc. Relative demand and supply influences from wages and inputs such as energy (oil and gas) contribute to inflationary effects. Consumers and workers influence inflation, and their behaviour matters, not just their numbers[20,27].

As populations age, automation is considered a solution, and many countries have adopted it to increase both labour productivity and labour participation rates. Acemoglu and Restrepo[28] model and provide empirical evidence to document the links between ageing and automation for the US and developed countries. They find that ageing leads to greater (industrial) automation, particularly to more intensive use and development of robots. Using US data, they find that robots substitute for middle-aged workers (those between 36 and 55). They show that an increasing ratio of older to middle-aged workers is associated with greater adoption of robots and other automation technologies across countries. They also provide evidence of more significant development of automation technologies in countries undergoing greater demographic change. Their model suggests a greater role for automation in industries and sectors with a higher proportion of middle-aged workers and those with greater automation possibilities.

A *Nature* briefing[29] on the impact of automation highlights that artificial intelligence and machine learning are likely to change not just the number of jobs but the types of jobs. Will this make us more productive? This is the open question that economists and technologists are discussing and debating, as tax, technology, and labour policies are critical determinants of the net productivity gains from technology.

Bryjnholfsson and McAfee, in *The Second Machine Age*[30], provide exceptional futuristic insights into the promise of digital technology in improving and transforming human lives and society. However, technological progress will bring with it challenges for individual workers, households, society, and governments. Technological progress and digital technology will pose a challenge to workers with ordinary skills. Avoiding this will require lifelong learning, skills training, and human capital development, as highlighted by the OECD and several researchers like me. Governments will have to get ahead of the game and influence the future through reforms in labour, tax, technology, mobility, and pensions: i.e. adopt progressively holistic policy reforms.

Intangible investments (investments in software, databases, research, and organisational processes), as opposed to tangible investments (machines and equipment), have been growing at an increasing rate. In *Capitalism without Capital*, Haskel and Westlake[31] outline the growing importance of intangible assets in explaining growth in economic inequality and stagnation of productivity.

This poses challenges for societies, businesses, and households as economic progress and development are different in an economy with growing intangibles. Additionally, Haskel argues that there are implications for monetary policy[32] since intangibles also influence the natural interest rate.

The OECD's Nedelkoska and Quintini[33] studied 32 countries to understand the interactions between automation, skills, and the future of jobs. They found that 66 million jobs are automatable, with another 140 million having a high probability of automation. There is high variance in automatability across countries, which is better explained by differences in the organisation of job tasks rather than sectoral differences. Automation risks are not distributed equally across workers or sectors.

3.4   Debt, Deficits, and Fiscal Sustainability

As people and countries age, the share of old dependents increases. Increasing life spans (not factored in well enough by pension promisors in the 1970s–2000s) are now coming to haunt individuals, households, institutions, and countries due to the cost of supporting increasing aged populations. Public pensions, public health, and the long-term care burden are becoming fiscally unsustainable. The $64 million question is, who will pay for ageing costs? It was raised by Peter Heller in the context of two critical issues converging upon countries and societies worldwide[34].

One of the earliest attempts to understand fiscal sustainability by bridging theory and practice was conducted by Craig Burnside[35], who addressed fiscal sustainability issues from a conceptual viewpoint against the backdrop of the enormous fiscal problems being faced by the Latin American countries. Burnside provides analytical tools to assess fiscal sustainability within the context of business cycles and their impact on fiscal positions and the role of fiscal rules.

Policymakers in Europe—and the European Commission, in particular—have devoted resources to analysing this issue, as the bulk of the oldest countries, excluding Japan, are in Europe.

A sequence of policy reports by the EU[36,37] provides very detailed country-specific and aggregative regional analysis using scenarios and the latest data to assess the fiscal sustainability of public debt and deficits along different horizons.

As per the EU ageing report, the EU OADR (people aged 65+ years to those aged 15–64 years) is projected to increase by 21.6 percentage points from 29.6% (2016) to 51.2% (2070); this results in a fall from 3.3 working-age people for each person aged 65+ years to only 2. The labour force will be significantly strained. The total EU labour force (20–64 years) is expected to fall by 9.6% between 2016 and 2070, while labour force participation rates are projected to rise from 77.5% in 2016 to 80.7% in 2070. This increase is particularly apparent among women and older workers. It would pressure public finances, posing a significant challenge to EU member states. The total cost of EU ageing (public spending on pensions, healthcare, long-term care, education, and unemployment benefits) is expected to increase by 1.7 percentage points to 26.7% of GDP between 2016 and 2070.

The evolution of ageing costs across EU member states will vary with costs: (i) falling in Greece, Croatia, France, Latvia, Estonia, Italy, Lithuania, and Spain; (ii) increasing by up to 3% of GDP in Portugal, Denmark, Cyprus, Poland, Sweden, Romania, Bulgaria, Finland, Hungary, and Slovakia; and (iii) increasing by more than 3% of GDP in the Netherlands, Austria, Ireland, Germany, the UK, Belgium, Czech Republic, Slovakia, Malta, and Luxembourg. Long-term care and healthcare costs are expected to contribute the most to the rise in age-related spending, increasing by 2.1 percentage points.

The EU Fiscal Sustainability Report (FSR)[37] provides a timely update of fiscal sustainability challenges faced by the member states. The FSR 2018 uses the latest available macroeconomic forecasts (based on the European Commission's autumn 2018 forecast). The projections rely on agreed long-term convergence assumptions for the interest-growth rate differential and the long-term budgetary projections of age-related costs from the European Commission 2018 ageing report. Over the medium and long term, the assessment mainly relies on macroeconomic and fiscal projections that differ from forecasts as they are based on conventional assumptions over a longer time horizon (typically two years).

The FSR 2018 adopts a revised approach to assess long-term fiscal sustainability risks, to better account for vulnerabilities associated with medium- and long-term high debt levels. Fiscal sustainability challenges remain, despite some overall favourable prospects in the EU as a whole. The EU and Euro Area (EA) government debt ratios are set to gradually decline over the next decade, under the baseline no-fiscal-policy-change scenario, from a peak of 88% of GDP in 2014 (respectively, 94% of GDP in the EA) to 72% of GDP in 2029 (respectively, 78% of GDP in the EA). Table 3.3 presents major age-related expenditures for the EU.

This table aggregates the age-related expenditures on the three major components for 2016 and depicts the changes forecasted by the EU on a long-term budget projection basis. This, along with the FSR, provides policy projections regarding short-term, medium-term, and long-term budgets. In "A Demographic Perspective of Fiscal Sustainability: Not Just the Immediate Term Matters"[38], I highlighted that policymakers need to assess fiscal sustainability from all horizons as there are generational impacts that vary from country to country; further, many rich countries are not strong on the fiscal sustainability front. Such analyses of fiscal sustainability are essential for countries to plan their future budgets. One of the crucial determinants of long-term age-related spending is the OADR, and it is important to note that labour reforms, skills enhancement, and lifelong training are likely to help mitigate fiscal burdens from ageing.

The European Commission ageing report and FSR consider different scenarios, projections, and variants by way of sensitivity analyses[39]. Many different parameters could change the pensions' burdens, such as OADRs, which vary with working-age definitions, coverage ratios of pensions, replacement rate promises, benefit changes, etc. Different growth projections, as well as cost changes in healthcare and long-term care, were also considered as part of the sensitivity analyses for long-term projections that the European Commission conducted over 2016–2070. The projections that are

Table 3.3 Age-related spending (% of GDP): 2016–2070.

Long-term budgets ageing report 2018—Baseline scenario

	Pensions		Healthcare		Long-term care		Total: Pensions + healthcare + LT care	
	2016 level	CH 16–70	2016 level	CH 16–70	2016 level	CH 16–70	Total 2016	Total 2070
Belgium	12.1	2.9	5.9	0.4	2.3	1.7	20.3	25.3
Bulgaria	9.6	1.4	5	0.3	0.4	0.1	15	16.8
Czech Rep	8.2	2.8	5.4	1.1	1.3	1.6	14.9	20.4
Denmark	10	-1.9	6.9	1	2.5	2.2	19.4	20.7
Germany	10.1	2.4	7.4	0.7	1.3	0.6	18.8	22.5
Estonia	8.1	-1.8	5.3	0.3	0.9	0.5	14.3	13.3
Ireland	5	1.6	4.1	1	1.3	1.9	10.4	14.9
Greece	17.3	-6.6	5	1.2	0.1	0.1	22.4	17.1
Spain	12.2	-1.5	5.9	0.5	0.9	1.3	19	19.3
France	15	-3.3	7.9	0.5	1.7	0.6	24.6	22.4
Croatia	10.6	-3.8	5.2	0.7	0.9	0.3	16.7	13.9
Italy	15.6	-1.7	6.3	0.7	1.7	1.2	23.6	23.8
Cyprus	10.2	2.3	2.8	0.4	0.3	0.3	13.3	16.3
Latvia	7.4	-2.6	3.7	0.6	0.4	0.1	11.5	9.6
Lithuania	6.9	-1.7	4.1	0.4	1	1	12	11.7
Luxembourg	9	8.9	3.9	1.2	1.3	2.8	14.2	27.1
Hungary	9.7	1.5	4.9	0.8	0.7	0.4	15.3	18
Malta	8	2.9	5.6	2.7	0.9	1.4	14.5	21.5
Netherlands	7.3	0.6	6.2	0.8	3.5	2.5	17	20.9
Austria	13.8	0.5	7	1.3	1.9	1.9	22.7	26.4
Poland	11.2	-1	4.3	0.8	0.5	0.8	16	16.6
Portugal	13.5	-2.2	5.9	2.4	0.5	0.9	19.9	21
Romania	8	0.7	4.3	0.9	0.3	0.3	12.6	14.5
Slovenia	10.9	3.9	5.6	1	0.9	0.9	17.4	23.2
Slovakia	8.6	1.2	5.6	1.2	0.9	0.6	15.1	18.1
Finland	13.4	0.6	6.1	0.8	2.2	2.1	21.7	25.2
Sweden	8.2	-1.2	6.9	0.7	3.2	1.7	18.3	19.5
United Kingdom	7.7	1.7	7.9	1.4	1.5	1.3	17.1	21.5
Norway	10.7	2.1	7.7	1.2	3.7	3.4	22.1	28.8
Euro Area	12.3	-0.4	6.8	0.7	1.6	1.1	20.7	22.1
EU28	11.2	-0.2	6.8	0.9	1.6	1.2	19.6	21.5
EU27 excl UK	11.9	-0.5	6.6	0.7	1.6	1.1	20.1	21.4
Unweighted EU average	10.3	0.2	5.5	0.9	1.3	1.1	17.1	19.3

SOURCE: European Commission, Economic Policy Committee.

broken down by 2016–40 and then 2040–2070 are subject to huge levels of aggregate uncertainty from individual, corporate, and country perspectives. The European Commission highlights that gross national product (GNP) may provide a better guide to debt sustainability than GDP; this is especially the case in Luxembourg and Ireland, where remittances are significant and GNP is smaller than GDP. Health expenditures are modelled with scenarios that incorporate ageing, morbidity, health technology, and incomes. Similarly, long-term care scenarios are a function of social care institutions and are not a consequence of ageing alone but are related to disability, frailty, and sickness. The report factors in different sensitivity factors to project long-term care expenditures, which are affected by complex interactions between demographics and disability.

The recent COVID-19 pandemic has added to short-term debt projections as governments have had to support the member states through fiscal stimulus of countries and EU support. These pandemic-related support expenditures have been targeted toward small businesses, households, and the vulnerable segments of society.

There are certain intergenerational implications of ageing that are discussed in terms of equity, with smaller generations of the working-age population to support growing groups of older people. In *The Coming Generational Storm*[40], Kotlikoff and Burns highlight the fact that if our government continues on the course it has set, we'll see skyrocketing tax rates, drastically lower retirement and health benefits, high inflation, a rapidly depreciating dollar, unemployment, and political instability. They propose bold new policies, including meaningful reforms of Social Security and Medicare. Their proposals are simple, straightforward, and geared to attract support from both political parties. They caution against spending more than the US has and promising to pay more than can be delivered. They also expound on the risk that the Baby Boomers face if the US faces a fiscal crisis and implicit debt default. As the pioneers of generational accounting, they lay bare the potential clash of the generations. They advocate the need for a consistent plan to manage and deal with rising entitlements as the Baby Boomers retire.

As shown in this discussion, these issues are relevant not just for the US but also for the European countries, based on public pensions, healthcare, and long-term costs, as shown in Figure 3.8. The sum of these promised costs acts as a drag on future growth. Social protection expenditures are on average 19.8% of GDP; the components related to ageing dominate and are the largest component of public expenditures.

Ageing strains and concerns have coincided with Japan's low growth and ballooning debt ratio over the last three decades (the "lost decades"). K.G. Nishimura[41] draws parallels with Keynesian analysis of the crisis, suggesting that potential market bubbles in advanced countries are related to demographic features. He highlights the change in population composition as inducing a significant swing in asset prices as a store of value. This has led asset prices to bubble and then collapse spectacularly in some countries, leaving us with severe balance-sheet problems and diminished expectations for investment returns. Nishimura discusses the role of technological innovation to cater to the unique needs of the old, financial innovation to cater to the needs of the young, and private-public partnerships to adopt socially desirable investments to avoid the boom and bust of asset price bubbles followed by their collapse.

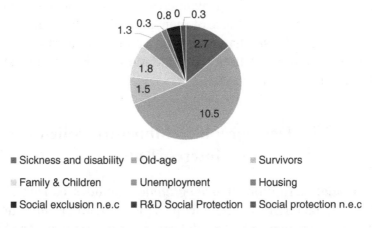

Figure 3.8 EU social protection expenditures (% of GDP): 2019.
SOURCE: European Commission.

In terms of Japanese fiscal sustainability, in a research column summarising their earlier research papers, Imohoroglu et al.[42] note that expenditures for age-related programmes—pensions, public healthcare, and long-term care insurance—are projected to rise significantly, far outpacing the projected revenues and insurance premiums collected as the working-age population shrinks rapidly. In the absence of reform, the net debt-to-GDP ratio would reach the unprecedented level of 230% by 2040 and 630% by 2070. Four components—expenditures for public pensions, health insurance, long-term care (LTC) programmes, and debt servicing—would contribute equally to the rising deficits and debt, with the interest payments rising more rapidly as more debt is accumulated. They state that a combination of policy reforms and changes in the labour market and productivity would solve the problem. More female participation and increased earnings would increase income tax revenues and the budgets of all three social insurance programmes. A significant obstacle is the work disincentive and what is essentially a severe penalty for more women working that is embedded in the current social insurance policy and tax system. To improve fiscal sustainability, they recommend a combination of policies such as raising the full retirement age to 67, reducing pension benefits, increasing the co-pays for public medical expenditures and LTC spending to 20%, increasing women's earnings and employment characteristics to match those of men, and raising the consumption tax rate to 15%; these changes would achieve fiscal sustainability and lead to significant fiscal consolidation, with a lower debt-to-GDP ratio in 2050 than in 2020.

3.5   Demographics, Monetary Policy, and Interest Rates

The broader definition of *demographics* includes consumer and worker characteristics. The incomes of individuals and households less what they consume determines their savings. As shown earlier, consumer expenditures differ by age; and by extension, empirical research shows that they vary by gender, education, race, etc. Incomes also vary by age and other demographic character-istics, as do savings. The level of savings relative to investments determines equilibrium interest rates. The role of central banks is to control inflation and unemployment as per their objectives, which set targets for both. Worker characteristics influence the labour supply, which interacts with labour demand to determine levels of employment and wages. Therefore, the broader definition of *demographics* influences the levels of inflation and unemployment, both of which are objectives of monetary policy and central banks.

The impact of ageing on debts, deficits, and fiscal sustainability has been studied and analysed by fiscal policy researchers. However, the impact on monetary policy was not extensively studied by economists as demographics was supposed to have long-term effects while monetary policy was intended to control short-term inflation and unemployment.

This is exemplified by a European Central Bank (ECB) working paper by Enkin and von Thadden[43], who use model frameworks and calibration to conclude that demographic changes, while contributing slowly over time to a decline in the equilibrium interest rate, are not visible enough within the time horizon relevant for monetary policy making to require monetary policy reactions. In a chapter "Should Monetary Policy Be Different in a Greyer World?" David Miles[44] finds that the generosity of the pension system is a crucial determinant of savings and investment choices and that therefore, monetary policy effects in an ageing world need to be considered alongside the existing pension system and its future changes. Lower equilibrium interest rates close to the zero lower bound may affect monetary policy effectiveness, but many contend that due to slow-moving changes of demographics on equilibrium interest rates, they should not be considered necessary in designing monetary policy.

Mester[45] argues for the need to understand the impact of demographics on the broader economy as a central banker influencing monetary policy to achieve its targets. She states that demographic change can influence economic growth, structural productivity growth, living standards, savings rates, consumption, investment, the long-run unemployment rate, equilibrium interest rate, housing market trends, and the demand for financial assets. Changing demographic trends across countries can be expected to influence current account balances and exchange rates, thereby necessitating an understanding of relative cross-country demographics.

Berg et al.[46] decompose the response of aggregate consumption to monetary policy shocks into contributions by households at different stages of the life cycle. They find that older households have a higher consumption response than younger households. Amongst older households, the consumption response is also increasing in income. This, along with data on net wealth, presents evidence for a wealth effect in driving response patterns. The model qualitatively explains the empirical patterns. They recommend that understanding the heterogeneity in consumption responses across age groups is essential for understanding the transmission of monetary policy, especially as the US population grows older. Another study by Lehigh and Thapar[47] examines the effect of monetary policy across US states that have different age structures. Income and employment responses to the same interest-rate changes are different. They find that when monetary policy is more effective, the greater the share of the 40–65 middle-aged population; and less effective, the greater the share of the young (aged 20–40). The share of the population over 65 has no discernible effect on the effectiveness of monetary policy.

As discussed earlier, Juselius and Takáts[24] find a sizeable and statistically stable demographic impact on low-frequency inflation suggesting that policy needs to understand the evolution of age structure in both advanced ageing countries and emerging countries.

Monetary policy is less effective in terms of its impact on older and aged economies. This was asserted by Imam[48], showing that the weakening of monetary policy effectiveness is due to demographic changes. This helps explain why changes in monetary policy have a more benign impact on advanced economies than in the past. In previous research, I highlighted that a reason for lower monetary policy effectiveness was that older people engage less in financial markets and are invested primarily in safe, risk-less assets. I also argued[49] that the impact of monetary policy is very mute and relatively ineffective based on conventional policy instruments as they do not take into account the age structure and changing behaviour of consumers and workers. Voting patterns of the old impart a disinflationary bias in their favour. Fiscal policy has a larger and more effective and targeted role to play in ageing economies where interest rates are low and monetary policy is less effective. The new generation of monetary models still falls short of incorporating demographic-related distributional and behavioural changes exhibited by consumers and workers. As a result, in an inter-connected real and financial world, the transmission mechanisms and dynamics are very different from those understood and modelled.

Favero et al.[50] modelled the age structure and related it to the US term structure, finding that the composition of age structure determines the equilibrium rate in the monetary policy rule and, therefore, the persistent component in one-period yields. Fluctuations in demographics are then transmitted to the whole term structure via the expected policy rate components.

3.6 Demographics and Unemployment

One of the important variables characterising the health of economies is the level of unemployment. Earlier, I presented data on age-specific unemployment and highlighted the challenges of gender differences across employment. Ageing, however, has implications for labour productivity, and technological progress has implications for the future of work.

The founding fathers of modern economics, Adam Smith and John M. Keynes, focused many of their economic discussions on employment levels alongside output (measured by GDP or industrial production) and prices (consumer prices, wages). In an earlier discussion, we showed that labour participation rates (women) have been increasing at all ages, with increases in older male activity rates. The potential available labour force for employment has also changed due to the changing structure of the economy and increased levels of education across countries. Young people are joining the labour force later due to more years of schooling across high school and college. While earlier acceptance of the working-age population between 15 and 64 years was the standard norm, we argued in earlier reports[14,20,38] that changing definitions of working age have implications for OADRs and fiscal strains.

One of the significant macro indicators targeted by central banks and many fiscal authorities globally is the unemployment rate. As shown in Figure 3.9, there is a large gap between the unemployment rates of working-age people versus youth aged 15–24. The measure of unemployment varies according to the range considered to be working age. High youth unemployment shows a significant potential to fully utilise the labour force, as youth have the highest labour productivity growth. Members of the young age group today are better educated and skilled in general than a decade or two ago, and that is observed to be true across all countries.

The risks of not dealing with youth unemployment were clearly observed during the youth revolts in the Arab world, also better

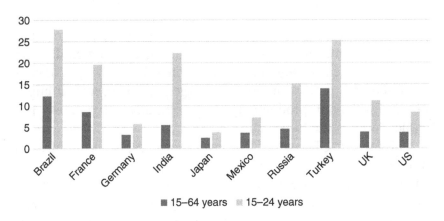

Figure 3.9   Unemployment and youth unemployment (%): 2019.
SOURCE: International Labour Organization.

known as the Arab Spring. As younger people become better educated, it is essential to create gainful employment for them. The
challenge often is that lower growth rates do not act as favourable
catalysts for new job creation. Creating jobs for younger[51], skilled,
and more flexible workers is a longer-term source of greater productivity growth as well as social stability.

3.7 Demographics, Capital Flows, and Current Account

Around the time Ben Bernanke was propagating his global savings glut hypothesis[52] as an explanation for the growing US current
account deficit, another recognised monetary economist and Federal Open Market Committee (FOMC) member, William Poole[53],
was highlighting the importance of demographics on US capital
flows and current account.

St Louis Fed President Poole argued that an ageing world with
faster increases in the old population relative to those of working
age would have numerous implications for current global accounts.
He stated that the demographic transition would lead to repercus-
sions for all the decisions that influence economic growth. While
research and policy attention was devoted to ageing implications
for US Social Security and Medicare programmes, more attention
to demographic effects on capital flows was needed. He concluded
by stating that "Saving and investment behavior are the keys to the
evolution of a country's current account. It is exactly these behav-
iors that the demographic perspective highlight".

As mentioned earlier, Cleveland Fed President Mester[45] highlighted that cross-country demographic trends and differences
are likely to drive capital flows, exchange rates, and current
account balances.

Brooks[54] modelled the global capital flows in a parallel world of
young and old countries, stating that demographic change effects
are intuitive. Fast-ageing regions will observe greater savings due
to increasing retirees' needs, while investment demand will fall due

to a declining workforce. In a world with perfect capital mobility, this will lead to capital outflows to regions with higher population growth until the return on capital is equalised across regions.

Borsch-Supan[55] modelled overlapping generations in multi-country models, highlighting that while ageing patterns are similar in many advanced countries, there are substantial differences in timing and initial conditions. He contended that in a world of international capital mobility, population ageing will induce capital flows. His framework finds that capital flows from fast-ageing regions to the rest of the world will initially be substantial but that trends are reversed when households decumulate savings. He also concludes that closed-economy pension reform missed out on the important effects of international capital mobility.

Higgins[56] addresses the relationship between age distributions, national savings, and the current account balance. His results point to substantial demographic effects, with increased youth and OADRs associated with lower savings rates. He highlights that demographics has differential effects on savings and investment, with an essential role in determining current account balance.

In similar research extended across many countries, we[57] discuss the importance of demographics in influencing savings, investment, and current account, while not finding a significant direct effect on exchange rates, which are influenced by higher frequency influences. We found evidence of statistically strong links between demographic variables and aggregate saving, aggregate investment, and the current account balance. We also found that demographic variables can enhance the explanatory performance of models for both real and nominal exchange rates if they are not strongly correlated with other macro variables.

3.8   Conclusions

In this chapter, I connected demographics to economic growth, living standards, inflation, public debts and deficits, monetary policy, capital flows, and exchange rates. This shows the impact of demographic variables on both short-term and long-term economic variables and investments. Demographics was therefore misunderstood earlier as having only long-term effects on economics.

Consumers, savers, and workers are essential decision-making individuals who, in aggregate, influence growth, employment, and inflation—the core macroeconomic indicators—at all horizons. Further, demographic heterogeneity and behavioural characteristics play a significant role in determining micro-differences underlying macro-aggregates and, consequently, prices in cross-section and over time.

Demographics is intimately linked to the fiscal sustainability pressures of a country, although similarly, old countries face different degrees of strain based on their fiscal planning, budgeting exercises, and other institutions. Voter preferences for inflation may be reflected in countries that have much older cohorts than younger ones. Also, in older countries, monetary policy plays a diminished role in terms of its effectiveness.

Demographics affects output, inflation, public debt, unemployment, and current account; its impact is pervasive across time, with short-term and long-term effects.

The consumption expenditures and savings behaviour of households and individuals during the COVID era has influenced GDP and inflation at short horizons. At the same time government deficits and debt increased too to support all segments of the population.

The future of the global macroeconomy over the next decade is linked to the growth of China and even more so to its living standards (GDP per capita). To grow on both these fronts, it is imperative for China to continue structural reforms of its labour market (especially Hukou reforms) alongside progressive reforms in education, health, insurance, and financial markets. That necessitates opening up in partnership with other regions of the world and fully exploiting its demographic dividend in conjunction with technology. Global economic leadership will require collaborative partnerships on other fronts like climate change, trade, intellectual property, financial markets, technology, etc. Demographics will be a key part in China's road to economic leadership. The one-child policy is not a major issue given that current Chinese fertility rates exceed those of the EU, Japan, Singapore, Korea, Hong Kong, and many others, as the policy was not implemented in rural China and has now been replaced by a two-child policy in law.

Chapter 4

Demographics and Asset Prices

People (both workers and consumers) care about their financial well-being. In today's connected world, with advances in finance, literacy, and technology, the range of opportunities to transform savings into future wealth or income has expanded dramatically. The democratisation of finance and the advent of FinTech are transforming every aspect of life, including payments, bank accounts, loans, mortgages, emergency assistance, savings choices, investment avenues, etc. But to grow wealth, financial assets need to generate returns, and their prices help generate capital gains. While most conventional thinking accepts these obvious facts, it often does not appreciate that individual behaviours also affect asset prices and returns. This chapter summarises disparate strands of research on how demographics affect asset prices and investment returns. In a later chapter, I connect this discussion to strategic asset allocation for pension funds that manage retirement money for individuals, corporates, and governments.

This chapter is the natural successor to Chapter 3 as it explores the impact of demographics on asset prices. In the previous chapter, we discussed and amplified links between demographics and macroeconomic indicators such as GDP, GDP per capita, inflation, unemployment, productivity, debt, and deficits, as well as capital flows and current account. It is important to acknowledge and understand that asset prices reside within the context of a macro-economy that affects interest rates and inflation. The depth of capital markets and behaviour of savers and investors help determine asset prices.

Our broader interpretation of demographics pertaining to consumer and worker characteristics means the behaviour of individuals, households, and families as both consumers and workers influence inflation and wages. Additionally, the consumption, savings, and investments of individuals and households help determine asset demand, whereas asset supply depends on the financing needs of institutions, corporations, and governments along with equity and bond markets, exchanges, index providers, trading structures, and regulation.

How much an individual consumer or household should consume and save depends on their preferences toward consumption (how they trade off a unit of consumption in the present versus a unit of consumption in the future), which is captured by their degree of impatience about consuming today versus in the future and their attitude about risk: their degree of *risk aversion*. Decisions are typically made with implications in terms of returns or future income. Savings decisions are made keeping in mind intergenerational considerations such as bequests.

4.1 Theories of Life-Cycle Consumption, Savings, and the Permanent Income Hypothesis

4.1.1 Life-Cycle Consumption Theory

As we discussed in the earlier chapters, life expectancy has dramatically increased since 1950 and continues to rise, although the rate of increase has slowed in the last two decades. Individuals and households make dynamic decisions about consumption and savings throughout their lives. Economists have been studying these decisions and devising tests of the decision-making processes. Individuals start consuming at birth, although until they are adults, their parents make consumption expenditure decisions for them. Once they start earning their income after working as adults, they have to decide how to allocate their income across consumption and savings.

The theory of consumption was an area of research in the 1950s and 1960s by leading macroeconomists like Franco Modigliani, Albert Ando, and Richard Brumberg[1,2]; they developed the *life-cycle hypothesis* (LCH) alongside Milton Friedman, who developed the *permanent income hypothesis* (PIH)[3]. Paul Samuelson[4] also pioneered research in the area of multi-period savings decisions. These theories also laid the foundations for many asset-pricing models, retirement decisions, and pension plan investments.

The life-cycle theory of consumption posited that individuals make consumption and savings decisions based on their income over their lifetime rather than their income at a single point or their current stage of life. Early in life, when they are earning, they tend to save part of their income (accumulate assets); later in life, they tend to draw down their assets (decumulate assets).

The life-cycle theory also led to predictions regarding (i) aggregate savings within an economy depending on the rate of growth of the national income of the economy, not its level; and (ii) the level of wealth in an economy depending on the length of retirement. Angus Deaton[5] stated that the LCH laid the foundation for the discussion of several issues such as private versus public provision of social security, the effects of the stock market on the economy, the effects of demographic change on national saving, the role of saving in economic growth, and what determines aggregate wealth. Many consider Modigliani one of the foremost economists on issues pertaining to pensions, pension systems, social security, and retirement.

The life-cycle theory was also a theory of aggregate wealth of an economy; it described how wealth is transferred across generations with the very young having little wealth, middle-aged people having more wealth, and peak wealth being reached just before retirement.

In retirement, retirees sell off their assets to provide food, housing, and recreation. The assets shed by older people are taken up by younger people who are still in the accumulation stage of life. In younger economies, there are more young people, and they tend to save more for consumption over the remainder of their lives; that exceeds the dissaving by the smaller group of old people. Further, if incomes grow, the savings of the young far exceed the dissaving of the old in the economy; economic growth leads to savings, and the greater the growth, the greater the rate of savings.

The inference was that the growth of aggregate national income leads to higher savings (not the income level), and it didn't matter if aggregate income grew because of population growth or growth in per capita incomes. Modigliani and Brumberg[1] theorised that wealth was related to the retirement period in the economy, and when the ratio of wealth to income was lower, the higher the income growth rate. Many decades later, the consumption, savings, and wealth implications were validated by empirical evidence and tests across many data sets in the US and other countries.

4.1.2   Permanent Income Hypothesis

Milton Friedman's *permanent income hypothesis* was based on the notion that consumer decisions depended on estimates of permanent income. He thus went beyond the typical Keynesian notion of consumption depending on income. Instead, he postulated consumption as a function of *permanent income*: the discounted value of income over the lifetime, akin to an annuity.

Meghir[6] states that Friedman's classic book *The Consumption Function* helped explain why traditional Keynesian demand management can have little or no effect on real consumption. The underlying intuition was that individuals would prefer level consumption that did not fluctuate with short-term income fluctuations. The model further explained important empirical facts such as why income is more volatile than consumption and why the long-run marginal propensity to consume at a level greater than income is higher than that in the short term.

A significant contribution of Friedman was his devising of empirical econometric tests for the PIH. He was one of the first to use *instrumental variables*, an econometric technique that is now well-established in economics and finance. Measured income was decomposed into a permanent component and a transitory component; likewise, measured consumption was decomposed into a permanent component and a transitory component. The average (marginal) propensity to consume from permanent income depended on the interest rate and taste-shift variables. The primary point was that the individual's consumption plan is uncorrelated to the transitory component.

The role of taste preferences is important in both theories of consumption (the LCH and the PIH). Friedman explained the differences in tests of the PIH in cross-section versus time-series. Income, race, and other characteristics also support our key points that **demographic characteristics other than age** influence aggregate consumption.

Friedman stated that average income reflects (average) permanent income, as over many observations, the law of large numbers applies and the transitory components average out to zero. This phenomenon is observed in many data sets and under varying conditions. One interpretation of why Blacks save more than Whites with the same observed income is that they have lower permanent income than Whites. When the tests are conditioned on Blacks being in the same observed income class, the transitory component of income (which does not affect consumption) is likely to be larger among Blacks than Whites. Similar arguments apply to comparing the self-employed to the salaried workers or farm to non-farm households, with the former in each pair having larger transitory components to their income.

The theory underlying the PIH shows that the marginal utility of consumption in each period is equal to the expected marginal utility of wealth multiplied by a factor depending on the interest rate and the rate of time preference.

4.1.3   Consumption, Savings, and Intertemporal Loans: Pioneer Paul Samuelson

In addition to the LCH of Franco Modigliani and the PIH of Milton Friedman, another pioneering and fundamental contribution toward understanding intertemporal consumption was Paul Samuelson's model[4] of consumption in response to changes in interest rates. He developed a three-stage life-cycle model across generations and then solved the model for a sequence of consumption and interest rates in equilibrium under assumptions made in his framework.

Samuelson argued the role of money in a world of transfer of income from the middle-aged to the young in return for income in retirement. He developed arguments for intergenerational contracts and collusion to explain how generations can intertemporally help smooth consumption through transfers facilitated by money as a medium of exchange. He found a role for money in an intergenerational world that facilitates transfers and explains an equilibrium out of many possible solutions where a social optimum (or close to it) is achieved. His article threaded through philosophical arguments alongside economic optimisation principles and demographics of multiple generations.

Samuelson's contributions to demographics and population dynamics were acknowledged and summarised by leading economic demographer Ronald Lee[7], who stated that he "illuminated issues of compelling policy importance, such as declining fertility and population aging. While his work in population economics has been very influential, his work in population and evolution appears to have been largely overlooked". Samuelson's fundamental work led to overlapping-generations models in monetary economics and fiscal policy building on the foundational issues of intergenerational exchange.

Samuelson[8] also read and followed many of the Malthusian predictions, incorporating into his frameworks the ideas of rapid population growth constraining the living standards. He considered the optimal population size and conjectured that there must be an intermediate rate of population growth (positive, zero, or negative), depending on the parameters of the problem, at which the disadvantages of further growth were cancelled by the advantages. This would lead to the optimal rate of population growth, which maximises per capita lifetime utility of consumption. He stated that if that optimal rate were mandated by propensities to procreate, voluntary life-cycle personal savings would suffice to support the equilibrium without recourse to social security alterations of life-cycle consumption.

A.K. Dixit[9] stated that Samuelson's work on the papers just listed opened up research areas for many other prominent economists such as Peter Diamond's seminal work on debt, Cass and Shell's research on sunspots, and Robert Barro's research work on Ricardian equivalence. In addition, Samuelson's paper laid the foundations for Robert C. Merton's contributions to life-cycle finance, optimal intertemporal portfolio selection, and capital asset pricing.

4.2 How Demographics Influences Equity Prices and Markets

I consider Andrew Abel and James Poterba pioneers for laying the foundations of how demographics and the ageing of the US population will affect asset markets. They both started by considering the public implications for debt and labour markets but extended the aggregate generational impacts on stock markets.

Extending the standard overlapping-generations models, Abel (in the 1980s and 1990s) studied the impact of demographics on savings by linking lifetime income, savings, and investments. James Poterba, in parallel, was examining the public and private implications of US ageing, linking consumers, savers, and stock markets. Both of them linked savings to Social Security, social insurance, and annuity markets.

Poterba[10] did detailed estimations to evaluate the impact of age structure (that captured population dynamics over time) on asset returns: the association between population age structure, particularly the share of the population in the "prime saving years" (40 to 64), and the returns on stocks and bonds. He found that most measures of demographic structure do not show a statistically significant correlation with asset returns. However, the findings do provide some evidence that the level of asset prices, measured as the price of corporate equities relative to corporate dividends, is related to demographic structure. The evidence is strongest when age-specific asset demands are used to construct time-varying projected asset demands, which are then related to prices.

Studies by Abel (2001, 2003) investigated the impact of retirement cohorts—especially the Baby Boomers—in aggregate on the stock market. He had previously published on altruism, intergenerational transfers, and the role of fiscal policy and savings. Baby Boomers—people born between 1946 and 1964—are one of the largest generations due to the post-WW2 boom in investments combined with a positive attitude toward peaceful prosperity. Abel[11] discusses the role of altruism and intergenerational bequests on the predicted stock market meltdown. His model projects a decline in the price of capital when Baby Boomers retire, assuming a bequest motive does not reduce the decline in capital prices.

Another extensive study on this issue was done by Bakshi and Chen[12], who studied the effects of age structure on capital market prices. They examined two theoretical hypotheses—*the life-cycle investment hypothesis and the life-cycle risk-aversion hypothesis*—regarding their influence on asset prices. The life-cycle investment hypothesis essentially states that at different stages of an investor's life, their investment needs vary in terms of types of assets to hold. When investors are in their 20s and 30s, housing is a desirable investment. At that stage, they will probably allocate a higher proportion of wealth to housing and other durables. But as the investor grows older, the demand for housing will stabilise or decrease, and the demand for financial assets will rise, as will the need to invest for retirement due to increasing life expectancy. If this hypothesis is true in a time-series sense, its implications are immediate: as the population ages, the aggregate demand (as a proportion of aggregate wealth) for housing decreases, which depresses housing prices, while that for financial investments increases, which drives up financial prices.

The life-cycle risk-aversion hypothesis asserts that an investor's relative risk aversion increases with age. If this is true, then equilibrium market risk premiums should be correlated with demographic changes. In particular, market risk premiums should be positively correlated with changes in the age of the "average" investor.

As per the life-cycle investment hypothesis, an investor's asset mix changes with their life cycle. When the population ages (average age *increases*), the aggregate demand for financial investments rises and that for housing declines; and when the population becomes younger (average age *decreases*), the opposite effect occurs. According to the life-cycle risk-aversion hypothesis, an ageing population means an increasing average risk aversion, leading to higher risk premiums.

Bakshi and Chen[12] found that demographic fluctuations have had a significant impact on capital market prices. They contended that the persistent influence of the Baby Boomers and increasing life expectancy on the general economy will continue for decades to come. They used average age to approximate demographics-driven asset demand functions, including real estate and investment demands. They incorporated behavioural characteristics like risk aversion, which varies with age. And they found that age structure and demographics could found future stock returns and post-WW2 risk premiums.

An illustration of the life-cycle investment hypothesis follows, assuming three stages of an individual's life. The first stage, between birth and T_1, is the young dependent phase with no independent income, traditionally age 0–15 but now typically 0–20 or even 25 years in some countries (due to military service and more years of high school and undergraduate education). The second stage, between T_1 and T_2, is the working stage, where income and resources increase from level Y_L (starting income) to Y_{Max}. When decumulation starts, post-retirement, the level of resources and income decreases until Y_B, which denotes the level of bequest. A testable intuitive argument is that as the number of savers in the second stage increases, more investment flows into the equity market through their asset demands, leading to higher stock prices and returns.

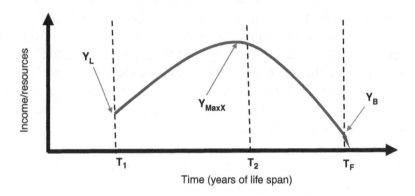

Figure 4.1 Typified life-cycle income/investment hypothesis.

Figure 4.1 is an over-simplified representation of an individual's life cycle over three stages. In the first five decades of the post-WW2 period, T_F—the last date of life—was not that different from T_2: i.e. the retirement period was much shorter than it is today, when retirement may extend more than two decades or as in some advanced countries like Japan and Italy, more than three decades. In terms of savings, when individuals are young and start working, their incomes are often lower than their consumption needs, and they borrow against their potential lifetime earning capacity. As they gain experience and their incomes exceed their consumption, they save and invest for housing, their children's education, and retirement. Just before retirement, most individuals face a small marginal decline from their maximum income or resource levels. Then, beyond the period T_2, individuals decumulate resources until their death and leave a bequest of Y_B.

The latest data from the US Consumer Expenditures Survey covering 2019 supports the life-cycle hypothesis, highlighting that younger households spend more than their income by borrowing. Income levels increase with age, peak, and then decline over the retirement period. Figure 4.2 shows the income trend after taxes and consumer expenditures based on the age of the head of household.

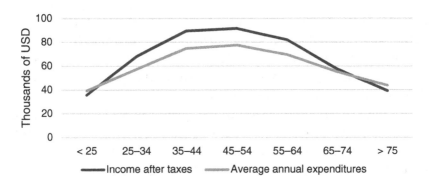

Figure 4.2 Income and consumer expenditures by age (based on age of head of household): 2019.

SOURCE: Bureau of Labor Statistics; Current Employment Statistics.

Sheshinski and Tanzi[13] documented that the share of interest income and dividend income held by the 65+ aged population had been steadily increasing. With ageing, the share of the 65+ age group was also projected to increase.

Poterba et al.[14] investigated the relationship between stock prices, equity-holder wealth, and consumption patterns, finding that stock prices reflect future consumption, although equity wealth does not immediately affect consumption. They also showed that consumption is not immediately and directly affected by equity wealth, as many theories posit. An important finding of theirs was that most American equities are owned by wealthy old people. This suggests that studying the consumption behaviour and habits of older people relative to the young may be useful. This was one of the initial papers that highlighted the unequal distribution of equities across the population, with the implication that while all individuals are consumers, few are holders of equities as a source of wealth.

Bergantino[15] conducted a detailed cohort analysis to examine the life-cycle savings of individuals and their patterns of drawdown post-retirement. Based on life-cycle investment behaviour, he posited that younger households (those below the age of 40) who borrow to buy their homes through mortgages are net borrowers, with their borrowings exceeding their total investments out of their savings or income; they are net negative investors. Middle-aged households (head of household age 40–60) become net positive investors in financial markets. Old households (head of household over 60) also draw credit from financial markets but, unlike young households, do so by drawing down their previous accumulated assets.

Using correlations between age structure and long-run asset prices (stocks, bonds, and house prices), Bergantino found that demographic factors accounted for approximately 59% of the observed annual increase in real housing prices between 1966 and 1986. Similarly, demographically driven changes in financial asset demands could account for approximately 77% of the annual increase in real stock prices between 1986 and 1997 and at least 81% of the annual increase in real bond prices. He suggested that annual growth in demographic housing demand would provide a positive stimulus of about 0.35% per year to real house price increases over 1997–2007 (down from 0.98% per year over 1986–1997 and 1.02% per year over 1966–1986. He forecasted that growth in demographic demand for assets would stimulate real stock and bond price appreciation of 8.76% per year over 1997–2007, up from about 6.62% per year over 1986–1997 and 1.34% per year over 1966–1986.

Poterba[16] further assessed various demographic measures related to asset returns, finding that age-specific projected asset demands correlated with asset prices rather than age shares. He argued that the projected asset demand variables placed roughly equal weight on retired individuals and prime-age workers because the age-wealth profiles do not show a substantial decline in old age. Thus, the variables that seem to track at least the level of equity prices do not distinguish between prime-age workers and older individuals. His results are consistent with those of Brooks[17] and Bergantino[15].

Poterba used the Survey of Consumer Finance data to construct age-specific asset profiles, providing richer insights than simple cross-section age-wealth holdings. His specification allowed for the existence of both cohort and time effects in asset holding patterns. He documented that the decrease in asset holdings is not as significant at older ages as the increase in asset holdings during middle age. For net financial asset demands, the peak holdings were between ages 70 and 74, whereas, with net wealth, the peak occurred between 65 and 69. He thus concluded that the dramatic rush to sell financial assets underlying a possible stock market melt-down in 2020–2030, as per most predictions, is overstated. The data and behaviour of older families in Japan, Italy, and the US thus far indicate similar patterns due to the uncertainty of life expectancy, as discussed earlier.

Figure 4.3, excerpted from my 2012 report[18], shows that live births differ over time, and extending them forward by 65 years gives a crude estimate of the number of 65-year-olds in the future. In advanced countries with low mortality rates, this calculation facilitates future planning and estimation.

Amit Goyal[19] studied the relationship between aggregate invest-ment flows and demographics by directly modelling stock market flows and testing model predictions using US data. He investigated the link between age structure, stock market outflows, and stock returns, finding that stock market outflows are positively correlated with the fraction of the population age 65+ and negatively corre-lated with those in the 45–64 age group. He found validation of the life-cycle model using a four-generation overlapping generations framework and found that the age structure also helps explain the variation in the equity premium. He stated that the international demographic structure helps explain the international capital flows.

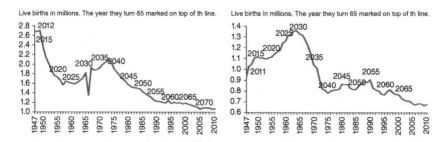

Figure 4.3 Annual live births and when they turn 65: Japan and Germany post-WW2–2010.
SOURCE: Roy et al.[18]

Geanokpolos et al.[20] attempted to explain the three distinct phases of boom and bust in post-WW2 US stock prices (the bull market of 1946–64, the bear market of the 1970s and early 1980s, and the bull market of the 1990s and 2000s) based on demographic changes. They found that US live births have gone through alternating 20-year periods of boom and bust, resulting in changes in the population's age composition. In their model, an increasing share of the middle-aged cohort leads to an increase in stock prices, and a decreasing share of the cohort leads to lower prices. However, the behaviour of the middle-aged cohort, either as myopic or rational regarding the demographic effects of cohort sizes, determines the magnitude of stock price increases—if rational, then the impact is amplified more than the size of the cohort. Their model gave rise to three testable predictions: (i) the price-earnings (PE) ratios should be proportional to the ratio of middle-aged to young adults (the MY ratio), (ii) real rates of return on equity and bonds should be an increasing function of the change in the MY ratio, and (iii) the equity premium should co-vary with the MY ratio (the reciprocal of the MY ratio). Figure 4.4, Figure 4.5, and Figure 4.6, from Geanokpolos et al.[20], show birth variations and the correlations between age structure and asset returns.

They modeled US birth rate trends, making assumptions regarding relative insensitivity of savings to interest rates and a fixed amount of land with endogenous capital, finding that the

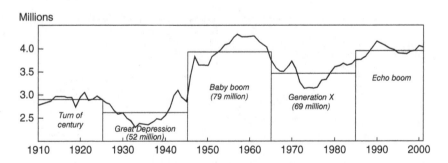

Figure 4.4   Live births and cohorts: 1910–2001.

SOURCE: Abridged from Geanokpolos et al.[20].

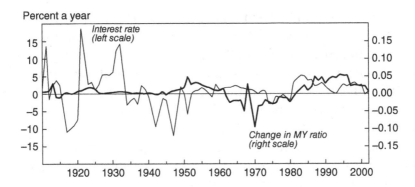

Figure 4.5   Short-term interest rates and the MY ratio: 1910–2001.
SOURCE: Abridged from Geanokpolos et al.[20].

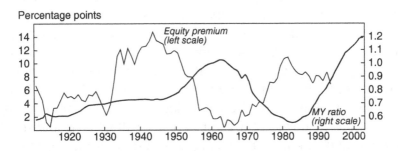

Figure 4.6   Equity premium and the MY Ratio: 1910–2001.
SOURCE: Abridged from Geanokpolos et al.[20].

demographic effect on PE ratios is larger than previous studies suggested. They also find that the equity premium is smaller when the population of savers is older. Figure 4.5 shows the co-movement of the MY ratio with real short-term interest rates according to the authors while setting up their model and framework.

Figure 4.6 displays the co-movement of equity premium with the MY ratio. They found that the maximum equity premium occurred in the early to mid-1940s, reflecting the fact that the excess return on equity was high during the 20 years of rising prices from 1945 to 1965. The minimum occurred around 1965, which means that the equity premium was small during the declining market of the

1970s and early 1980s. Then there is a local maximum in 1980 arising from the high rate of return on equity from the beginning of the 1980s up to 2000. They found that qualitatively the equity premium movements were consistent with the predictions of their model.

The authors found that the turning points of stock prices and PE ratios are well synchronised with the demographic cycle, as measured by the MY ratio, which favours the demographic hypothesis. They also stated that changes in equity prices are accompanied by changes in rates of return and interest rates linked to the change in, rather than the level of, the MY ratio.

However, I believe this is based on the conventional arguments of counting people: shares of people in the cohort over time without accounting for changes in the behaviour of consumers and workers or their behaviour as savers and investors in changing capital markets. Globalisation and changes in the knowledge and information sets of consumers make them different today than people two decades ago or four decades ago, at all ages—not just when they are young or old. Their opportunity sets for consumption and investment are different, as is the technology for transforming savings into income or investment returns. I have illustrated and drawn attention to changing consumers and workers[21] in the past and in earlier sections.

We quantitatively examined demographics and asset price linkages[18], we showed strong relationships between long-term government bond yields and demographics for five developed countries (the US, the UK, Japan, France, and Germany). For PE ratios of stocks, the results were strong only for the US. We found significant differences across countries for the predictability of the PE ratio equity index based on demographic variables, and we believe these differences emanate from a mix of demographic and institutional features. *Investors in various countries differ in terms of stock and bond market participation, size and length of the baby boom, retirement ages, retirement income provision, risk aversion, institutional structure, etc. These investor differences affect asset allocation and asset prices.*

We used our statistical estimations based only on demographic variables to forecast up to 2025 broad PE ratios in the US and long-term bond yields for the US, Germany, Japan, France, and the UK. A strong note of caution is that many other variables, which we did not quantitatively include in our estimations (both demographic and non-demographic), also influence asset price variables. As people live longer, life-cycle stages are delayed, and asset accumulation and decumulation patterns are likely to differ significantly from the past. We believe that age ranges typically used in past studies to represent savers and dis-savers will not work as well in the future.

The use of age-based demographic ratios has been advocated and tested in a few of the papers cited earlier, and that is why I examined some of these ratios across different countries. The results are shown in Figure 4.7 and display the variations across countries. These ratios also vary based on the definitions of age ranges, as discussed in Chapter 2. The two popular ratios we present are the *Yuppy-Nerd ratio* and the *Middle-Old ratio*, using different age ranges for the numerator and the denominator. The *Middle-Young ratio* is also used sometimes; these are all variations on dependency ratios and support ratios that we discussed in Chapter 2. The patterns across countries look similar over some periods but are not synchronous. In some studies, asset returns are considered to evolve with a correlation to changes in these ratios rather than levels, as Geanokpolos et al. also described[20].

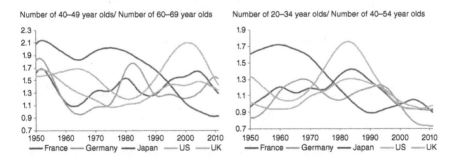

Figure 4.7   Variations in demographic ratios across countries.
SOURCE: Abridged from Roy et al.[18].

Liu and Spiegel[22] examined how the ageing of the US population creates headwinds for the stock market. They looked at the ratio of the middle-aged cohort (40–49) to the old-age cohort (60–69) (MO) ratio. They estimated that the MO ratio explained about 61% of the movements in the PE ratio of the S&P 500 from 1954 to 2010 and concluded that the MO ratio predicts long-run trends in the PE ratio fairly well. Their model-generated path for real stock prices in the future implied by demographic trends is quite bearish. As per their model, real stock prices are expected to follow a downward trend until 2021, cumulatively declining about 13% relative to 2010. Real stock prices are not expected to return to their 2010 level until 2027. Their calculations suggested that by 2030, the real value of equities will be about 20% higher than in 2010.

Favero et al.[23] studied the predictability of long-run stock returns using demographic variables. They documented a slowly evolving trend in the log of the dividend-price ratio, determined by the middle-aged to young (MY) ratio. Deviations of the dividend-price ratio from the long-run component explain transitory but persistent fluctuations in stock market returns. They stated that the joint significance of the MY ratio and the dividend-price ratio in long-horizon forecasting regressions for market returns explains mixed evidence on the ability of dividend price ratio to predict stock returns. They asserted that demographics are a natural input into a forecasting model of long-horizon returns and a long-horizon investor's optimal asset allocation decision. They interpreted the MY ratio as the information component that drives long-horizon stock market fluctuations after the noise in short-horizon stock market fluctuations subsides.

4.3   Will There Be an Asset Market Meltdown When the Baby Boomers Retire?

As mentioned earlier, the Baby Boomer generation is defined as those born between 1946 and 1964 and therefore expected to retire beginning in 2011, leading to a stock market meltdown. The asset price meltdown hypothesis states that when Baby Boomers retire, they will reduce their asset holdings, and asset prices will be adversely impacted. This is a big question with implications that affect the retirement industry, mutual funds, equity investors, and equity indices, to name just a few. The average household invests in stocks in the US as part of their 401K plans and their savings plans.

Poterba[10] rejected the asset price meltdown hypothesis, using data on the age-wealth profile of US households. He showed that while asset holdings increase sharply when households are in their peak saving years, they fall slowly when households retire. He projected that asset demand will not decline sharply between 2020 and 2050.

Abel[11] re-examined the asset price meltdown hypothesis based on Poterba's work[10], noting that even if the demand for assets does not fall when Baby Boomers retire, that does not imply that the price of assets will not fall. Taking into account both supply and demand of assets, he showed that the equilibrium price of assets may fall when Baby Boomers retire even if the demand for assets by retired Baby Boomers remains high.

Jeremy Siegel[24] noted that the ageing population of the developed world will put downward pressure on stock prices. His model showed that if the productivity rise is modest and taxes, retirement age, immigration, and life expectancy are as currently expected, retirees won't be able to maintain the living standard they seek and hence will try to sell their assets. However, there will not be enough young Americans to demand all the stocks that Baby Boomers will want to sell during retirement, which could drive down stock prices unless foreign buyers step in. Siegel stated that rich young people in the developing world (China, India, Mexico, Brazil) will buy the stocks American Baby Boomers will want to sell, creating enough demand to increase stock prices. The developing world is getting richer faster, and if it continues to grow and buy shares, asset prices in the developed world will not fall.

In contrast, Brooks[25] stated that wealthy individuals who own a large share of US stock won't need to sell, and companies may boost dividends so retiree investors can maintain their shares.

He contended that the hit to retiree living standards would be to those without savings and depending on government assistance. Milton Friedman also expressed that rather than selling assets, typical retirees will be happy to hold their stocks and bonds and live off whatever dividends, interest, and pensions they receive.

Brooks used an overlapping generations model to examine the effect of financial markets of Baby Boomer retirement and tried to reconcile the opposing views of a large stock market meltdown when Baby Boomers retire to sell their assets to a smaller generation versus the view that forward-looking markets will anticipate this and therefore no meltdown will occur. He found that age distribution changes significantly affect asset returns even when agents are rational and forward-looking. Changes in the age distribution affect savings and the real interest rate—a baby boom pushes up return on capital and riskless assets, while a baby bust pushes down the returns on capital and riskless assets. Demographic shifts also change the differential return between stocks and bonds, with larger populations depressing the rate on bonds. Wage income moves inversely with the size of the population or labour force. The paper argues for a redistributive role for the government in smoothing out interest rate effects over time.

A US Government Accountability Office (GAO) report[26] also did not find evidence that Boomers' retirement asset drawdowns will cause a stock market meltdown. The report stated that while many Boomers have few financial assets to sell, a small minority own most of the assets held by this generation and will likely need to sell few assets in retirement. Most current retirees spend down their assets slowly, with many continuing to accumulate assets. Therefore, as per the GAO, if Boomers behave the same way, a rapid and large sell-off of financial assets appears unlikely. Other factors such as increased life expectancy may reduce the likelihood of a sharp and sudden drop in asset prices due to spreading asset wealth over a longer period and the possibility that many Boomers will work past traditional retirement ages.

Lim and Weil[27] also analysed the baby boom relative to the stock market boom, finding that the effect of demographic shifts on the stock market depends on the installation costs of capital—if the costs are high, then the effects on the stock market are significant.

In our previous research[18], we showed that the population growth rate, the MO ratio, and GDP per capita growth can effectively explain the variation in the S&P 500 PE ratio for the US market. Similar specifications work for the DAX index PE and Tokyo Stock Exchange PE, leading us to conclude that differences in risk preferences, stock market access, stock market development, education, and other socioeconomic characteristics of investors are plausible factors that explain the strength of results and specifications across the three markets.

4.4   Demographic Changes and Interest Rates (Bond Yields)

Earlier in this chapter, I summarised studies that highlighted demographic variables and their impact on stock prices, stock returns, and equity markets. Some of these studies also focused on interest rates, risk-free rates, and government bond yields. A few additional studies focusing on bond yields and interest rates are discussed in this section.

In previous research, we highlighted global demographic linkages to GDP growth, debt, inflation, savings, capital flows, etc. These macroeconomic factors affect countries' growth and sustainability prospects. In the aftermath of the credit crisis, we extended our analysis[28] to see whether macro-underpinned demographic variables could explain sovereign bond spreads. To a large degree, real GDP growth, government budget balance, current account, external debt to exports ratio, household savings, and household debt explain the variation in sovereign bond spreads (relative to Germany) for countries in our study. These macro variables are affected by demographic factors. Hence demographic factors affect sovereign spreads through macro-fundamental variables.

According to our reasoning, high real GDP growth, household savings, government fiscal balance, and current account balance imply lower risk and lower sovereign bond spreads. Therefore, their expected regression coefficient signs should be negative. Similarly, low household debt and a low gross external debt to exports ratio imply lower risk and lower sovereign bond spreads. Hence their expected signs should be positive.

The combined explanatory power and significance of these variables differ across countries, with the adjusted R^2 of the regressions ranging from 41% in the UK to 96% in Spain. As expected, macroeconomic fundamentals affect sovereign bond yield spreads differently across countries. Fundamental macro factors need to be followed closely to understand countries' sovereign ratings, spreads, and fiscal sustainability.

Favero et al.[29] studied the well-established persistence of bond yields using demographic-based factors and, based on that, constructed bond-yield forecasts. They stated that empirical models feature a very high level of persistence that makes long-horizon predictions inherently inaccurate. They related the common persistent component of the US term structure of interest rates to population age composition. The age structure composition determines the equilibrium rate in the monetary policy rule and, therefore, the persistent component in one-period yields. Fluctuations in demographics are then transmitted to the whole term structure via the expected policy rate components. They built an affine term structure model that exploited demographic information to capture yield dynamics and produced forecasts of bond yields and excess returns of value for long-term investors.

Gozluklu and Marin[30] studied the strong co-movement between real stock and nominal bond yields at generational frequencies. Using a stochastic decomposition of nominal bond yields, they found that demographic changes affect nominal yields mainly through real bond yields and have a moderate effect on both the inflation risk premium and expected inflation. Based on a cross-country panel, they found empirical support for their theoretical predictions. The empirical evidence illustrates that the strength of demographic effect on real yields explains cross-country differences in the co-movement between stock and bond markets. They also noted that other explanations using alternate demographic channels failed to explain such cross-country heterogeneity.

Carvalho et al.[31] studied the various channels through which demographics affect interest rates. According to them, demographic changes can affect the equilibrium real interest rate in three ways. (i) Increased longevity or increased longevity expectations puts downward pressure on the real interest rate as individuals build up their savings in anticipation of a longer retirement period. A decrease in the population growth rate has two opposing effects: (ii) Capital per worker increases, leading to lower real interest rates through a reduced marginal product of capital and (iii) eventually leading to a higher old-age dependency ratio (the fraction of retirees to workers). As retirees save less than workers, this reduces the aggregate savings rate and pushes up real rates. The authors stated that demographic trends have important implications for monetary policy, especially regarding the zero-lower-bound on nominal interest rates.

In the earlier report "How Demographics Affect Asset Prices"[18], we used demographic variables to predict 10-year bond yields in the US, Germany, and Japan. We found the results from regressing 10-year government bond yields for the three countries on their respective Yuppie-Nerd ratio (the ratio of the number of 20–34-year-olds to the number of 40–54-year-olds), and inflation provided a good regression fit. We noted there that the development and access of government bond markets for both individuals and pension funds, directly and indirectly, are fairly similar. We highlighted the need to consider foreign investor demand for sovereign bonds of developed countries in a globalised world. We stated that demographic ratios would change with changes in longevity and lifecycle changes to work entry changes and retiremeny.

Gagnon et al.[32] studied the role of demographics in a world characterised by many as the "new normal". Their model indicates that post-WW2 baby boom demographic factors influenced real interest rates and real GDP growth from 1960 to the 1980s. Since the 1980s, the model accounted for a little more than a 1-percentage-point decline in real GDP growth and real interest rates—much of the permanent declines in those variables. Their model predicted GDP growth and interest rates will remain low by historical standards, consistent with a "new normal" for the US economy.

Demographic factors alone accounted for a little more than a 1-percentage-point decline in the equilibrium real interest rate in the model since the 1980s—much, if not all, of the actual permanent decline in real interest rates over that period according to time-series estimates of Johannsen and Mertens (forthcoming) and Holston et al.[33]. The model is also consistent with demographics having lowered real GDP growth by 1.25 percentage points since the 1980s, primarily through lower growth in the labour supply in line with changes in estimated GDP trend growth over that period.

Ho[34] employed a Bayesian estimation framework to investigate the robustness of a range of estimates regarding demographic effects on interest rates. He showed that these magnitudes are not well-identified without data on capital and life-cycle consumption, which are often omitted. Without these data, small changes in the prior for the discount rate, intertemporal elasticity of substitution, and capital depreciation rate can shift the estimates of the effects of demographics by up to 1.5 percentage points. He stated that Data on the capital-output ratio and life-cycle consumption help identify the models and generate more robust estimates.

A recent review of demographics and interest rates by researchers at actuarial associations (Society of Actuaries, Institute & Faculty of Actuaries, and Canadian Institute of Actuaries)[35] looked at the stability over time of the relationship of age structure to longer-dated bonds and the sovereign bonds of various countries. Their general conclusion from the empirical analysis was that the results hold in many (but not all) circumstances. An increase in the demographic MY ratio is associated with a reduction in bond yields at various points on the yield curve from 3 months to 30 years. An increase in the demographic MO ratio is associated with an increase in those bond yields. When they examined shorter sub-periods within the data, these relationships were not nearly as strong. Generally, they still hold for the sub-period 1960–1974. In some instances, particularly for Canada, they hold for the sub-period 1990–2015.

The authors stated that the bond market turmoil during 1975–1989 resulted in unstable relationships between bond yields and demographic ratios. They found that the demographic ratios are very slow-moving, whereas bond yields (and inflation) moved very rapidly during this period. They emphasised that the relationship is not quite as stable when looking at the circumstances of the UK, Germany, and Japan. They suggested that the smaller (or absence of a) baby boom in these countries precludes us from finding a stable relationship.

Gozluklu and Morin[30] investigated the co-movements in stock and bond yields, relating them to life-cycle savings patterns and the age structure. In their overlapping generations with money model, life-cycle patterns in savings behaviour made both real stock and nominal bond yields move together with the changing population age structure. Their nominal bond yields analysis showed that while moderately influencing the inflation risk premium and expected inflation, demographic changes affect nominal yields mainly through real bond yields. Using US data and also a cross-country panel, they found empirical support for these theoretical predictions. They also showed that the strength of the demographic effect on real yields explains cross-country differences in the co-movement between stock and bond markets, while alternative demographic channels fail to explain such cross-country heterogeneity.

The authors noted that stock yields and real bond yields are negatively correlated with the MY ratio, as are inflation and the inflation risk premium. They found that demographic changes affect nominal yields mainly through real bond yields, and hence, on average, nominal bond yields and real stock yields co-move positively at generational frequencies.

They concluded by highlighting that decomposition of nominal bond yields reveals that the real channel via real bond yields and inflation risk premium play the primary role in explaining stock-bond yield correlation. While the demographic channel cannot explain all of the time variations in stock and bond yields, the first-order effects of the population age structure on financial markets are too significant to be dismissed.

4.5   Demographics and Risk Premiums

Thus far, our discussion has focused on consumer and investor decisions over their life cycle. Demographics and age structure have been shown to affect the individual components of the equity risk premium (the excess return for investing in stocks relative to treasury bills or bonds).

There is an extensive literature on the equity premium. The historical equity premium is best documented in the financial history classic *Triumph of the Optimists*[36] by Dimson, Marsh, and Staunton and its recent updates, as in the Credit Suisse Investment Yearbook(s). However, theoretical explanations and conceptual arguments cannot explain the empirical behaviour of the equity premium in the US and other countries. As several underlying explanations have been found inadequate to explain the level and variability of the equity premium, researchers have named it the *equity premium puzzle*[37].

Ang and Maddaloni[38] conducted a detailed empirical investigation across major developed markets and a sample of 15 countries over a shorter time span to ascertain the effects of demographic changes on risk premiums, specifically the equity risk premia. They found that demographic changes indeed predict risk premia internationally. The relationship between changes in average age and risk premia of the US (found by other studies such as Bakshi and Chen[12] and others) is unique and not observed in other countries. However, they found that the change in the proportion of retired adults is a significant predictor of excess returns. Also, unlike the US experience, increases in the proportion of retirees as the proportion of the total adult population decreases excess returns. Their results are consistent with models that include a retirement state for retirees who receive no income shocks. Since retirees face no labour market risk, they are less averse to bearing aggregate risk and hold substantial amounts of equities—an increasing share of old people would see decreasing risk premiums.

The authors investigated whether their results of increasing growth rates of retirees decreasing future excess returns were related to different levels of social security benefits or participation in securities markets across countries. These factors influence the saving-investment choice of economic agents, especially retirees. They found a similar pattern of demographic predictability across countries with smaller or larger social security benefits and well- or less-developed financial markets. A growing proportion of retired people significantly forecasts decreases in the equity premium over one-, two-, and five-year forecasting horizons. Their international empirical results back up the predictions of Abel[11], who suggested that, as the Baby Boomer generation enters retirement and leaves the middle-aged peak-saving years, future realised excess returns on equity will be low. This demographic predictability of risk premiums by changes in the proportion of retirees is strongest for countries with high levels of social security benefits and countries with less-developed financial systems.

A recent paper by Kopecky and Taylor[39] investigates the impact of population ageing on the equity premium. The authors state that while population ageing has been linked to global declines in real interest rates, it also leads to rising equity risk premiums. By calibrating a heterogeneous agent life-cycle model with equity markets and aggregate risk, they show that aging demographics can simultaneously account for the majority of a downward trend in the risk-free rate and increase the return premium attached to risky assets. Projecting forward to 2050, they show that persistent demographic forces will continue to push the risk-free rate further into negative territory while the equity risk premium remains elevated.

4.6   Asset Holdings and Age

A feature related to how demographics affect asset prices is how asset holdings vary by age. Or, more explicitly, how do individuals vary their portfolio of assets with their age? Many investors and analysts subscribe that the younger population holds more stocks in their portfolio than older people. However, there has not been total agreement on the reasons why this is so.

Jagannathan and Kocherlakota[40] asked why older investors should invest less in stocks and showed that the only consistent explanation was the longer working life of younger investors, against which they could better apportion their risks. They evaluated three alternative explanations given by financial planners, using theories of investor behaviour: (i) that substantial risk in stock holdings can be reduced by holding them over the longer term, (ii) that asset allocation is governed by the needs of large midlife obligations, and (iii) that a younger person "can use wages to cover any losses from increased risk" while an older person cannot. Only the final explanation is viable as a reason for stock-holding advice varying with age—younger people have many years of wages available to them, while the old do not.

Ameriks and Zeldes[41] studied US portfolio holdings over 1982–2001, finding that: (i) although stock holding has increased over decades, nearly 50% of people own no stocks; (ii) there is significant heterogeneity in stock-holding behaviour, with seemingly similar individuals making different portfolio-holding choices regarding wealth in stocks; and (iii) individuals rarely take direct actions to change their portfolio allocations over time.

Figure 4.8 and Figure 4.9 from the Federal Reserve Board show US asset holdings by age and race. Figure 4.8 highlights that age has a bearing on the asset breakdown of individual portfolios. Similarly, Figure 4.9 shows a difference across *race* characteristics in how portfolios are allocated across asset groups.

Similarly, other characteristics also matter, such as *education and income*. Therefore, I reiterate my original assertion that demographics is about consumer and worker characteristics beyond just age. People's behaviour reflects their psychology, background, experiences, and consumer and worker characteristics. This is also easily understood by a quick glance at the appendix at the end of this chapter: the US Survey of Consumer Finances (SCF) 2019 shows that asset holdings vary with income levels, age, family structure, and education. Inequality is highlighted, with the top 1% of

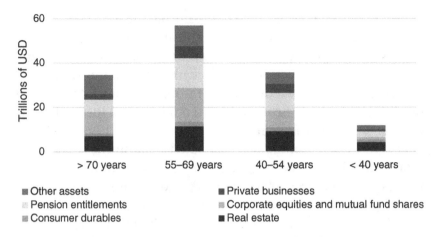

Figure 4.8   US assets by age: Q4, 2020.
SOURCE: US Federal Reserve.

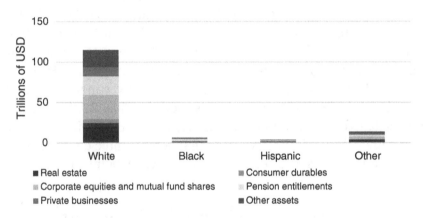

Figure 4.9   Assets by race: Q4, 2020.
SOURCE: US Federal Reserve.

households owning 38% of overall equity and 51% of directly held equity. The pandemic has been good for equity market holders and has worsened inequality, with lower-income groups, women, self-employed people, and minorities being relatively worse off.

Poterba et al.[14] investigated stock-holding patterns for the US, reporting significant changes in the aggregate and cross-sectional patterns of corporate stock ownership during the post-WW2 period. There has been a gradual but significant trend toward greater ownership of equity through mutual funds and thrift plans and defined contribution pension plans, with direct individual ownership replaced by indirect ownership through a financial intermediary. The rise of IRAs, thrift plans, and other related institutions led to an increase in stock ownership during the 1987–1995 period.

Pew Research[42] summarised the latest data on the demographics of stockholders, reporting that among those with annual family incomes of less than $35,000, about 20% have assets in the stock market. The shares increase as income rises; among those with incomes above $100,000, 88% own stocks (directly or indirectly). The amount of assets families hold in stocks also varies considerably by income. Among those with incomes less than $35,000, the median amount held is less than $10,000. For those at the higher end of the income scale, the median amount is more than $130,000. Families headed by White adults are more likely than those headed by Black or Hispanic adults to invest in the stock market. A majority (61%) of non-Hispanic White households own some stock, compared with 31% of non-Hispanic Black and 28% of Hispanic households. Median investments vary here as well: among Whites, the median is about $51,000. By comparison, the median for Black families is $12,000, and for Hispanic families, it is just under $11,000. Thus we note that demographic characteristics of investors such as race and education influence their asset holdings.

4.7   Demographics and Equity Sectors

Thus far, the discussion has focused on demographic influences on life-cycle investments, equity returns, bond yields, risk premiums, and asset holdings, but there is another very significant influence of demographic trends on industries and equity sectors. This allows for the fundamentals of creating demographic-based portfolios, funds, baskets, certificates, and exchange-traded funds, to name a few instruments and investment vehicles.

Dellavigna and Pollet[43] studied the impact of demographic information based on cohorts and demonstrated the potential to earn risk-adjusted returns of 5–7% p.a. using long-term cohort-based information. They considered demographic information, showing that changes in cohort size produced forecastable demand changes for age-sensitive sectors such as toys, bicycles, beer, life insurance, and nursing homes. These demand changes are predictable once a specific cohort is born. They used lagged consumption and demographic data to forecast future consumption demand growth induced by changes in age structure. They found that demand forecasts predict profitability by industry, and future demand forecast changes 5 to 10 years ahead predict annual industry stock returns. One additional percentage point of annualised demand growth due to demographics predicts a 5–10 percentage point increase in annual abnormal industry stock returns, but forecast demand changes over shorter horizons do not predict stock returns. The predictability results are more substantial for industries with higher barriers to entry and more pronounced age patterns in consumption. A trading strategy exploiting demographic information earns an annualised risk-adjusted return of 5–7%.

A similar exercise in 2001 allowed me to predict that the Chinese auto industry would grow and overtake the US between 2010 and 2015, using crude population growth and GDP per capita growth forecasts to drive automobile demand. Another exercise considering mobile phone demand was also very good at making similar forecasts over 10–15 years, assuming simple growth scenarios.

Another very relevant investment question related to the discussion in this section is whether demographics can help predict positively which sectors to invest in for the medium and long term. I asked a similar question about two decades ago to predict sectors positively aligned to future demographic changes.

We extended our focus on consumers by attempting to predict the industry sectors that would emerge as winners from demographic changes. In one of my earlier reports, I developed my thinking of many years, answering this client request: "Please tell us which sectors we should invest in based on your view of forthcoming and future demographic changes". This report formed the foundation for my collaboration with Credit Suisse's HOLT team, which helped choose stocks within the sectors we had identified to create a basket of stocks. A similar analysis with a demographic component underlay the construction of Megatrend Funds.

We stressed in our research that our characterisation of demographic change is different from others in the field, and we see demographic changes as having short-term, medium-term, and long-term effects on macroeconomic and financial variables. We believe that unprecedented demographic changes will impact macroeconomic variables such as GDP, aggregate consumption, the current account, inflation, and specific industrial and service sectors.

We emphasised that ignorance of the effects of such demographic change is likely to prove costly in the future to economies, societies, companies, and individuals, as we have seen over the past decade. We have been bullish on the following sectors: pharmaceuticals and biotech, retirement real estate, leisure and travel/tourism, financial services, commodities, emerging markets, infrastructure, and technology. Investors who agree with our views should assess the correlations of these sectors with their existing allocations and create portfolios that take advantage of these demographic trends. Some academic research also supports our conclusions, as mentioned earlier in this section.

The demographic sectors[44] that are clearly advantaged in my view (first formed in 2002) remain the same, and the underlying reasons have grown stronger over time. I discuss next all six sectors in terms of their relative importance, with technology being a common sector underlying all the other sectors as a disruptor and improver:

- *Health services and pharmaceuticals:* This, in my view, is the most critical sector broadly and includes genomics and biotechnology. As discussed in the next chapter, the overarching importance of health and healthy life expectancy emanates from the quality of life and cost concerns. Individuals, families, companies, and governments will need a renewed focus on newer dimensions of health—mental and occupational health come to mind, and attention on them is growing. The advent of Alzheimer's, Parkinson's, Multiple Sclerosis (MS), Myalgic Encephalomyelitis (ME), newer diseases and afflictions amongst the old, and newer diagnoses for the young related to allergies and diet mean a stronger emphasis on changing health trends. Mark Penn's *MicroTrends* books[45,46] highlight the newly emerging health trends. The COVID outbreak showcases the emphasis of individual and public health in both advanced and emerging countries that face challenges of avoidable deaths due to diphtheria, malaria, tuberculosis, chicken pox, typhoid, cholera, etc.

Researchers have studied how household portfolios change after retirement and how health shocks such as the death of a spouse or a heart attack/stroke affect the composition of household portfolios. They found that ownership rates for homes and vehicles fall dramatically with age, whereas bank account holdings and certificates of deposits (CDs) increase with age. Health shocks predict home sales, vehicle sales, transfer of money into bank accounts, and CD holdings. Poor mental and physical health amplify these responses. New pharma and biotech research into mental health disorders and gerontological disability is needed, as we are seeing the initial effects of increased longevity accompanied by many more mental disorders than in the past.

The challenge of genomics, pharma, and biotech is to invent and discover new drugs and treatments that cost-effectively enable the older population to enjoy a better quality of life in their post-retirement years. Delivering services efficiently and effectively is crucial, as the COVID pandemic is teaching us.

- *Financial services:* As humans live longer and better than ever before, they need their wealth and income to keep pace with their desires and needs. Financial services broadly are critical to serving their needs from loans to individuals and families, health insurance, life insurance, auto loans, credit cards, etc. The growth of FinTech has facilitated better, efficient delivery of such services. As individuals evolve in their human relationships, use of technology, modes of consumption, and work life, a necessary complement is the evolution of financial services.

The investment, insurance, banking, and reinsurance sectors are changing in response to the needs of consumers and workers, regulation, cost pressures, and their desire to innovate and modernise. The growth of new asset classes, alternative investments, and improved technology has meant that financial services firms and fund managers have had to innovate to develop new return-generating strategies and products to generate business revenues and profits in an increasingly competitive world.

We see financial product innovation, risk management, and active asset allocation as the cornerstones of growth in financial services, much of which will occur in catering to the older retiring population whose needs and perspectives are not known with certainty and could evolve over time. The transition trend from defined benefit (DB) to defined contribution (DC) pension plans will create a demand for financial planning unlike any we have seen before. This will occur when individuals may not have enough human capital to diversify against the financial risks they face during retirement. Even Baby Boomers or pre–Baby Boomers may not have felt the need to plan for such long horizons in the face of reduced or no income.

- *Leisure, luxury, and travel:* Growing wealth and increasing inequality keep stimulating this sector and providing a great fillip from demands for luxury yachts and personal cruise ships, residential luxury homes valued at billions, space trips, ownership of islands, and ownership of global corporates. This demand is here to stay as long as market-based capitalist enterprises and democracies exist. The list of billionaires with more than $10 bn in net assets continues to expand in the US and worldwide. According to *Forbes* (https://www.forbes.com/billionaires), "the number of billionaires on Forbes' 35th annual list of the world's wealthiest exploded to an unprecedented 2,755– 660 more than a year ago. Of those, a record high 493 were new to the list–roughly one every 17 hours, including 210 from China and Hong Kong. Another 250 who'd fallen off in the past came roaring back. A staggering 86% are richer than a year ago". From earlier generation family industrialists and oil-based billionaires to newer wealthy billionaires in tech, real estate, and other sectors, as well as those in emerging China, Russia, Brazil, Mexico, and India, the number of uber-rich has grown. But most importantly, their needs, aspirations, and behaviour are different from those of billionaires 20 years ago.

For retirees who have worked for most of their lives, advances in longevity have led them to expect a longer post-retirement life span along with more free time in which to pursue leisure activities. The work-leisure trade-off will become a critical factor for most people in old age. The ease of booking travel, the travel itself, and post-travel processing of experiences, videos, photos, etc., appears to have enhanced the desire for and satisfaction from travel for the older population. Technology plays a significant part in enabling easier travel, cheaper insurance, and better communications with family and loved ones or doctors in the home country when seniors travel abroad.

- *Retirement real estate:* The number of retirees and their life spans keeps increasing globally, and the current generation of retirees are in general much better off than their counterparts in previous generations. What about housing demand? Will they need the same type and size of houses that they lived in during their peak years? It is safe to surmise that they will not, for various reasons: smaller family size, lesser demands for work, avoiding congestion and traffic, a preference to be closer to nursing and healthcare, weather, and locational preferences.

The current generation of retirees—those retiring after 1995—are amongst the wealthiest on average in the developed world, as they participated in the macroeconomic growth of the 1980s and 1990s and benefited from the best asset performance decades while they were in the highest-earning periods of their working life. Data from US and European country surveys supports the fact that the wealth of the 65+ age cohort is amongst the top two groups of all age cohorts. But that wealth needs to last longer for an average retiree. Many retiree households could use that wealth to buy retirement homes or relocate to smaller, manageable homes or buy houses as a retirement asset with their surplus savings. In our view, housing and real estate markets are easier for the average retired population to understand, follow, and invest in than many other financial assets. Therefore, we believe that retirement real estate catering to the growing and different demands of the old will be a positive sector. Real estate developments in the sunshine belt of the US and southern parts of Europe are being placed closer to leisure, health, educational/IT, and shopping facilities for the growing number of retired people. We think the retirement real estate sector is positively related to the demographic changes based on an increasing number of retirees, an increase in retirees' wealth, and housing being used as an asset in individual and family portfolios.

- *Emerging markets:* The projected ageing and decline of populations in advanced developed countries has increased the appeal of younger emerging markets as potentially greater growth targets for the largest retail firms globally. This extends beyond food and beverages to sports, technology, furniture, cars, and even houses in a globalised world where information is easier and cheaper to acquire for decision-making. In terms of numbers, given the income and wealth of the uber-rich in emerging markets, consumers and workers are attractive target pools for global firms selling or hiring. The aspirations and expenditure patterns of billionaires in China, Russia, Brazil, and India garner the attention of leading wealth managers, retail and tech firms, and luxury and infrastructure service firms.

  The increasing focus of global brands and manufacturers is not just on drawing labour from emerging markets but also on gaining the attention and purchasing power of consumers in those markets toward goods made in the advanced developed world. The growing middle classes in China, India, Brazil, Mexico, and other emerging markets will more than likely offset the decreased or diminished demand resulting from fewer consumers in the developed world. The number of consumers in emerging markets is increasing, as is their relative purchasing power, with the middle classes in those markets trying to emulate their richer middle-class cousins in the developed world. This is an essential point as aggregate private consumption expenditures account for the largest component of GDP by expenditures.

- *Infrastructure:* The growth in demand for infrastructure goes hand in hand with the growth and development of an economy. Changing consumers and workers, along with multiple generations co-existing and wanting a greener, more sustainable world (as we discuss in Chapter 7), naturally create a demand for new infrastructure, including roads, airports, waterways, railway tracks, and space vehicles. This demand plays another important role by creating infrastructure as an asset class with longer-term matches to liability cash flows held by insurers, pension funds, and reinsurers. The growth of megacities and major global production centres in the emerging-market countries further fuels the need for good infrastructure to attract financial and real capital. Nearly all population growth until 2030 will be in urban areas of the world, in our view. Most major urban cities and centres are very strained and struggle to cope with blackouts (New York), snow and ice (London), flooding (Mumbai), and smog (Delhi, Mexico City).

The suppliers and creators of new infrastructure will need to cope with the changing needs of older retirees and the next generations of post-Millennials. Today, most of the world's urban population lives in urban settlements with fewer than 1 million inhabitants. More precisely, in 2018, two billion people lived in urban settlements with fewer than 500,000 inhabitants, and another 400 million in settlements between 500,000 and 1 million, totalling 58% of the urban population. According to the World Urbanization Prospects[47], "In 1990 there were 10 cities with more than 10 million inhabitants, hosting 153 million people, which represents less than 7 per cent of the global urban population. Today, the number of megacities has tripled to 33, and most of them are in Asia, including fiver that have recently joined the group: Bangalore, Bangkok, Jakarta, Lahore and Madras. Globally, the population megacities contain has grown to 529 million". The challenge is to create sustainable, green, affordable, and liveable infrastructure for the changing world and its population as they demand different infrastructure.

4.8   Demographics and Real Estate

As we discussed earlier, life cycles are changing, and so are consumers, savers, and investors in this modern, ageing, globalised world. The implications for life-cycle asset allocation and consumption are complex, because careers, personal lives, and retirement and health paradigms are undergoing radical shifts. We have discussed the impact of pensions for long-bond yields and individuals' retirement savings and bequest motives.

One of the most significant financial decisions for individuals, households, and families is home ownership; a house is the biggest asset of a typical individual or household. Real estate markets have done well, and investors have gained from real estate appreciation in the Western world over the last four decades. Real estate has been used by ageing retirees to help provide income/collateral when their liquid retirement savings have been strained and stretched by financial needs in a longer post-retirement phase than they had planned for or anticipated. The effects of demographic factors on the housing market have also been studied in past academic and policy studies.

Mankiw and Weil[48] found that significant demographic changes induce large (and mostly predictable) changes in the demand for housing. These fluctuations in demand appear to have a substantial impact on the price of housing in the US. They also concluded that the recent demographic patterns (from baby boom to baby bust) imply that housing demand will grow more slowly over the next 20 years. If the historical pattern continues, their estimates suggest that real housing prices will fall substantially. As they noted then and we saw later, the housing bust turned out to be a housing boom and eventual bust.

Using post-WW2 Canadian data, Engelhardt and Poterba[49] examined the links between demography-induced changes in housing demand and real house prices. They stated that although Canadian demographic patterns are very similar to those in the US, real house prices have exhibited a substantially different trajectory: they rose in the early 1970s and then fell nearly 40% between 1975 and the mid-1980s. They estimated simple time-series models relating house prices to demographic factors; and unlike Mankiw and Weil's previous estimates for the US[48], they found a statistically insignificant and (in most cases) negative association between demographic demand and house prices. Their results suggest caution in extrapolating historical US trends to the next century and highlight that substantial real declines in house values are not impossible.

Green and Hendershott[50] analysed age-related influences on housing demand and real house prices. They argued that real house prices are directly determined by the willingness of households to pay for (and willingness of builders to supply) a constant-quality house. Changes in the quantity of housing demanded affect real prices only to the extent that the long-run housing supply schedule is positively sloped. In their paper, they used 1980 census data to measure the impact of the age structure, education, and income on the willingness of households to pay for a constant-quality house. They computed total and partial derivatives for the effect of age on housing demand, and the total derivatives looked much like the Mankiw-Weil age-demand[48] results. They found that the partial derivatives suggested the demand for housing tends to be flat or rise slightly with age, and they believed their partial derivatives more accurately depicted the age-demand relationship. They concluded that the ageing of the population should not be expected to lower real house prices. Credit Suisse Economics Research[51] also highlighted the interaction between US demographics and the real estate market. Around 1965, a critical mass of baby bulgers (born in 1935 or soon after) began buying real estate to house their families. House prices, which had been falling relative to CPI inflation, began to rise in real terms.

Takats[52] showed that demographic factors affect real house prices significantly, using real house price data from 22 advanced economies between 1970 and 2009. His paper showed that 1% greater real GDP per capita corresponds to around 1% higher real house prices. Similarly, a 1% larger population implies around 1% higher real house prices, and a 1% higher dependency ratio is associated with around 2/3% lower real house prices. According to his paper, ageing will lower real house prices substantially over the next 40 years. Based on a more detailed analysis, Takats stated that demographic tailwinds of the past decades are switching fast to strong demographic headwinds in the coming decades: around 80 basis points per annum in the US and much stronger in ageing Europe and Japan. This switch will be large and economically significant across all regions that have seen rapid ageing.

A paper from the US Congressional Budget Office[53] discussed the underlying demand for new housing units (the demand that prevails when cyclical and financial conditions are normal and vacancy rates are at long-run levels). Over long periods, this underlying demand is the main factor that determines housing starts. It has five components:

- The change in the number of households (occupied units) due to population growth
- The trend change in the number of households due to other factors
- The trend change in the number of vacant units for sale or rent
- The change in the number of other vacant units, such as second homes
- The net scrappage (removal) of existing units

According to this paper, increased household formation due to population growth would cause most of the increase in the underlying demand for new housing units from 2008 to 2012.

The demand for housing is primarily driven by demographics. During the post-WW2 housing boom, this was due to incentives given to US armed forces personnel returning from war to peace and contributing to new household and family creation. Population growth, the movement of people, and the formation of households determine the need for housing. Urbanisation also plays an essential role in shaping the real estate market. In addition, income and savings trends influence the willingness and ability to pay for houses.

D. Miles of the Bank of England[54] studied the implications of demographics on house prices and mortgage design. His paper modelled the housing market, accounting for population density, to assess the impact of population changes on the value and size of the housing stock. The model implied that if population density is on an upward trajectory, rising population and income increasingly generate price responses and diminishing growth in the stock of housing. This has implications for the optimal structure of housing finance: it makes equity financing of home purchases more desirable. He stresses that hybrid debt-equity contracts for financing house purchases have micro and macro benefits. At the micro household level, they allow more effective risk-sharing, generating larger benefits with higher house prices. Hybrid contracts may be a stabilising force at the macro level because they generate funding costs that increase as house prices accelerate.

Gevorgyan[55] tested the linkages between demographics and house prices. Her model predicted that economies with a higher fraction of old people in the overall population have lower house prices. She tested this hypothesis using data on house prices and demographic variables from the Organization for Economic Cooperation and Development (OECD), finding that if population growth increases by 1 percentage point, house price growth increases by 1.4 percentage points.

The US Census Bureau's surveys of home-ownership by age in 2019, relative to those from 1982 and 2001, displays the following trend: an increase in the share and number of older people aged 65+, with the peak of home-ownership stretching into their late 60s or early 70s. As in Fig 4.10, the wealthier older age groups continue buying homes in their later years.

Older people often buy a second home or buy a home on behalf of their children or grandchildren to transfer as a gift or later as a bequest. The trend toward older people owning more homes has to

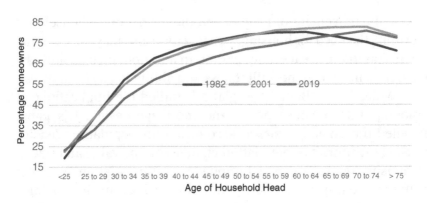

Figure 4.10 Homeownership rates by age of head of household.
SOURCE: US Census Bureau.

do with their wealth and the lack of affordability of homes by some members of younger age groups. These younger age groups have lower incomes relative to house prices and exhibit a preference to buy houses later in life, somewhat in line with delayed marriages and parenthood. The newer generations—Millennials and post-Millennials—believe more in renting and sharing than the Baby Boomer generation.

The US Census Bureau also reported home-ownership rate differences by race for 2021 Q1: against the US average of 65.6% home-ownership, Whites had ownership rates of 73.8%, Blacks 45.1%, Hispanics 49.1%, and all other races 57.1%. Similarly, home-ownership rates vary based on income: of those with income higher than the median, 79.4% own homes, while of those with below-median incomes, 51.7% own homes. The national average is 65.6%.

4.9   Demographics and Commodities

Population numbers and demand for commodities by consumers and workers influence commodity prices and, consequently, inflation. While commodities as a group cover a vast expanse of commodity types, we would be remiss not to recount a few critical features of commodity price increases—especially food and oil, gold, silver, and copper—along with their availability. The study of demographics in economics owes a lot to the Malthusian theories that we discuss here. This is related to two fundamental issues: climate change and sustainable development goals.

Over the last five decades, world oil prices have influenced inflation and, by extension, the level of savings (disposable income minus consumer expenditures) by households and individuals. This has been particularly true of low-income oil-importing countries. Food demand is inelastic, as food is an essential part of consumer expenditures. Higher expenditures on food imply less to save or spend on non-food discretionary consumer expenditures. Demand for soft commodities like grains, cereals, and edible oils influence their prices depending on storage capacity and transport costs. Chinese pork and soybean prices and Indian onion prices have been drivers of overall inflation over the last couple of decades.

In the eighteenth century, population and economics came to the attention of policymakers thanks to Thomas Malthus's treatise highlighting the connection between population growth and growth in resources, focusing primarily on food. In *An Essay on the Principle of Population* (1798), Malthus warned of future difficulties based on the population increasing in a geometric progression (doubling every 25 years) while food production increased in an arithmetic progression, resulting in famine unless birth rates decreased. This was in contrast to the prevailing popular view that living standards were improving in Europe. In his book, considered one of the classics of demography, Malthus wrote that "the increase of population is necessarily limited by the means of subsistence"; "population does invariably increase when the means of subsistence increase"; and "the superior power of population is repressed by moral restraint, vice and misery".

Two centuries later, biologist M.S. Swaminathan[56] raised the issue of facing a Malthusian crisis following a rapid global population increase from 6 billion in 1998 to more than 7 billion, alongside (i) decreased arable land and water availability per capita, (ii) expanding food demand due to urbanisation and increased living standards, (iii) environmental damage and increased sea level, (iv) stagnant marine production, and (v) decline in world per capita grain production. He asked if recent advances in molecular genetics, information, space, renewable energy, and management technologies could help promote sustainable food security.

According to the UN's Food and Agriculture Organization (FAO), food security exists when all people, at all times, have physical and economic access to sufficient, safe, nutritious food that meets their dietary needs and food preferences for an active and healthy life. The dimensions of availability, access, utilisation, and stability are considered vital.

The International Food Policy Research Institute's "The Global Report on Food Crisis (GRFC) 2020" reported the highest global number of acutely food-insecure people on record. It revealed that in 2019, some 135 million people in 55 countries and territories urgently needed food, livelihood, and nutrition assistance due to conflict, weather extremes, economic shocks, or a combination of all three drivers. This figure reflected not only worsening levels of acute food insecurity in many countries but also the broader availability of food security data, including in previously inaccessible areas and in contexts that had previously yielded poor-quality data. In these 55 food-crisis countries and territories, an estimated 75 million children were stunted and 17 million were suffering from acute wasting.

Deaton and Laroque[57] investigated the volatility of commodity prices for 13 commodity groups. They used a model incorporating myopic demand and supply and inventories of competitive speculators who held commodities for profits. They summarised the evidence for commodity prices over 1900–1987, stating that the commodity prices for the commodity groups they studied were autocorrelated and volatile and displayed skewness and kurtosis. The volatility of consumer prices affects household savings and expenditure patterns.

In the COVID era, uncertainty drove up demand for gold and silver, and their prices were high in 2020. Oil prices gyrated wildly due to fluctuating economic demand caused by industrial shutdowns and lockdowns. The 2021 economic recovery in developed countries post-COVID has also led to a recovery in oil prices, and a shift toward clean energy driven by climate change has led to a rapid increase in demand for copper. Copper price appreciation and silver were notable in the period from onset of COVID to 2021Q2.

According to Goldhub[58], in 2021, Q1 gold demand (excluding OTC) was 815.7 t, virtually on a par with Q4 2020 but down 23% compared with Q1 2020. Jewellery demand of 477.4 t was 52% higher year over year, a strong improvement compared with the historically weak Q1 2020; and the value of jewellery spending—US $27.5 bn—was the highest for the first quarter since Q1 2013. Demand remained muted on a longer-term basis, 6% below the five-year quarterly average of 505.9 t. India and China were the engines of recovery, generating the vast majority of global year-over-year growth. With an annual demand equivalent to about 25% of the total physical demand worldwide, India is one of the largest consumers of gold Its retail demand for gold (jewellery, and bar and coin combined) is related to income, desire for adornment, and gold being considered an inflation hedge.

Silver had the best performance in terms of commodity price gains in 2020 as demand dominated. Silver was trading around $27 an ounce in mid-May 2021, a 74% rise from a year earlier when the spot price was around $15.5 per ounce. In comparison, gold prices rose 6.4% in a year. From electrical switches and solar panels to chemical-producing catalysts, silver is an essential component in many industries. Its unique properties make it nearly impossible to substitute, and its uses span a wide range of applications. Almost every computer, mobile phone, automobile, and appliance contains silver. It is the perfect substance for coating electrical contacts—like those in printed circuit boards—because of its high electrical conductivity and durability.

The impact of demographics through household demand (relative to supply) on food prices, the feedback effect on household savings, and the retail demand for precious metals illustrate how consumers are affected by and influence commodity prices.

4.10   Conclusions

This chapter discussed the ways demographics (consumer and worker behaviours) affects asset prices. Starting with pioneering macro theories of intertemporal consumption, savings, and borrowing, we discussed the impact of demographics on equity prices in the context of changing age structures. In this chapter, I summarised several academic research papers that studied the effects of demographics on equity returns, bond yields and risk premia.

Then we highlighted the asset meltdown hypothesis of the 1990s, which posited a stock market meltdown that never materialised. Demographic forecasts based solely on age or age structure ignored behaviour, and institutional contexts turned out to be wrong. The chapter also focused on stockholders and stock owners versus those who do not hold equity or stocks. We also highlighted mistakes made by researchers who ignored the behaviour of consumers and investors and looked only at their age. A 30-year-old consumer or investor today is not the same as in the 1980s and 1990s, and neither is a 65- or 70-year-old; their opportunities, income, wealth, and preferences are different.

We discussed the link between sovereign bond yields and equity risk premiums. The section on house prices reflected the changes in the behaviour of homeowners over time, especially the growing proportion of older homeowners. Finally, the section on commodity prices highlighted the broader Malthusian concerns of food shortages and food security.

Consumer demands are affected by food prices, and food prices in turn influence consumer expenditures and savings. In addition to food commodities and oil, the retail demand for precious metals is worth noting, especially in China and India, which boast huge populations with preferences that differ from those of advanced countries. Demographics—consumer and worker characteristics that are reflected in their behaviour and demands—will continue to affect asset prices but need to be assessed in the context of institutional structure, taxes, capital markets, and regulatory structure. The appendix shows asset holdings against various demographic characteristics; but as highlighted earlier, these relationships evolve as investor risk preferences and other characteristics evolve in response to the environment and opportunities. Behaviour matters, and insights from the intersection of behavioural finance with asset pricing and derivatives will see future growth. Increased life spans and changing asset horizons and preferences are having an effect on the profiles of household, corporate and government debt (Chapter 3) being held.

Appendix: Demographic Characteristics and Asset Holdings

Family characteristic	Savings bonds	Bonds	Stocks	Pooled investment funds	Retirement accounts	Cash-value life insurance
			Percentage of families holding asset			
All families	**7.5**	**1.1**	**15.2**	**9.1**	**50.5**	**19.0**
Percentile of income						
Less than 20	2.3	*	5.3	2.1	10.7	9.7
20–39.9	5.5	*	7.9	3.6	32.8	16.3
40–59.9	7.7	*	11.5	6.2	53.7	18.0
60–79.9	8.2	.8	17.0	9.0	69.6	23.2
80–89.9	13.0	*	24.8	14.1	80.8	26.5
90–100	14.6	5.1	43.7	34.7	90.5	28.9
Age of reference person (years)						
Less than 35	6.3	*	13.8	4.8	45.3	9.9
35–44	8.9	*	14.3	7.0	55.8	12.7
45–54	7.9	.6	14.5	9.6	57.9	16.8
55–64	7.4	1.5	15.6	10.6	54.5	22.4
65–74	7.2	1.7	15.3	13.3	48.1	27.8
75 or more	7.6	2.7	19.2	10.8	37.7	30.7

Family characteristic	Savings bonds	Bonds	Stocks	Pooled investment funds	Retirement accounts	Cash-value life insurance
Family structure						
Single with child(ren)	5.0	*	5.9	4.0	33.8	13.9
Single, no child, age less than 55	5.2	*	13.4	5.4	40.3	7.7
Single, no child, age 55 or more	5.0	1.8	11.5	7.4	35.9	19.8
Couple with child(ren)	10.6	.9	16.7	10.0	63.4	19.2
Couple, no child	8.2	1.6	20.6	13.0	59.0	26.2
Education of reference person						
No high school diploma	*	*	2.5	1.8	18.7	11.7
High school diploma	4.8	*	7.8	4.0	41.2	18.1
Some college	6.5	.7	12.8	5.0	44.4	18.4
College degree	11.7	2.1	25.8	17.8	71.0	22.1
Race or ethnicity of respondent						
White non-Hispanic	9.8	1.5	18.6	11.9	57.2	20.8
Black or African-American non-Hispanic	2.7	*	6.7	1.8	34.9	21.5
Hispanic or Latino	*	*	4.3	*	25.5	5.8
Other or multiple race	5.3	.8	15.6	8.5	52.7	16.3

SOURCE: US Federal Reserve.

Chapter 5

Health and Longevity

As illustrated and discussed in the previous two chapters, demographics affects macroeconomic variables and asset prices. However, a large and increasing part of individuals' life spans is the post-working-life retirement period. The share of retirement in life spans increases due to increases in longevity. However, labour markets in most countries have not adjusted retirement ages upward with the changes in longevity. Another development influencing labour markets is the later entry of young individuals into the workforce; this has been caused by increasing years of education beyond high school and some entrants having further educational qualifications beyond an initial undergraduate degree. In this chapter, we discuss health, longevity trends, longevity risk, and longevity risk management[1]. We introduced increased longevity in Chapter 2 using data on increased life expectancies across selected countries. We further discussed the implications for growth and monetary and fiscal policy in Chapter 3.

Economic historian and Nobel laureate Robert Fogel studied different cohorts of US army personnel based on several waves to understand the social implications of increased longevity[2]. He stated that the lessons from longitudinal household data set analyses of developed countries would provide ideas and guidance to countries in South and East Asia regarding how to meet the demands of the increasing number of people who survive to old age.

In another paper, Fogel[3] argued that the advanced (Organisation for Economic Cooperation and Development [OECD]) countries generally face crises in their pension and healthcare systems not because they are poor but because they are exceedingly rich by historical or Third World standards. He remarked, "It is the enormous increase in their per capita incomes over the past century that permitted the average length of retirement to increase by five-fold, the proportion of a cohort that lives to retire to increase by seven-fold and the amount of leisure time available to those still in the labour force to increase by nearly four-fold".

The demand for leisure in retirement in advanced countries has led to a drop in potential GDP growth due to ageing, as shown in Chapter 3. In addition, precommitments to health, social security/pension, and long-term care expenditures by governments have led to unsustainable long-term fiscal burdens that need renegotiation (as these promises cannot be fulfilled). This is the theme I have been advocating over the last 15 years but articulated best in a review of fiscal sustainability[4].

As the ongoing COVID crisis has shown, countries that invested well in public health infrastructure and systems have been better able to withstand the effects of the pandemic in terms of number of cases, number of deaths, and—on a positive note—rates of recovery. Those countries have adapted by creating additional beds, deploying ventilators and oxygen cylinders, testing, and manufacturing and using protective equipment for nurses and doctors. As expected, large emerging economy countries with poor infrastructure and high population density have fared worse: Brazil, Mexico, Russia, and Turkey. China has been a surprising exception for many reasons, including effective lockdowns early in the pandemic. The heterogeneity of impact, responses, and recovery reveals more than just the state of public health; it reflects governance, education, diet, life expectancy, and individual, household, private sector, and public sector responses to health emergencies like the COVID pandemic.

The pandemic has also demonstrated that those with fewer underlying health conditions have had faster recovery rates. Health will be a key indicator of development in a world where biosecurity risks are likely to become more prominent. Part of the Malthusian hypothesis of population may be coming true. Better health outcomes require a combination of individual behaviour, public incentives, health insurance, and effective, resilient public health systems.

Nobel laureate Angus Deaton[5] examined how some parts of the world experienced sustained progress, opening gaps and setting the stage for today's disproportionately unequal world. He took an in-depth look at the historical and ongoing patterns behind the health and wealth of nations. He described the successes of antibiotics, pest control, vaccinations, and clean water on the one hand, and disastrous famines and the HIV/AIDS epidemic on the other (a bit of a Malthusian reckoning). He considered how economic growth in India and China had improved the lives of more than a billion people. Deaton argued that reforming incentives to drug companies and lifting trade restrictions would allow the developing world to bring about its own Great Escape. That might prove more effective than international aid, which had not helped much.

5.1   Health Issues, Expenditures, and Measures

This section discusses global health systems, presents health expenditure trends, and discusses measures of preparedness and resilience to deal with epidemics and pandemics. Each individual adult is ultimately responsible for behaviours that are associated with good health or at least preventive toward disease, infections, and ill-health. The old adage of "health is wealth" is very appropriate as the world deals with the second year of COVID-19 via lockdowns, vaccinations, social distancing measures, etc. It is vital to understand the interactions between health, longevity, and pensions from different perspectives: individual, family, corporate, and societal.

Nearly a decade ago, I highlighted the significance of a holistic understanding of consumer and worker behaviour in terms of their universal impact on every individual in the world[6] and their market, economic, and societal impacts[7]. Our research-based advisory and advocacy stated that governments need to adopt a holistic policy making framework that includes health, education, benefits, taxes, pensions, and employment to achieve success in dealing with life-cycle changes. Opportunities exist for new financial services products across banking, insurance, reinsurance, derivatives, and multi-strategy asset allocation. Real estate, infrastructure, hedge funds, and private equity will also have rich new roles to play amidst changing consumers and workers.

5.1.1   Health Expenditures

Advanced countries tend to spend a lot on health as a share of GDP. However, both the expenditures and the split between public and private (out of pocket) costs vary.

Figure 5.1 and Figure 5.2 show the variations in health expenditures as well as health expenditures per capita in the G6 advanced countries. The US leads in health expenditures as a share of current GDP and health expenditures per capita but lags in median age and

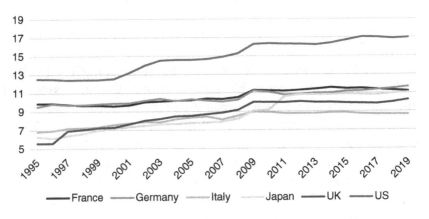

Figure 5.1   Health expenditures (% of current GDP).
SOURCE: OECD.

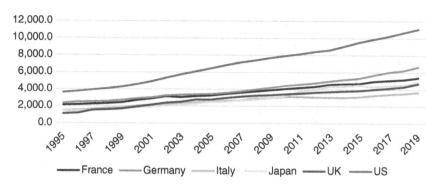

Figure 5.2 Health expenditure per capita (current prices, current purchasing power parity [PPP], USD).
SOURCE: OECD.

life expectancy at birth (shown in Chapter 2). This reflects divergences in terms of inequality and health access across different regions of the US, as well as inefficiency in the delivery of healthcare based on each dollar spent.

The last 25 years (1995–2019) have seen health expenditure shares increase over time across all the countries. The increases reflect not only greater healthcare expenditures but also increases in the range, quality, and availability of health treatments. Advances in pharmaceutical drugs, new surgical procedures, and genomics-related improvements, all based on biomedical progress, have gone hand in hand with the increased prosperity of individuals, households, and certain sectors.

An alternative view is to assess health expenditures per person adjusted for population size. This is shown in Figure 5.2, where increases in health expenditures per capita show the differences across the G6 countries: the US leads the group, with health expenditures per capita more than tripling of over the period 1995–2019. A noticeable trend is that health expenditures over time have grown from essential and critical care to cosmetic and optional treatments for a select minority of richer people.

The aggregate expenditures displayed in Figure 5.2 mask the inequality within countries and the efficiency of expenditures translating into better health outcomes. Another way to look at health expenditures is the share of private out-of-pocket expenditures as a share of total health expenditures: as shown in Figure 5.3, this is less than 20% for all of the countries except Italy. The balance of the expenditures is defrayed by government and compulsory health insurance schemes.

5.1.2   Global Health Security

The ongoing pandemic is a wake-up call for the entire world to focus on health security for citizens' health, economic, and social welfare. Biological threats create risks for global health, international security, and the global economy irrespective of whether they originate from natural, accidental, or intentional causes. Infectious diseases know no borders in a globalised world, so all countries must prioritise and exercise the ability to prevent, detect, and rapidly respond to public health emergencies. Every country must also have the resilience to tackle biological and health risks from infectious diseases by identifying, preventing, and responding to national health

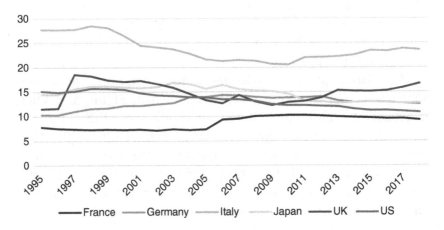

Figure 5.3   Out-of-pocket health expenditures as a share of the total (%).
SOURCE: OECD.

emergencies. Countries need to assure neighbours that they can stop an outbreak from becoming an international catastrophe. In turn, global leaders and international organisations bear collective responsibility for developing and maintaining a robust global capability to counter infectious disease threats. This includes ensuring that financing is available for building epidemic and pandemic preparedness. These steps will save lives and achieve a safer and more secure world.

The Global Heath Security (GHS) Index[8] is the first comprehensive assessment and benchmarking of health security and related capabilities across 195 countries. It was created in 2019 as a joint project of the Nuclear Threat Initiative (NTI) and the Johns Hopkins Center for Health Security (JHU) and was developed with the Economist Intelligence Unit (EIU)—and it should have served as a warning indicator regarding risks from the pandemic. The vision of its creators was that the GHS Index will spur measurable changes in national health security and improve the international capability to address one of the world's most omnipresent risks: infectious disease outbreaks that can lead to international epidemics and pandemics.

The GHS Index assesses countries' health security and capabilities across 6 categories, 34 indicators, and 85 sub-indicators. The average overall GHS Index score among all 195 countries assessed was 40.2 of a possible 100. Among the 60 high-income countries, the average GHS Index score was 51.9; 116 high- and middle-income countries do not score above 50.

The GHS Index analysis found that no country is fully prepared for epidemics or pandemics. Collectively, global international preparedness is weak. Many countries do not show evidence of the health security capacities and capabilities needed to prevent, detect, and respond to significant infectious disease outbreaks. *Overall, the GHS Index finds severe weaknesses in countries' abilities to prevent, detect, and respond to health emergencies*; severe gaps in health systems; vulnerabilities to political, socioeconomic, and environmental risks that can confound outbreak preparedness and response; and a lack of adherence to international norms.

The countries were categorised into three tiers based on score: countries scoring between 0 and 33.3 were in the bottom tier, those scoring between 33.4 and 66.6 were in the middle tier, and those that score between 66.7 and 100 were in the upper tier. Category scores underlying the index are summarised here:

- *Prevention:* Fewer than 7% of countries scored in the highest tier for the ability to prevent the emergence or release of pathogens.
- *Detection and reporting:* Only 19% of countries were in the top tier for detection and reporting.
- *Rapid response:* Fewer than 5% of countries scored in the highest tier for their ability to rapidly respond to and mitigate the spread of an epidemic.
- *Health system:* The average score for health system indicators is 26.4 of 100, making it the lowest-scoring category.
- *Compliance with international norms:* Fewer than half of the countries have submitted confidence-building measures under the Biological Weapons Convention (BWC) in the past three years, indicating their ability to adhere to important international norms and commitments related to biological threats.
- *Risk environment:* Only 23% of countries score in the top tier for indicators related to their political system and government effectiveness.

In terms of overall GHS Index scores, the top 10 countries were the United States (83.5), the United Kingdom (77.9), the Netherlands (75.6), Australia (75.5), Canada (75.3), Thailand (73.2), Sweden (72.1), Denmark (70.4), South Korea (70.2), and Finland (68.7).

In terms of *early detection and reporting of epidemics*, the top-ranked countries were the United States (98.2), Australia (97.3), Latvia (97.3), Canada (96.4), South Korea (92.1), the United Kingdom (87.3), Denmark (86.0), the Netherlands (86.0), Sweden (86.0), and Germany (84.6).

In terms of *rapid response to and mitigation of epidemic spread*, the top-ranked countries were the United Kingdom (91.9), the

United States (79.7), Switzerland (79.3), the Netherlands (79.1), Thailand (78.6), South Korea (71.5), Finland (69.2), Portugal (67.7), Brazil (67.1), and Australia (65.9).

In retrospect, these scores are a validation of why we have seen the US economy recover quickest from global pandemics and biosecurity threats in terms of labour force, production, and sales.

5.1.3   Global Burden of Disease

Another indicator to assess health systems is the Global Burden of Disease (GBD) created by the Institute for Health Metrics and Evaluation (IHME, www.healthdata.org). This is a continuation by the authors of a World Health Organization (WHO) project[9] in 1990, projected until 2020. The latest GBD 2019 findings, released in October 2020[10] in the medical journal *The Lancet* stated that this was a comprehensive global study that analysed 286 causes of death, 369 diseases and injuries, and 87 risk factors in 204 countries and territories. It also provided insights into how well the world's population was prepared in terms of underlying health for the impact of the COVID-19 pandemic.

The GBD 2019 key findings were as follows:

- The global crisis of chronic diseases and public health failure to stem the rise in highly preventable risk factors have left populations vulnerable to acute health emergencies such as COVID-19.
- Urgent action is needed to address the global syndemic of chronic diseases, social inequalities, and COVID-19 to ensure more robust health systems and healthier people, making countries more resilient to future pandemic threats.
- The GBD study provides a roadmap to where the need is greatest, with country-specific data on risk factors and chronic disease burden.

The GBD 2019 study (http://www.healthdata.org/gbd/2019) highlighted that the interaction of COVID-19 with the continued global rise in chronic illness and related risk factors (including obesity, high blood sugar, and outdoor air pollution) over the past

30 years created a perfect storm fuelling COVID-19 deaths. The study revealed that the rise in exposure to key risk factors (including high blood pressure, high blood sugar, high body-mass index [BMI], and elevated cholesterol), combined with increasing deaths from cardiovascular disease in some countries, may lead in certain areas to a turning point in life expectancy gains.

The study found that the promise of disease prevention through government actions to promote and enable healthier behaviours and access to healthcare resources is not being realised globally. The authors emphasise that most of these health risk factors are preventable and treatable, and tackling them will bring enormous social and economic benefits. They state, "We are failing to change unhealthy behaviours, particularly those related to diet quality, caloric intake, and physical activity, in part due to inadequate policy attention and funding for public health and behavioural research".

The risks associated with the top 10 leading causes of death in 2019 globally for both sexes were as follows.

1. High systolic blood pressure (10.8 million deaths)
2. Tobacco (8.71 million deaths)
3. Dietary risks (e.g. low fruit, high salt) (7.94 million deaths)
4. Air pollution (6.67 million deaths)
5. High fasting plasma glucose (6.50 million deaths)
6. High BMI (5.02 million deaths)
7. High LDL cholesterol (4.40 million deaths)
8. Kidney dysfunction (3.16 million deaths)
9. Child and maternal malnutrition (2.94 million deaths)
10. Alcohol use (2.44 million deaths)

The latest results from GBD 2019[11] also highlight the impact of risk factors on disability-adjusted life years (DALYs). In most health and life-expectancy policy discussions, DALYs are a standard metric for comparison and evaluation. The WHO's rationale for using DALYs (https://www.who.int/data/gho/indicator-metadata-registry/

imr-details/158) is as follows: "Mortality does not give a complete picture of the burden of disease borne by individuals in different populations. The overall burden of disease is assessed using the disability-adjusted life year (DALY), a time-based measure that combines years of life lost due to premature mortality (YLLs) and years of life lost due to time lived in states of less than full health, or years of healthy life lost due to disability (YLDs)".

5.1.4 Health in Emerging Countries

The earlier discussion of health focused on advanced G6 countries and the world overall. But the majority of the world's population live in non-advanced countries, with China and India together contributing a third of the world's population. The issues, concerns, and costs dominating health in emerging markets differ from those in developed countries. Many diseases, infections, and conditions that are very easily treatable in the developed world still account for the lion's share of fatalities and deaths in emerging countries.

In a globalised world where people can travel through and across countries using multiple modes of transportation and applicable documentation, the health of world citizens in emerging countries is also an essential factor to monitor and consider while considering the state of global health conditions and potential risks. In many developing countries, health conditions interacts with environmental conditions, creating circumstances inimical to good health.

A large proportion of environmental impact is concentrated in a few risk areas: poor water quality and availability, sanitation, vector-borne diseases, poor indoor air quality, toxic substances, and environmental change. Systematic incorporation of preventive measures to deal with such risks has been a challenge and impacts both life expectancy and quality of life in emerging countries. Many poor emerging countries are still affected by high infant mortality and maternal mortality rates due to the lack of adequate facilities in rural areas and very crowded pockets in many large cities. With the bulk of megacities concentrated in emerging markets, the interplay of environmental and health factors is an essential policy area that requires urgent attention.

As per the WHO, global estimates of deaths from most significant environmentally related causes or conditions and from certain diseases with a significant environmental component include the following:

- Unsafe water and poor sanitation and hygiene kill an estimated 1.7 million people annually.
- Indoor smoke, primarily from the use of solid fuels in domestic cooking and heating, kills an estimated 1.6 million people annually.
- Malaria kills over 1.2 million people annually, predominantly African children under the age of five. Poorly designed irrigation and water systems, inadequate housing, poor waste disposal and water storage, deforestation, and loss of biodiversity may contribute to the most common diseases such as malaria, dengue, etc.
- Urban air pollution generated by vehicles, industries, and energy production kills approximately 800,000 people annually.
- Road traffic injuries are responsible for 1.2 million deaths annually, with low- and middle-income countries bearing 90% of the death and injury toll.
- Lead exposure kills more than 230,000 people per year and causes cognitive effects in one-third of all children globally, with more than 97% of those affected living in the developing world.
- Climate change, including extreme weather events, is estimated to cause over 150,000 deaths annually.
- Unintentional poisonings kill 355,000 people globally each year and are closely associated with excessive exposure to, and inappropriate use of toxic chemicals and pesticides.

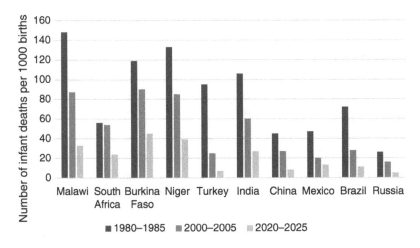

Figure 5.4 Infant mortality rates: EM.
SOURCE: UN Population Division.

The largest category of preventable deaths in the poorest countries is infant mortality. Figure 5.4 shows the progress made in reducing infant mortality rates. In addition to the EMG6 countries, the poorest African countries are included to highlight the magnitude of differences relative to Russia, China, and Turkey. Advances in reducing the infant mortality rate would indicate progress toward achieving one of the UN's Sustainable Development Goals, which we discuss later in Chapter 7.

In addition to infant mortality rates, adverse conditions in childhood with poor parents lead to many early childhood deaths, a significant loss to humanity and individual countries. These deaths are also a reflection of public health systems that do not guarantee a normal childhood beyond infancy. If infants survive but succumb to diseases and infections such as malaria or diarrhoea, that is sadly a loss of potential life, experiences, and contributions to family and society that the young child was deprived of through no fault of their own.

Figure 5.5 illustrates the progress made due to public health improvements and fewer under-five deaths over time across the selected EM countries, including the poorest countries: Malawi,

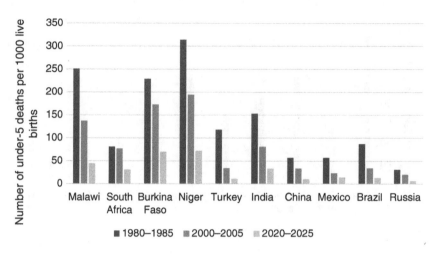

Figure 5.5   Under-five mortality per 1000 live births.
SOURCE: UN Population Division.

Niger, and Burkina Faso. Even the latest figures from 2020 to 2025 show the differences across the range of EM countries. While many charities and philanthropies contribute resources and efforts to save animal species from extinction and help the planet, it is essential for humanity worldwide to save human child lives in the poorest of countries. Improved education, sanitation, health, and environment standards are essential complementary factors in reducing the loss of lives in early childhood.

Better Public health and better infrastructure would lead to longer, fuller lives for children born in poorer countries. There is a moral and social imperative for advanced richer countries to support basic living conditions worldwide. A joint report by the World Bank and the WHO[12] found that despite some progress on universal healthcare (UHC), at least half of the world's population still cannot obtain essential health services. And each year, close to 100 million people are being pushed into extreme poverty because they must pay for health expenses out of their own pockets. The report is a sobering wake-up call if we are serious about reaching the global goal of UHC by 2030.

The differences in median ages across countries and regions depict the vast inequality in health outcomes when we compare Japan to Niger on the one hand and the high-income countries to the low-income countries on the other hand. If the world has to combat inequality, then a good measure that reflects progress, opportunity, or choice available to the average citizen is a comparison of median age or life expectancy at birth. Median age differences are evident in Figure 5.6: Niger had a median age in 2020 that was less than a third of that in long-living Japan. The inequality is similarly visible by comparing the median ages of low-income countries with those of high-income countries.

An examination of health indicators from the World Bank's world development indicators database highlights the under-provision and inadequacy of health resources even in large emerging economies, not to mention the poorest such economies. (Data is available on a comparable, consistent basis only for 2018.) The focus on health needs to be centre-stage as the world recovers from a pandemic that has seriously affected the economy's formal and informal sectors. In emerging economies, the informal sector is a larger employer than the formal sector. Figure 5.7 shows the vast

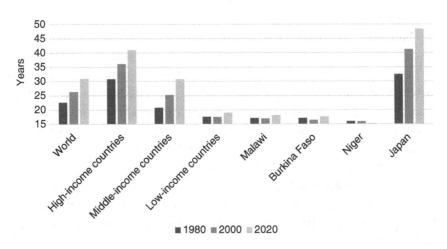

Figure 5.6 Median age: country/region variations.
SOURCE: UN Population Division.

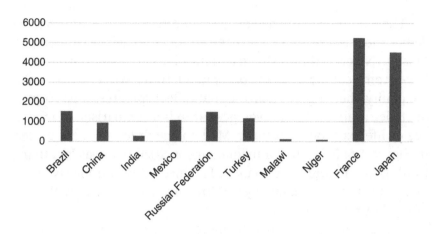

Figure 5.7   Current health expenditure per capita (international PPP): 2018.
SOURCE: World Bank world development indicators.

differences between poor countries (EMG6, Niger, and Malawi) and two of the best health systems worldwide: Japan and France. This figure spans nearly the entire range from the poorest to the richest, with the US excluded (as argued earlier, it is an outlier due to features specific to its system), and it lays down a marker based on the wide disparity among countries in health expenditures per capita.

Across these countries, a similar pattern emerges when comparing doctors, nurses, or hospital beds per thousand people. If health is wealth, some of these countries appear even poorer when measured on dimensions of health expenditures. Therefore, many of these poorest countries rely on grants from multilateral agencies, health projects, and charitable aid from the Red Cross, Gates Foundation, and Médecins Sans Frontières, to name just a few directly connected with health, vaccinations, and access to basic drugs. Figure 5.8, based on 2017 data, shows the same picture: a glance at India and Niger relative to Japan and France highlights inequality in access to hospital beds for the general population.

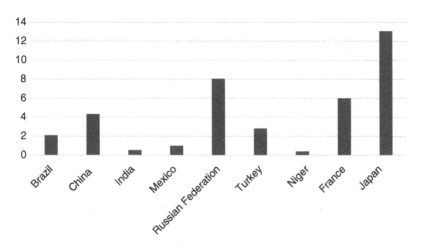

Figure 5.8 Hospital beds per thousand: 2017.
SOURCE: World Bank world development indicators.

5.2 Longevity

There is an English saying, "Be careful what you wish for", and this comes to mind while remembering Nobel laureate Robert Fogel's pioneering research in economic history work on longevity across US cohorts. He had noted that at the beginning of the twentieth century and during WWI, most people and citizens in the Western world—notably, the US and the UK—would have wished to live until 100 years of age and be centenarians. In an article titled "Can We afford Longevity? Our Future as the New Leisure Class"[13], Fogel argued for self-realisation through good health and extensive leisure. This would create demand for healthcare and lifelong learning in the twenty-first century. He argued for the equitable spiritual realisation of individual and collective nature to foster equality by distributing immaterial resources.

However, as we noted earlier, while longevity is very desirable it comes with a much longer post-retirement period due to long life and a trend toward early retirement spurred by periods of aggregate prosperity in terms of income as well as asset prices in the three decades of the 1980s, 1990s, and 2000s. The most significant uncertainty faced by retirees and pensioners is how to manage a long, uncertain period of retirement with fixed or slowly growing wealth at the end of working lives. *In other words, how will we pay for increased retirement, and who will pay?*

5.2.1   Increases in Life Expectancy and Conditional Life Expectancy

This section links health to increased longevity: as countries and societies advance and progress economically, there are associated gains in good health and longer lives due to better nutrition, available medical resources, awareness, and education. As illustrated and discussed in earlier chapters, longer life expectancy and population growth have accelerated since 1950, particularly in the last three decades of the twentieth century.

Figure 5.9 shows that life expectancy at birth has increased most dramatically in low-income countries from a much lower level; however, the most significant benefits accrue to higher-income countries that are also dealing with increased longevity. The difference between high-income and low-income countries is more than a decade and a half.

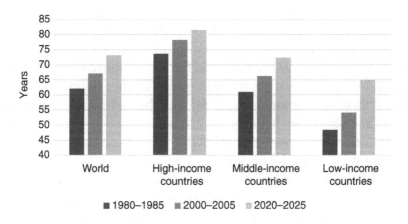

Figure 5.9   Increasing life expectancy at birth.
SOURCE: UN Population Division.

Expenditures on the old in ageing Europe average 20%+ of GDP, and very few countries can afford these expenditures in an ageing, low-growth era. Therefore, along with others, I have been advocating that all countries and their citizens need to save more, with a recommendation that a 15% savings rate by households could ameliorate the strains faced by public finances due to spending for the old. It is, however, easier to save more in an era of growth, and growth can be boosted (as argued in earlier chapters) by increasing productivity with the use of technology, furthering full inclusivity of female and younger labour force groups, labour reforms embracing working longer as we live longer, and flexible working part-time and part-years. Policies are needed to bolster high growth and would also partly mitigate concerns regarding debt sustainability.

Countries and societies, as well as individuals and families, should also pay much closer attention to life expectancies at older ages—the focus should be on conditional life expectancy at higher ages and, furthermore, on healthy life expectancies. Living longer with afflictions, medical conditions, limited mobility, and limited cognitive ability is not what most people would want when they wish for a long life. In contrast to the early twentieth century, today's wish should be for a healthy, active long life, not just a long life. Working longer should go along with living longer, and that goes hand in hand with keeping people mentally engaged and active into their later years.

It is crucial to understand global longevity, factoring in the data presented in Figure 5.10, which displays life expectancy at age 60. The difference between low-income and high-income countries is 7.5 years (24.8 years for high-income and 17.3 years for low-income countries).

The tone of the message is mixed: while low-income countries are catching up with high-income countries once people reach age 60, they are significantly underprepared for a growing proportion of older people, as the common perception is that "the country is still young". It takes years to shrug off such misperceptions. A similar one is that Asia is still young and growing, whilst the truth is that it

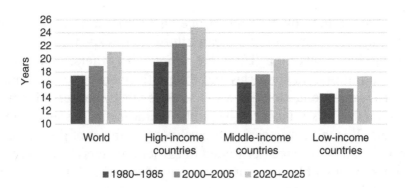

Figure 5.10   Life expectancy at age 60.
SOURCE: UN Population Division.

is ageing faster than the world average and growing more slowly in terms of numbers.

5.2.2   Life Expectancy vs. Healthy Life Expectancy

It is advisable to monitor healthy life expectancy at older ages. Healthy life expectancy estimates how many years a person might live in a "healthy" state. Both life expectancy and healthy life expectancy are key summary measures reflecting the health of a population. Figure 5.11 illustrates the stark differences between life expectancy (LE) and healthy life expectancy (HALE) for the G6 (developed) and EMG6 (developing) countries, using the latest WHO database. The differences extend up to 10 years for some countries.

Economies and societies should focus on reducing periods of morbidity for their citizens, primarily when they are inactive or semi-active. As discussed in Chapter 2 and earlier in this chapter, LE estimates how many years a person might be expected to live; it is commonly measured at birth and later ages. The greater the old-age DALYs, the lower the costs associated with poor quality health and morbidity.

Figure 5.12 presents the analogous differences between LE and HALE at age 60 for the G6 and EMG6 countries. Even at age 60, the

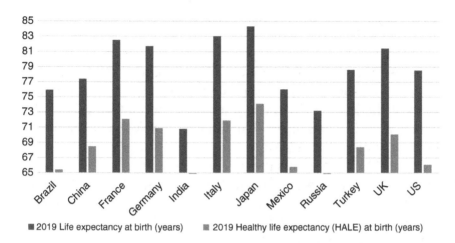

Figure 5.11 Life expectancy vs. healthy life expectancy at birth (years): 2019.
SOURCE: WHO.

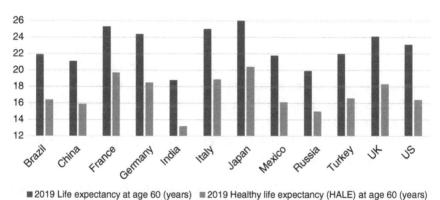

Figure 5.12 Life expectancy at 60 vs. healthy life expectancy at 60 (years): 2019.
SOURCE: WHO.

differences extend six to eight years. The expenditures at an older age are also greater due to associated long-term care and increased caution applied during medical procedures to avoid complications. Recovery periods are also longer, requiring follow-ups and more careful monitoring.

5.2.3 DALYs and Their Causes

In the first section of this chapter, we discussed DALYs and defined them as an alternative to understand the burden of disease. The disability-adjusted life year is a time-based measure that combines years of life lost (YLLs) due to premature mortality and YLLs due to time lived in states of less than full health, or years of healthy life lost due to disability (YLDs).

One DALY represents the loss of the equivalent of one year of full health. Using DALYs, the burden of diseases that cause premature death but minor disability (such as drowning or measles) can be compared to diseases that do not cause death but do cause disability (such as cataracts causing blindness). It is worth re-emphasising that DALYs are calculated as the sum of the YLLs due to premature mortality and YLDs due to prevalent cases of a disease or health condition in a population.

The latest WHO findings on DALYs over 2000–2019 can be summarised as follows:

- DALYs due to communicable diseases such as HIV/AIDS and diarrhoeal diseases have dropped by 50% since 2000.
- DALYs from diabetes increased by more than 80% between 2000 and 2019.
- DALYs from Alzheimer's disease have more than doubled between 2000 and 2019.

As per the WHO's GBD, using death and disability disaggregated by sex, annual global deaths and DALYs among women were around 15% lower than men. But women spent about 20% more YLDs. In the past two decades, the greatest increase in female deaths has been from Alzheimer's disease and other dementias, with nearly a threefold increase. These neurological disorders kill more females than males, with about 80% more deaths and 70% more DALYs for women than for men. *As women live longer than men on average but have higher YLDs, it is essential for health policy to focus on treating and preventing or mitigating such neurological disorders.*

DALYs from breast cancer were also amongst the most prominent causes of lower healthy lives for women.

In the medical journal *Lancet*[14], the authors of a study sponsored by the Bill and Melinda Gates Foundation summarised their findings on age-specific mortality, HALE, and DALYs and arrived at these conclusions: with increasing LE in most countries, the question of whether the additional years of life gained are spent in good health or poor health has been increasingly relevant because of the potential policy implications, such as healthcare provisions and extending retirement ages. In some countries and regions, a large proportion of those additional years are spent in poor health. Significant inequalities in HALE and disease burden exist across countries in different sociodemographic classifications and across sexes. The burden of disabling conditions has serious implications for health system planning and health-related expenditures. This is a warning for all countries' health systems dealing with the ageing of their populations.

5.2.4 Longevity and Mortality: More Than Just Births and Deaths

Longevity is how long somebody can reasonably expect to live (i.e. LE), while *mortality* is the probability that somebody will die over the next year. Mortality and longevity might seem to be opposite sides of the same coin, but there is a third, connecting concept: mortality improvements of future cohorts.

To the extent that mortality and longevity involve the same concept of "life or death", they are influenced by the same factors. The measurable factors affecting mortality are age, gender, medical history (and related medical aspects, such as BMI and blood pressure), smoking habits, and socioeconomic status. An individual's genes are also likely to be very influential, and so ideally would feature in such a list, but genetic make-up is just starting to be quantified scientifically.

The risks corresponding to mortality and longevity[15] are generally used from the perspective of the financial institutions bearing the risk rather than the individuals whose lives are being implicitly discussed here. The *mortality risk* is the risk of adverse mortality movements from the perspective of an insurer or reinsurer with a portfolio of life insurance policies. If mortality increases, they pay out more than expected. *Longevity risk*, rather than being the opposite of mortality risk, is the risk that longevity increases more than assumed—in other words, the risk that mortality improvements end up being greater than assumed. This is clearly good for the underlying individuals but is likely to be financially adverse for insurers or pension schemes.

The two risks are also not the same because their underlying assumptions are different: mortality rates are relatively easy to estimate reliably and objectively, and hence the risk is about a rare event occurring to make mortality suddenly jump over the year—for instance, a pandemic. But longevity calculations rely on subjective mortality improvement assumptions, and those improvement assumptions may (with the benefit of hindsight in the future) be found to have been, overall, too low. Hence there is a substantial market in managing longevity risk.

While longevity increases have been ongoing for few decades, the focus from an economic, finance, and actuarial perspective has been on retirement and life insurance. Longevity increases have implications from social, health, training, unemployment, income, and wealth perspectives for a generation and across multiple generations. I believe that just as demographics pertains to all individuals who are consumers (the entire population), longevity increases also have multidimensional implications for them. Our earlier research reports[6,7] outlined and discussed the implications of increased longevity in greater detail.

Longevity has been increasing at historically unprecedented rates since 1950, and this reflects the progress of humankind on many fronts: science, society and economics, to name just a few. The increases are nearly universal, from the richest to the poorest countries. But longevity trends have become increasingly uncertain to predict, and the burden of ageing is more difficult to budget. Longevity is increasing at different rates across countries and age groups and between males and females. Longevity increases due to increases at older ages have been more dominant in developed countries due to medical advances and better living conditions, extending lives at the higher end; but longevity increases at birth and in childhood have been foremost for developing countries.

There has been global interest in the causes and differential trends of longevity, leading to the establishment of the Human Mortality Database (HMD). The HMD was created to provide detailed mortality and population data to researchers, students, journalists, policy analysts, and others interested in the history of human longevity. Two teams of researchers have had primary responsibility for the creation of this database; they are based in the Department of Demography of the University of California, Berkeley (UCB) and the data laboratory of the Max Planck Institute for Demographic Research (MPIDR). There are many regional versions of HMD for the large developed countries.

A recent report using the HMD for Germany[16] shows that despite a large disparity in income inequality across regions of Germany, the same trend is not borne out in mortality. This is an interesting avenue with policy implications for good practices across both developed and developing countries. The report records that Germany's regional inequalities in LE are comparatively low internationally, particularly among women, despite high state-level inequalities in economic conditions. These low regional mortality inequalities emerged 5–10 years after reunification. Mortality is converging over most ages between the longest- and shortest-living German state populations and across the former East-West political border, except for an emerging East-West divergence in mortality among working-aged men. This German example shows that significant regional economic inequalities are not necessarily paralleled by large regional mortality disparities.

As populations live longer, they should work longer[17], as advised and advocated by researchers like us and the OECD. While people are working longer in countries like Japan, recent research on US working patterns at later ages indicates the opposite[18]. The results show that there has been no overall expansion of the length of working life, partly due to the recent crisis, which has led to a decline in working LE. The differences in working LE across subpopulations are substantial, with gender, race/ethnicity, and the intersection of these factors playing important roles. This heterogeneity is a cause for concern, as the working LE of some groups, particularly Blacks, is markedly lower than it is for others. The authors suggest that policies aimed at increasing the length of working life should better address this heterogeneity.

In a more detailed paper, Dudel and Myrskylä[19] use the US Health and Retirement Study for 1992–2011 and multistate life tables to analyse working LE at age 50 and study the impact of the Great Recession in 2007–2009. Despite declines of one or two years following the recession, in 2008–2011, American men aged 50 years still spent 13 years, or two-fifths of their remaining life, working, while American women of the same age spent 11 years, or one-third of their remaining life, in employment. Although educational differences in working LE have been stable over the past 20 years, racial differences started changing after the Great Recession. The results showed that while Americans generally work longer than people in other countries, considerable sub-population heterogeneity exists.

5.2.5   Longevity Risk and the Uncertain Future of Longevity

In a significant portion of the literature on pensions and insurance asset allocation, longevity is considered a given based on expected LE generated from models. However, even the experts disagree on the future of longevity—will the large increases continue into the future? After all, longevity has economic, market, and social implications, as we have been showing in our research. Various stakeholders need to take longevity and its manifest implications into account based on their differing interests, objectives, and time horizons.

For individuals and families, longevity increases pose challenges to existing frameworks of asset allocation, time allocation, and resource management and affect their relationships—internally and externally, as well as intergenerational dynamics within societies. This requires a significant change in their thinking to develop solutions to deal with longer-term investments and longer-term risks.

Governments and societies will need to appreciate the increased LE of their citizens alongside the changing intergenerational challenges of four to five generations co-existing with differing needs and preferences for consumption vs. saving, saving vs. investment, and labour vs. leisure. Policy changes in labour, health, pensions and retirement, education, and social benefits are necessary. Governments need to promote securities markets, which insure against longevity and inflation risk by, for example, issuing longevity bonds.

Fund managers, pension funds, and life insurance companies also need to reassess their current frameworks, assumptions, and views to develop new solutions for current and future clients. Newer approaches to understanding, measuring, and monitoring LE and its implications for consumers and workers are a *must*.

The implications for sovereign wealth funds, which have largely apolitical mandates in maximising the wealth of a nation, are different from those of countries governed by political leaders. They face longer horizons for optimising wealth and resources, subject to constraints from national objectives, and must recognise the global flows of physical and human capital.

Will we live to reach 100 years of age on average by the 2030s? This is the question posed by *National Geographic Magazine* in a 2015 cover article, "This Baby Will Live to Be 120". The answer is uncertain, as biological and longevity experts cannot agree on the limits of LE. In a March 2005 Watson Wyatt/Cass Business School lecture, "The Uncertain Future of Longevity", two world-leading experts—James W Vaupel of the Max Planck Institute of Demographic Research; and Jay R Olshansky, from the University of Illinois—from opposite camps regarding how high future LE may go in the future, presented their views on whether past LE increases would repeat into the future or fall after tapering off[20].

In the optimists' camp, Vaupel argued that the pace of centenarians at least doubling each decade since 1950 will not slow down and that LE is not approaching a limit. He stated that improvements in old-age survival are primarily responsible for increases in

LE. Advances in prevention, diagnosis, and treatment of age-related diseases will lead to the continued rise of LE; and if the trend continues, the first half of the twenty-first century may see European LE exceed 90 years, in contrast to lower official estimates, which may lead to severe consequences for public and private decision-making.

In the camp of the realists, Olshansky was sceptical of the prediction by Oeppen and Vaupel that human LE will rise to 100 years in the twenty-first century, given the lack of scientific evidence to support it and some evidence to the contrary. Due to the important public policy predictions associated with the conjecture of Vaupel and others, Olshansky felt compelled to present his multifaceted objections. The foundation for such forecasts was the presumption that the past increases in world LE across low mortality countries over the last 150 years would continue into the twenty-first century. But the straight-line forecasts are not based on the trend of any single country's longevity, particularly the forecast that US LE at birth will reach 100 by 2060.

The problem is that past increases were driven by one-time decreases in early age mortality that will not soon be repeatable. Further, continuing the pace of advances in biomedical technology that drove dramatically lower death rates would require (i) developing new technologies that do not exist, including non-existent technologies that slow the ageing process; (ii) significant technologies to reduce death rates from heart disease, cancer, and stroke; and (iii) distribution and availability of these non-existent technologies. Lastly, Olshansky emphasised that the proponents of naïve extrapolation ignore the underlying biology of ageing and death, assuming no biological or demographic reasons can prevent death rates from converging to zero.

5.2.6 Longevity Forecasting Models: Countries and Regions

As discussed earlier, several medical, biodemographic, and actuarial approaches to forecasting longevity have been adopted due to the possible effects on beneficiaries and stakeholders. The longevity debate has implications for individuals and families and pharmaceutical, health, biotechnology, insurance, and other consumer sectors. The ramifications of greater longevity extend to the private and public sectors with policy and industry effects.

An article in *The Lancet* in 2017 presented findings of increased longevity across 35 industrial countries[21]. Mortality and LE projections are needed to plan for health and social services and pensions. Their aim was to forecast national age-specific mortality and LE using an approach that considers the uncertainty related to the choice of forecasting model.

They developed an ensemble of 21 forecasting models, all of which probabilistically contributed to the final projections. They applied this approach to derive age-specific mortality projections to 2030 in 35 industrialised countries with high-quality vital statistics data. They used age-specific death rates to calculate LE at birth and age 65 and the probability of dying before age 70, using life table methods. Their findings were as follows:

- Life expectancy is projected to increase in all 35 countries with a probability of at least 65% for women and 85% for men. There is a 90% probability that LE at birth among South Korean women in 2030 will be greater than 86.7, the same as the highest worldwide LE in 2012, and a 57% probability that it will be greater than 90. Projected female LE in South Korea is followed by those in France, Spain, and Japan.
- There is a greater than 95% probability that LE at birth among men in South Korea, Australia, and Switzerland will surpass 80 in 2030, and a greater than 27% probability that it will surpass 85. Of the countries studied, the US, Japan, Sweden, Greece, Macedonia, and Serbia have some of the lowest projected LE gains for both men and women.
- The female LE advantage over men is likely to shrink by 2030 in every country except Mexico, where female LE is predicted to increase more than male LE. In Chile, France, and Greece, the two sexes will see similar gains. More than half of the projected gains in LE at birth in women will be due to enhanced longevity above age 65.

The UN Population Division's Population Prospects 2019's latest Medium Fertility Variant Projections have data on LE for the world and its regions. Figure 5.13 and Figure 5.14 present life expectancies at birth and at age 60.

Figure 5.13 highlights the enormous increases in LE at birth across all regions, but increases in the highest LE regions of Europe, North America, and Oceania are lower than in the low LE regions

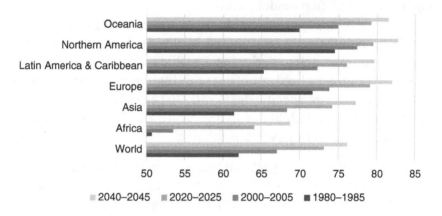

Figure 5.13 Life expectancy at birth, world and regions: 1980–2040 (years).
SOURCE: UN Population Division.

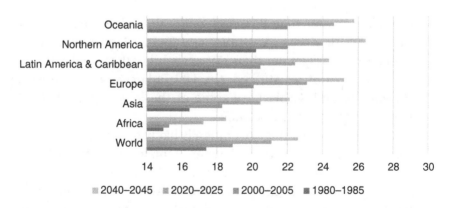

Figure 5.14 Life Expectancy at age 60, world and regions: 1980–2040 (years).
SOURCE: UN Population Division.

of Asia, Africa, Latin America. The ranges of LE increases (over six decades) range between 8.25 years in North America and 18 years in Africa, evidencing a projected convergence in life expectancies.

Figure 5.14 shows that life expectancies at age 60 are projected to increase differently over 1980–2040 for various regions. The contrast between Figure 5.13 and Figure 5.14 reveals that LE at older ages is projected to increase more in advanced countries and regions like Europe, North America, and Oceania than in the poorer regions of Africa, Asia, and Latin America. The older age increases in LE rely on medical and care improvements due to new technologies, as highlighted in the *Lancet* study and also based on probabilistic models of LE improvements. The LE improvements range from 3.5 years for Africa to nearly 7 years for Oceania.

5.2.7 Short Summary of Longevity Models

This subsection and the next draw heavily on the Asian Development Bank Institute (ADBI) working paper[22] and keynote presentation on longevity that I delivered at the annual conference in November 2011. In broad terms, three common approaches to forecasting mortality are discussed[23,24]:

- *Expectation:* This is based on the subjective opinions of experts. It is not generally a good basis for mortality forecasting as expert expectations are invariably conservative.
- *Explanation:* These are structural or epidemiological models of mortality derived from specific causes of death with known determinants. Decomposition by cause of death poses problems and is subject to data difficulties. However, it can provide a better understanding of the factors behind overall changes in mortality.
- *Extrapolation:* Most developments in mortality forecasting have been in extrapolative forecasting. This approach calculates estimates of future mortality using the current level of mortality and an estimate of the rate of change in future mortality, which is based on changes observed in the past. This observed trend

in mortality changes is assumed to continue over the forecast horizon. The extrapolative models can be either deterministic or stochastic. Deterministic models don't calculate forecast probabilities as they directly extend past trends.

Stochastic models attach probabilities to each forecast value. Since longevity has become uncertain, it is better to use the stochastic approach to calculate probability distributions rather than point estimates, in my opinion. Within the extrapolative approach, models have been developed that incorporate zero, one, two, or three underlying factors:

- Zero-factor models of aggregate measures, notably LE, provide no information about changes in the age pattern.
- One-factor models are also inadequate. Although they have the advantage of smoothness across age, they present serious problems for forecasting.
- Two-factor models incorporate time, which—being fundamental to forecasting—is a significant advantage. Methods using two-factor models (age-period or age-cohort) have been most successful. One type is the Lee-Carter model, in which a log-linear trend for age-specific mortality rates is assumed for the time-dependent component. The equation describing the Lee-Carter model is as follows:

$$\ln\left(m_{x,t}\right) = a_x + b_x.k_t + \varepsilon_{x,t}$$

$m_{x,t}$ denotes the central mortality rate at age x in year t, a_x denotes the average log-mortality at age x over time, b_x denotes the response at age x to a change in the overall level of mortality over time, k_t denotes the overall mortality level in year t (time-varying component of interest), and $\varepsilon_{x,t}$ denotes the residual.

The shortcoming of the Lee-Carter model is that it assumes the ratio of the rates of mortality change at different ages remains constant over time, whereas evidence of substantial age-time interaction has been found.

- Regression-based (generalized linear model [GLM]) methods, including dynamic parameterisations, have been less successful in forecasting because nonlinearities in time can lead to implausible forecast trends.
- Three-factor methods are more recent: the Lee-Carter age-period-cohort model appears promising. The Renshaw-Haberman model was the first to incorporate a cohort effect parameter to model variations in mortality among individuals from different cohorts. Cohort models involve heavy data demands.

These models generally model mortality rates for the underlying national population. However, insurers and pension funds are interested in the mortality rates of specific members. Barrieu et al.[25] proposed a model that looks at the links between insured specific mortality and national population mortality by studying the long-term relationship of the behaviour of these two series. For a complete analysis of this specific basis risk, we need to consider individual characteristics: income, education, professional status, etc.

Caution is needed when applying these models. There is a trade-off between goodness of fit and forecasting accuracy. There are limitations in time-series methods and their application to long forecasting periods. And there is a lack of appropriate data sources for particular applications and modelling error as not all sources of uncertainty can be quantified, making it essential to investigate more than one modelling framework. Beyond models, we need to understand the causal factors underlying longevity, the ageing process, and the characteristics governing different populations. Will these past longevity increases continue in the future? Recent forecasting errors have largely undermined various models, and mortality is now recognised as a stochastic process.

Shkolnikov et al.[26] researched best-practice LE, defined as the highest LE observed among national populations representing the best global health experiences. The trends in best-practice LE show to what extent developed countries as a group can lower mortality; these values then set the aspiration levels of longevity for developing countries. Conventional *period LE* is a statistic that can be interpreted as a measure of the average level of the hazard of death in a given calendar year, whilst *cohort LE* reflects the actual survival experiences of people born in a specific calendar year. For a given calendar year, cohort LE can be lower or higher than period LE. The authors state that the shapes of mortality decrease over time determine cohort longevity patterns. The elongation of life into old and oldest-old ages changes the traditional balance between the different stages of the life cycle and has large-scale socioeconomic and intergenerational consequences. Therefore, mortality forecasts are of great importance to the provision of policy-relevant information. The levels of survival to advanced ages reached by recent cohorts have been substantially higher than would have been expected from period mortality regimes when these cohorts were young. Governments making institutional arrangements for retirement and healthcare could have been unaware of the real prospects of cohort survival. The authors reiterate that increases in younger cohorts' LE depend on future mortality reductions. Referring to the best practice national trends, they find optimism based on extremely low levels of sub-national groups' mortality and other research. They suggest that considerable available resources exist for further mortality decreases. Figure 5.15, adapted from an earlier report of mine[6] and drawing on the extensive historical analysis by Shkolnikov et al.[26], depicts the country leaders in global LE.

Norway, Sweden, Iceland, Denmark, Australia, New Zealand, and Japan dominate the highest cohort life expectancies observed globally. The highest average life expectancies across both sexes have been observed only for Japan and Sweden. Other countries that have consistently had amongst the highest life expectancies include Italy, Germany, and Greece, as highlighted in yet another research report of mine discussing the heterogeneity and differences across the oldest five countries[27].

In a recent article presenting demographic perspectives on longevity, Vaupel et al.[28] review some past trends in human longevity and explore future trends in LE at birth. Demographic data on

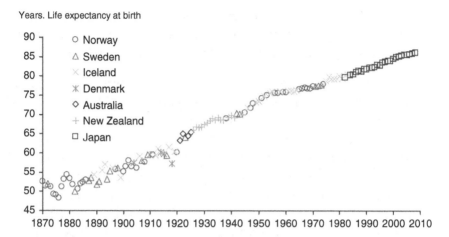

Figure 5.15 Historical highest female life expectancies (years).
SOURCE: Adapted from Roy et al.[6].

age-specific mortality is used to estimate LE, and validated data on exceptional life spans are used to study the maximum length of life. In the countries doing best each year, LE started to increase around 1840 at a pace of almost 2.5 years per decade. This trend has continued until the present. The authors emphasise that contrary to classical evolutionary theories of senescence and many experts' predictions, the frontier of survival is advancing to higher ages. They state that individual life spans are becoming more equal and reducing inequalities. They suggest that if the current pace of progress in LE continues, most children born this millennium will celebrate their 100th birthday.

However, considerable uncertainty clouds forecasts: LE and maximum life span might increase very little, if at all, or longevity might rise much faster than in the past. Substantial progress has been made over the past three decades in deepening understanding of how long humans have lived and how long they might live. The social, economic, health, cultural, and political consequences of further increases in longevity are so significant that the development of new models of mortality and longevity must become a priority.

The UK's Longevity Science Panel (LSP)[29] studied mortality trends in developed countries to understand the recent slowdown in mortality improvements over 2011–2015. They concluded that

- Mortality improvements after 2010 in most countries have been lower than in previous years. The magnitude of the changes varies by country, gender, and age.
- The LSP has used historical international data from 1965 to 2010 to project a mortality improvement rate beyond 2010 for people over 50. For women, the observed mortality improvements after 2010 have been less than projections, except in Denmark.
- For men, the situation is less clear-cut. Out of 16 countries investigated with observed data from 2011 to 2015, 10 countries, including the UK, have experienced lower mortality improvements than projected.

A recent modelling and forecasting paper[30] based on multi-country analysis found that formulating the multi-population mortality forecasting problem based on three-way (age, year, and gender/country) decompositions improves the out-of-sample forecasting performance. Forecasting is improved both for individual and aggregate populations compared with using the single-population mortality model (based on rank-1 singular value decomposition or the Lee-Carter model). The results also shed light on international patterns of mortality similarity and differences.

Studying older-age longevity, researchers from Stanford University and China[31] found that over five decades in 20 developed countries, old-age survival follows an advancing front like a wave. They make and test several predictions that support the existence of this front. Their unexpected result underscores the plasticity of old-age human mortality, with deaths steadily delayed as societies develop and an ongoing increase in the age of transition to disability. They find no evidence of an impending limit to the human life span.

As shown here and as we have been stressing, the focus should pivot and study LE at retirement or older ages. A few recent papers have begun to evaluate alternative models for generating retirees' mortality forecasts. An essential input for annuity pricing is future retiree mortality. From observed age-specific mortality data, modelling and forecasting can follow two routes: (i) truncate the available data to retiree ages, and then produce mortality forecasts based on a partial age-range model, or (ii) with all available data, first apply a full age-range model to produce forecasts and then truncate the mortality forecasts to retiree ages. By evaluating and comparing the short-term point and interval forecast accuracies, Shang and Haberman[32] recommend the first strategy by truncating all available data to retiree ages and then producing mortality forecasts.

5.2.8   Annuities as a Longevity Risk Management Tool

The previous sections have focused on the uncertainty of LE, forecasting approaches, needs for new models, and, most importantly, the impact of longevity and mortality risk for public policy makers and private sector businesses and individuals. As mentioned earlier, longevity risk is the risk that future outcomes in mortality and LE will differ from expectations. It manifests as either a characteristic or specific risk unique to each individual or aggregate risk, which is due to uncertainty about overall rates of population mortality increase. Specific longevity risk can be diversified by pooling; however, aggregate longevity risk cannot be diversified away.

Individuals, annuity providers, corporate pension funds, and governments are all carriers of longevity risk. Individuals risk outliving their assets post-retirement, life insurance providers risk not meeting their actuarial assumptions, and corporate pension plans and state and federal governments risk promising overly generous benefits that they cannot afford. A number of risks have materialised in the Western world. Many defined benefit pension plans have increasingly large liabilities, outstripping assets and constraining corporate operational performance.

Annuities are one of the significant instruments to hedge longevity risk. Individual retirees face the risk of outliving their resources if they spend aggressively or under-consuming their wealth if they spend conservatively. The primary appeal of annuities is that they offer an effective solution to the possibility of retirees out-living their assets by exchanging assets for a lifelong stream of guaranteed income.

An *annuity* is a contract offered by insurers guaranteeing a steady stream of payments for either a fixed term or the lifetime of the annuity owner in exchange for an initial premium charge. Its history can be dated back to ancient Rome when speculators who dealt with marine and other lines of insurance offered contracts promising payments for a fixed term in return for an up-front charge.

Sheshinski[33] provides a rigorous and conceptual discussion of the economic theory of annuities, highlighting their more than 2000-year history. He stresses that annuities have the financial characteristic that their holder is entitled to a certain return per period for as long as the annuitant is alive. These products are sold by insurance companies to individuals who depend on payout stipulations and individual characteristics like age. The demand for annuities comes from individuals to ensure an income flow in retirement against longevity risks. This is because while hazards to survival have been eliminated, increases in survival rates after age 60 have been much slower, leaving substantial uncertainty for those older than 60.

Uncertainty about the age of death poses a challenge to individuals as to how to allocate resources over their lifetime without access to insurance markets. Conservative consumption may lead to oversized bequests relative to foregone consumption. Life insurance and annuities can jointly serve this problem. A life insurance policy that pools many mortality ages creates a bequest value independent of the age of death. Annuities are sometimes referred to as *reverse life insurance*, as they pool individual mortality risks, thereby ensuring a steady consumption flow during life. This access is welfare-enhancing for individuals. Annuity payouts as a share of combined life insurance and annuity payouts were less than 10% pre-WW2 but now are more than 50%, according to the latest data covering 2020 from the Insurance Information Institute of the US[34].

Today, annuities have evolved into a multitude of forms: payouts can commence immediately or be deferred until later, payments can be fixed or vary with underlying factors such as inflation, and the policy can cover a single life or multiple lives or have an embedded bequest option that allows payments to continue to a beneficiary after the annuitant's death. Annuity contracts can also be purchased by pension funds for their members, as is the case with group annuities. Group annuities were initially associated with defined benefit (DB) pension plans to manage longevity risk and cash flows for plan sponsors and were recently used in defined contribution (DC) pension plans to mitigate longevity risk for individuals.

The annuity market grew very fast in the US from the 1980s until the recent financial crisis. However, the annuity market remains small relative to the magnitude of risk that individuals are exposed to. Several impediments have led to this under-annuitization. First, for annuity providers, the pricing of such products can be an onerous task. They are exposed to substantial mispricing risk, especially without appropriate financial instruments to further hedge longevity risk. Second, the annuity market suffers from asymmetric information, as those exposed to higher risk will be more willing to seek annuities, but insurers will not be able to distinguish between high-risk and low-risk types. The extent of adverse selection adds to the cost of annuities, making them unattractive to low-risk individuals. The consequence of the recent European ruling against gender discrimination for EU insurers has yet to be seen. Third, the demand for annuities is further tamed by retirees' bequest motives, the reluctance to lose discretionary control, etc.

A group of retirement experts[35] provide one of the most lucid introductions on the role of annuities in financing retirement. They highlight the different types of annuities that (i) ensure periodic payments for a fixed number of years or (ii) provide periodic payments for the duration of lives. Annuities help provide indemnity to individuals against the risks of running out of resources over their lifetime.

Annuity payouts depend on the individual annuitant's prospective mortality risk and the rate of return that annuity providers can earn on invested assets. Younger individuals receive lower annuity payouts than older ones for the same amount invested as they are expected to receive payments for a longer period. Except for single-premium immediate annuity, most annuities have an accumulation phase and a liquidation phase. The long accumulation phases of annuities make them similar to savings vehicles as they compete with other financial products for asset accumulation.

The authors provide a taxonomy for different types of annuities based on the number and timing of premiums, the number of lives covered, the nature of the payouts, and the date at which payouts begin. Different modes of paying premiums include single premium, fixed annual premium, and flexible premiums. Annuities can insure single or multiple lives jointly; they can begin payouts immediately (immediate) or after some period (deferred). Payouts can be a life annuity without refund or guaranteed minimum payout or a flexible payout structure. Characteristics of annuities that lead individuals to buy them include tax benefits, attractive long-term savings plans, and the ability to use a lump sum income inflow.

Group annuity contracts can also vary considerably. (i) With a deferred group annuity contract, the employer pays the insurance company periodically, and that is applied by the insurance company to purchase deferred annuities for covered employees; the purchase price for annuities is specified by the employer's contract with the insurance company, which indemnifies the employer against changes in mortality risk, rate of return, and other factors influencing pricing. (ii) A deposit administration contract is more flexible for employer payments with direct links between employer cost and mortality experience of employees. (iii) An immediate participation guarantee contract is a variant of (ii) but with more direct, explicit links to covered employees' mortality experience, investment returns, and employer pension costs.

Employee participation rules in private defined benefit pension plans (plans where employers guarantee benefits based on years of service, salary levels, and a multiplicative factor) vary from one plan to another, affecting participation in associated group annuity programs. The growth trend in variable annuities has continued since the 1980s as they combine mutual fund-like features with certain insurance elements that qualify for tax deferrals. The growth of private annuity markets is dependent on guaranteed public sector retirement income programs that already exist in several countries.

Cannon and Tonks[36] provide a comprehensive discussion of supply and demand of life annuities, factors influencing the growth of annuity markets in several countries, the history of annuity markets, and the role of annuities in changing pension systems. They discuss types of annuities, the annuity prices quoted by providers, and the movement of annuity prices.

A study of national annuity markets by Rusconi[37] investigated the demand and supply motivation differences across various countries. He argues that the demand for annuities continues to be low due to (i) poor consumer understanding and (ii) inflexible product design. Ironically, efforts to address these two factors may work against one another. Additionally, supply-side problems continue in mature immediate annuity markets, where provider numbers are shrinking. The same problems do not appear to exist in the newly opened immediate annuity markets or in their mature deferred annuity counterparts. He suggests that if customers are well informed and able to make sound decisions across a range of options, carefully limited product options may provide the means to expand the demand for and supply of annuity products.

Rusconi concludes that annuity markets differ from country to country; their customers, suppliers, and products vary; and therefore policymakers must seek to understand the issues in their own country before applying apparent solutions from others. Therefore, it is important to understand consumer and saver behaviour if policies and incentives of insurers and governments are to foster the growth of an efficient and fairly priced annuity market.

5.2.9   Other Longevity Risk Management Tools and Instruments

Longevity-linked instrument longevity indices and longevity bonds provide hedging tools for aggregate longevity risk of the overall population at an institutional level. However, the global financial crisis (GFC) regulation by authorities based on risk-based capital has provided headwinds for many innovative longevity products developed by investment banks[22].

Longevity indices: A longevity index indicates the probability of LE for individuals of a certain age to increase by a certain number of years over a period of time. Longevity indices not only provide a hedging tool for pension plans, insurers, and reinsurers to transfer their longevity risk to other participants in the capital market but also improve the understanding, visibility, and transparency of longevity risk.

A longevity index must be based on credible national data to be accepted as a transparent common reference. Therefore, governments and national statistical institutions, in particular, can play an essential role in promoting the development of longevity-indexed products by developing a standardised index for longevity risk to be used as a benchmark in markets for longevity bonds and annuities. The market for longevity indices is still in an embryonic stage.

Longevity bonds: also known as *survivor bonds*, these generally pay a coupon linked to the survivor rates of a selected birth cohort. If a higher-than-expected proportion of this cohort survives, the coupon rate will increase, offsetting some of the provider's cost and hedging aggregate longevity risk. Longevity bond issuance has so far been very limited. The most obvious reason is that very few market participants would gain from an unexpected rise in LE.

Pharmaceutical companies have been suggested as potential candidates, but the supply capacity of such companies is likely to fall short of potential demand. Some suggest that governments are better positioned to issue such longevity bonds even though they are already exposed to longevity risk through social security provision. Governments can use fiscal tools to share the risk across generations and have the option to increase the official retirement age. The development of longevity bonds will improve the efficiency of annuity markets and, in turn, reduce the need for governments to provide means-tested old-age entitlements.

The first attempt at longevity bond issuance was unsuccessful. In 2005, the European Investment Bank issued a £540 million longevity bond. The deal was structured by BNP Paribas and reinsured by PartnerRe. The coupons were linked to the survivorship of a cohort of males age 65 in 2003 in England and Wales and should have been of great interest to UK pension schemes and life insurers. However, it failed to attract sufficient demand and was withdrawn. The failure has been attributed to a lack of understanding of longevity risk, the product's utility among pension funds, and problems with the design of the issue.

In 2010, Swiss Re successfully launched a series of eight-year longevity-based insurance-linked securities notes worth $50 million. The DB legacy has captured the attention and efforts of pension plan sponsors as they have realised the amount of risk they have taken on: longevity risk are the key but not the only risk. Expectancy increases the length of the payment period. Recent capital market developments have offered a few solutions for DB plans to offload these risks, including pension buyouts, pension buy-ins, and longevity hedges. Pension buyouts and pension buy-ins are also called *bulk annuities*:

- *Pension buyouts:* In a pension buyout, the plan assets and liabilities are transferred from the plan sponsor to the insurer, enabling the sponsor to be fully discharged of liabilities and uncertainties of asset returns. Hence buyouts transfer all demographic and market risks. The insurance policies are written in the names of individual members, who then become completely disconnected from the scheme and receive payments from the insurer. A pension buyout allows the scheme to get rid of longevity risk and the risk of uncertain asset returns and inflation. However, members are exposed to counterparty risk from the insurer. Pension buyouts can be fully or partially structured, covering all or a selected group of members. Full buyouts are usually followed by the wind-up of the pension scheme. Pension buyouts are relatively small in the current state of the insurance market and are more attractive to smaller plans looking to eliminate otherwise disproportionally high running costs.
- *Pension buy-ins:* Pension buy-ins are an investment for pension schemes and are similar to pension buyouts, allowing the pension plan to transfer longevity risk, inflation risk, and the risk

of uncertain asset return. The key difference between pension buyouts and pension buy-ins is that in a pension buy-in, the insurance policy is written in the name of the pension trustee, and the liabilities remain in the pension scheme. Liabilities are insured, but the pension plan is still directly liable to its members. Assets are transferred from the pension plan to the insurer but are generally used as collateral against the insurance policy to reduce counterparty risk.

5.3   Conclusions

Health is wealth, and this is probably best realised now as we face a global pandemic unlike any other event in the history of mankind. As humans live longer, we need to live longer and healthily—mentally, physically, and spiritually—to exemplify good well-being. The causes of mortality are changing not only in the wealthiest countries but also in the poorest countries. While longevity is increasing in advanced countries due to elongation of life at older ages, it has increased in poor countries due to elongation at younger ages, thanks to advances in maternal and infant mortality.

Understanding and dealing with longevity has improved thanks to actuarial, biomedical, genetic, and scientific knowledge. Longevity models and forecasts at both the cohort level and a period basis have improved almost annually, contributing to better quality of life overall. The health, insurance, and pension industries have transformed themselves to deal with the uncertainties caused by longevity. The financial side of longevity consists of the liabilities to be defrayed by pension funds (corporate, industry-wide, or national) and requires proper planning. Financial innovation, novel modelling, and creating instruments to manage longevity risk are still growth areas in a world facing global ageing.

Disability-adjusted LE and HALE at older ages are the right metrics to monitor as quality-of-life indicators. Health and pensions are both essential to enjoy retirement. It is not just about retirement income—at least as important is retirement health.

A lesson from the ongoing COVID crisis is that advanced countries must improve their sharing of information, data, and technological findings on health, to advance global health and welfare while dealing with future health threats like epidemics and pandemics.

Chapter 6
Pensions and Retirement

One of the most important issues facing human society is ageing (notwithstanding climate change, which affects humans and the entire planet). This chapter is a natural successor to the previous one on health and longevity. Whenever I discuss ageing or demographics, the immediate sub-topics that are naturally referred to by most of my clients and colleagues, including my mentors, are pensions, retirement, and insurance. In writing this book, I have had to cut down many topics and issues and consolidate or merge other related topics in some chapters. But after much deliberation, I have decided that the area of pensions deserves a separate chapter. Many of the issues underlying ageing, pensions, retirement, and insurance have been covered in previous chapters, but this chapter will focus on aspects of pensions that I believe require holistic, coordinated actions. This chapter will discuss institutional pensions, pension systems, and pension policy (drawing on my policy advisory, academic, and investment research rather than individual or retail pensions, which are best advised on by IFAs and individual advisors).

As mentioned in the book's introduction, the perspective of demographics that I believe in is predicated on a focus on people's characteristics as consumers and workers. In terms of my perspective on demographics, pensions are related to people's life decisions as consumers and workers. Workers earn income for their labour over their working life, and whatever is not consumed is saved and grows over time to provide income and resources during the inactive, retired phase of life. On an individual basis, pensions connect working life to the retirement phase and, in more formal terms, connect the accumulation of assets during work life to decumulation of assets during retired life.

This chapter provides a macro perspective of pensions and covers the history of pensions, public pension challenges, pension finance theory, asset allocation, pension system design, and pension trends. It ends with the need for radical change in mindsets, tools, and asset allocation.

6.1   A Brief History of Social Security and Pensions

Certain inevitable facets of life, such as unemployment, illness, disability, death, and old age, are said to be threats to economic security. The ancient Greeks stockpiled olive oil, which was very nutritious and could be stored for relatively long periods; this was their form of economic security. In medieval Europe, the feudal system was the basis of economic security, with the feudal lord responsible for the economic survival of the serfs working on the estate. The feudal lord had economic security as long as there was a steady supply of serfs to work the estate, and the serfs had economic security only so long as they were fit to provide labour. Each family also had resources to draw upon; they were often a source of economic security, especially for the aged or infirm. And the land itself was an essential form of economic security for those who owned it or lived on farms.

Formal systems and organisations that provided economic security to their members during tough times included the guilds in medieval Europe, friendly societies in England, and fraternal organisations in the US and England in the late nineteenth century.

The first modern-day *public pension system* is attributed to German Chancellor Otto Von Bismarck. He created the first old-age social insurance program in 1889 at the suggestion of German Emperor William the First, who suggested to his parliament that the state care for those disabled due to age or invalidity. Chancellor von Bismarck introduced social insurance to promote the well-being of workers and the efficiency of the German economy and avoid calls for more radical socialist alternatives.

The German system provided contributory retirement benefits and disability benefits. Participation was mandatory, and contributions were taken from employees, employers, and the government. Coupled with the workers' compensation program established in 1884 and the "sickness" insurance enacted the year before, this gave the Germans a comprehensive system of income security based on social insurance principles. Germany started with a retirement age of 70 years when Bismarck instituted the system but later changed it to 65 years.

6.1.1   Pre–Social Security

A precursor to the US Social Security program was a program in the post–Civil War period that saw a higher proportion of disabled and survivors of deceased in the population than ever before. This led to the development of a generous pension program, with interesting similarities to later developments in Social Security[1].

The first national program for soldiers was passed in early 1776, prior to the signing of the Declaration of Independence, and limited pensions were paid to veterans of America's various wars. The creation of Civil War pensions led to a full-fledged pension system in America for the first time. This program began shortly after the start of the Civil War, with the first legislation in 1862 providing for benefits linked to disabilities "incurred as a direct consequence of military duty". In 1890, the link with service-connected disability was broken, and any disabled Civil War veteran qualified for benefits. In 1906, old age was made a sufficient qualification for benefits. By 1910, Civil War veterans and their survivors enjoyed a program of disability, survivor, and old-age benefits similar in some ways to later Social Security programs. Over 90% of the remaining

Civil War veterans were receiving benefits under this program in 1910, although they were barely 0.6% of the total US population. Civil War pensions were also an asset that attracted young wives to elderly veterans whose pensions they could inherit as the widow of a war veteran.

In terms of the chronology of US pensions before the end of WWI, a few landmark dates are as follows[2]:

- *1875*—The American Express Company established the first private pension plan in the US.
- *Late nineteenth century*—Roughly 75% of all males over age 65 were working. If a male over 65 was not working, it was likely because he was disabled.
- *1899*—There were 13 private pension plans in the country.
- *1900*—Life expectancy was approximately 49 years at birth. Individuals who reached age 60 could expect to live, on average, an additional 12 years.
- *1913*—Congress enacted the first federal income tax law.
- *1914*-The Internal Revenue Service ruled that pensions paid to retired employees were deductible, similar to wages, as ordinary and necessary business expenses.
- *1919*—Over 300 private pension plans existed, covering approximately 15% of the nation's wage and salary employees. The growth of pension coverage was attributed to employers' desire to attract workers, reduce labour turnover, and (more humanely) remove older, less productive employees.
- *1926*—The Revenue Act of 1926 exempted trust income from pension plans from an employee's current taxable income. This act also established that pension plans must be established for the exclusive benefit of "some or all employees".

6.1.2   Committee on Economic Security

On 8 June 1934, President Franklin D. Roosevelt announced his intention to provide a program for Social Security. He subsequently created the Committee on Economic Security (CES), which was instructed to study the entire problem of economic insecurity. It was tasked to make recommendations that would serve as the basis for legislative consideration by Congress. The CES did a comprehensive study of the whole issue of economic security in America and an analysis of the European experience. The committee's comprehensive report in January 1935 was the first of its kind, and it stood as a landmark study for many years. On 17 January 1935, the President introduced the report to both Houses of Congress for simultaneous consideration.

The Social Security Act was signed into law by President Roosevelt on 14 August 1935. In addition to several provisions for the general welfare, the act created a social insurance program designed to pay retired workers age 65 or older a continuing income after retirement. The significance of the new social insurance program was that it sought to address the long-range problem of economic security for the aged through a contributory system in which the workers themselves contributed to their own future retirement benefit by making regular payments into a joint fund.

In 1939, amendments made fundamental changes to the Social Security program by adding two new categories of benefits: payments to the spouse and minor children of a retired worker (*dependents benefits*) and survivor benefits paid to the family in the event of the premature death of a covered worker. This change transformed Social Security from a retirement program for workers into a *family-based* economic security program. The 1939 amendments also increased benefit amounts and accelerated the start of monthly benefit payments to 1940.

It was not until the 1950 amendments that Congress first legislated an increase in benefits to compensate for cost-of-living adjustments. Beneficiaries' payments were recomputed in two stages in 1950 and 1952. In 1972, the law was changed to provide, beginning in 1975, automatic annual cost-of-living allowances (COLAs) based on the annual increase in consumer prices.

The Social Security amendments of 1954 initiated a disability insurance program that provided the public with additional coverage against economic insecurity. On 1 August 1956, the Social

Security Act was amended to provide benefits to disabled workers age 50–64 and disabled adult children. In September 1960, President Eisenhower signed a law amending the disability rules to permit payment of benefits to disabled workers of any age and to their dependents.

The Medicare bill signed on 30 July 1965 made the Social Security Administration (SSA) responsible for a new social insurance program that extended health coverage to almost all Americans aged 65 or older. And in the 1970s, SSA became responsible for a new program, Supplemental Security Income (SSI).

A few other important landmark dates on the timeline of US pensions and retirement are as follows:

- *1974*—The Employee Retirement Income Security Act of 1974 (ERISA) required more plan disclosures to participants and the government (summary plan description, material modification notices, annual reports, and a statement of the participant's accrued benefits upon request), strengthened participation requirements, established vesting rules and the rule of 45 (at least 50% vesting when the employee's age and service add to 45), required joint and survivor annuity provisions, set minimum funding rules for plans, and set fiduciary standards for plan sponsors. ERISA established the Pension Benefit Guarantee Corporation to provide mandatory insurance for defined-benefit (DB) plans.
- *1978*—The Revenue Act of 1978 established qualified deferred compensation plans (Code Section 401(k) plans), which allow for pre-tax employee contributions to such plans (known as *elective deferrals*). Employees are permitted to withdraw their contributions from such plans after age 59½ or upon separation from service (currently "severance from employment"), or because of hardship or disability.
- *1978*—The 1967 Age Discrimination and Employment Act (ADEA) was amended to prohibit discrimination against individuals up to age 70. The law does not prohibit discrimination

against individuals age 70 and over; nor does it prohibit mandatory retirement.

- *1982*—The Tax Equity and Fiscal Responsibility Act of 1982 limited the number of annual additions (employer contributions,
employee contributions, and forfeitures) for each participant in
a defined-contribution (DC) plan.

- *1983*—The Social Security amendments of 1983 gradually raised
the normal retirement age from 65 to 67. For all individuals born
after 1959, the normal retirement age is age 67. (For example,
per the graduated system, for individuals born in 1959, the normal retirement age is 66 and 10 months).

To understand the historical contexts of retirement, in the
Oxford Handbook of Pensions and Retirement Income[3], Thane
(Chapter 3) and Steven Sass (Chapter 5) present different historical
perspectives on retirement and employer retirement income plans.
Arza and Johnson (Chapter 4 of the *Handbook*) trace the history
of the growth of international public pension plans between 1889
and the 1990s, illustrating reasons for differences across countries
and the role of the political context within which public pensions
evolved over more than a century. Thane states that governments'
and employers' need to win the trust of people and workers, respectively, drove employer and state pensions forward. Mass retirement
at earlier ages combined with longer life spans and expectations of
maintaining living standards required pensions to be subsidised
by taxpayers or employers. She mentions how workplace gender
inequality extends into pension gender inequality and advocates
greater attention to improving access to employment, income, and
pensions for women. Sass discusses the costs of employer pensions
and how many employers began to question the benefits of funding
these plans given the increasing costs.

A good history of UK pensions from historical times until
recently, covering both state and occupational pensions, is found in
the UK Pensions Archive Trust[4]. A more recent and detailed briefing note traces the history of state pensions between 1948 and 2010
as an Institute for Fiscal Studies (IFS) briefing note[5]. Perhaps the

most significant recent UK pension developments were triggered by the Pensions Commission report recommendations chaired by Adair Turner. The commission's first report, on 12 October 2004, provided a comprehensive analysis of the UK pension system; its second report, on 30 November 2005, presented the commission's recommendations for a new policy direction; and the final statement, on 4 April 2006, detailed its response to specific issues of pension reform since the publication of the second report[6].

6.2   Evaluating Pension Systems: Indicators and Cross-Country Comparisons

One of the interesting indicators is when people actually retire relative to official or normal retirement ages. The OECD's *Pensions at a Glance 2019* covers the period until 2018[7]. In a modern world with retirement ages and practices no longer as rigid, combined with acceptance of older individuals embarking on new careers, there have been some changes to when people actually retire—some before the usual retirement age, some at the retirement age, and some beyond it. Many of these decisions are voluntary rather than employer forced or mandated.

More than two decades ago, we advocated the concept of flexible retirement in a digital world. Work-from-home practices over the last two years have provided an added spur.

The *average effective retirement age* is defined as the average age of exit from the labour force during a five-year period. Labour force (net) exits are estimated by taking the difference in the participation rate for each five-year age group (40 and over) at the beginning of the period and the rate for the corresponding age group aged five years older at the end of the period. The official age corresponds to the age at which a pension can be received irrespective of whether a worker has a long insurance record of years of contributions. Tables 6.1–6.3 are based on assumptions made by OECD models to enable the computations and comparability. Table 6.1 illustrates that effective retirement ages are higher than the normal retirement ages in many countries partly due to uncertainty regarding long post-retirement life.

Table 6.1 Average effective retirement age vs. normal retirement age: 2013–2018.

Men Retirement Age			Women Retirement Age		
	Effective	Normal		Effective	Normal
Korea	72.3	61.0	Korea	72.3	61.0
Mexico	71.3	65.0	Japan	69.1	64.0
Japan	70.8	65.0	Chile	66.7	65.0
Chile	70.0	65.0	United States	66.5	66.0
New Zealand	69.8	65.0	Mexico	66.5	65.0
Israel	69.4	67.0	New Zealand	66.4	65.0
Portugal	68.5	65.2	Israel	66.0	62.0
Iceland	68.1	67.0	Iceland	65.9	67.0
United States	67.9	66.0	Estonia	65.7	63.3
Sweden	66.4	65.0	Portugal	65.4	65.2
Switzerland	66.4	65.0	Sweden	65.4	65.0
Turkey	66.3	51.0	Switzerland	65.0	64.0
Norway	66.1	67.0	Turkey	64.9	48.0
Latvia	65.7	62.8	Latvia	64.7	62.8
Ireland	65.6	66.0	Australia	64.3	65.0
Estonia	65.5	63.3	Ireland	64.1	66.0
Canada	65.5	65.0	Norway	64.1	67.0
Australia	65.3	65.0	Canada	64.0	65.0
Netherlands	65.2	65.8	Germany	63.6	65.5
Denmark	65.1	65.0	United Kingdom	63.6	62.7
United Kingdom	64.7	65.0	Finland	63.4	65.0
Lithuania	64.3	63.6	Lithuania	63.0	61.9
Finland	64.3	65.0	Netherlands	62.5	65.8
Germany	64.0	65.5	Denmark	62.5	65.0
Austria	63.5	65.0	Italy	61.5	66.6
Hungary	63.4	63.5	Czech Republic	61.3	62.7
Italy	63.3	67.0	Luxembourg	61.3	62.0
Czech Republic	63.2	63.2	Spain	61.3	65.0
Slovenia	63.1	62.0	Austria	60.8	60.0
Poland	62.8	65.0	France	60.8	63.3
Spain	62.1	65.0	Poland	60.6	60.0
Greece	61.7	62.0	Belgium	60.5	65.0
Belgium	61.6	65.0	Slovenia	60.1	61.7
Slovak Republic	61.1	62.2	Greece	60.0	62.0
France	60.8	63.3	Hungary	60.0	62.0
Luxembourg	60.5	62.0	Slovak Republic	59.9	62.2
OECD	65.4	64.2	OECD	63.7	63.5

SOURCE: OECD.

Among the standard indicators to understand the generosity of the provisions of a pension are the gross pension replacement rate and the net pension replacement rate as a percentage of current wages or earnings. The old-age pension replacement rate measures how effectively a pension system provides a retirement income to replace earnings, the primary source of income before retirement.

The *gross replacement rate* is defined as gross pension entitlement divided by gross pre-retirement earnings. Often, the replacement rate is expressed as the ratio of the pension to final earnings (just before retirement). Under the baseline assumptions, workers earn the same percentage of average worker earnings throughout their career. Therefore, final earnings are equal to lifetime average earnings revalued in line with economy-wide earnings growth. Replacement rates expressed as a percentage of final earnings are thus identical to those expressed as a percentage of lifetime earnings.

The *net replacement rate* is defined as the individual net pension entitlement divided by net pre-retirement earnings, taking into account personal income taxes and Social Security contributions paid by workers and pensioners. It measures how effectively a pension system provides a retirement income to replace earnings, the primary source of income before retirement. This indicator is measured as a percentage of pre-retirement earnings. Table 6.2 presents both gross and net replacement rates for the average male worker for 2018.

As per the OECD 2019 report, whilst the gross replacement rate gives a clear indication of the design of the pension system, the net replacement matters more to individuals, as it reflects their disposable income in retirement compared to when working. For average earners with a full career, the net replacement rate from mandatory pension schemes at the normal retirement age averages 59% across the OECD, 10 percentage points higher than the average gross replacement rate. This reflects the higher effective tax and social contribution rates that people pay on their earnings than on their pensions in retirement, primarily due to the progressivity of tax systems, tax advantages of pensions, and lower social contributions on pension benefits. Net replacement rates vary extensively,

Table 6.2 Pension replacement rates: 2018.

	Gross pension replacement rate (average male wage earner)	Net pension replacement rate (average male age earner)
	%	%
France	60.1	73.6
Germany	38.7	51.9
Italy	79.5	91.8
Japan	32	36.8
United Kingdom	21.7	28.4
United States	39.4	49.4
OECD—Average	49	58.6

SOURCE: OECD.

from around 30% in Lithuania, Mexico, and the UK to 90% or more in Austria, Luxembourg, Portugal, and Turkey for average wage workers.

While replacement rates indicate the pension promise relative to individual earnings, they are not a comprehensive indicator of cumulated pension payments. They only consider the benefit level relative to individual earnings at retirement. For a more complete view, life expectancy, normal retirement age, and indexation of pension benefits must be accounted for. Together, these determine the length of pension benefit payment and its evolution. An alternative indicator, pension wealth—a measure of the stock of future discounted flows of pension benefits—accounts for these factors. It represents the lump sum needed at retirement age to buy an annuity giving the same flow of pension payments promised by mandatory retirement-income schemes.

The OECD's *Pensions at a Glance 2019* reports that gross pension wealth (at individual earnings equal to the average wage) is highest in Luxembourg at 18.7 times individual annual earnings for men and 20.6 times for women. The lowest pension wealth for men is found in the UK and for women in Mexico at 4.1 and 4.3, respectively, due to low replacement rates. This indicator is built based on the average (gender-specific) mortality rates within countries. It thus assumes away differences in life expectancy across income levels. Hence, higher individual replacement rates for low earners than for average earners means that the computed pension wealth relative to individual earnings is also higher for low earners. For men with individual earnings equal to half average earnings, pension wealth is 10.9 times their annual earnings on average, compared with 8.9 times for average wage workers, and 12.1 and 9.8 times, respectively, for women. We present the variation in gross pension wealth across G6 countries and by income levels in Table 6.3.

It is important to note that pension wealth reflects differences in pension wealth across average earners, low earners, and high earners (relative to average) and between males and females. This shows that pension wealth incorporates the combined effect of life expectancy, normal retirement age, and indexation of pension benefits.

The effects of life expectancy on pension wealth can be noted in the OECD's comments, which show that in countries where the duration of retirement is shorter, such as Estonia and Hungary, the individual pension wealth is smaller. The effect is the opposite in Switzerland and some Nordic countries, where life expectancy is high. Pension wealth is also affected by indexation rules at a given initial replacement rate level. Although most OECD countries now index pensions in payment to prices, there are exceptions:

Table 6.3   Gross pension wealth by earnings (males and females).

| | Individual earnings, multiple of mean | | | | | |
	0.5	1.0	1.5	0.5	1.0	1.5
		Men			Women	
France	11.0	11.0	9.9	12.5	12.5	11.3
Germany	7.7	7.7	7.7	8.5	8.5	8.5
Italy	12.5	12.5	12.5	14.1	14.1	14.1
Japan	8.1	6.1	5.4	9.6	7.2	6.4
UK	8.2	4.1	2.7	9.2	4.6	3.1
US	8.4	6.7	5.5	8.9	7.1	5.8
OECD	10.9	8.9	8.1	12.1	9.8	8.9

SOURCE: OECD[7].

Germany, Ireland, Luxembourg, and the UK link their basic, DB systems to average earnings. As earnings tend to grow faster than prices, pension wealth is higher with wages than price indexation for a given replacement rate. If Luxembourg, for example, indexed to prices rather than wages, the pension wealth for an average male earner would decrease from 18.7 to 15.7 with an unchanged initial benefit based on the OECD pension model. The calculation of pension wealth uses a uniform real discount rate of 2%. Since the comparisons refer to prospective pension entitlements, the calculations use country-specific mortality rates by age and sex at the year of retirement. *Pension wealth is expressed as a multiple of gross annual individual earnings.*

The counterpart to the gross pension wealth indicator after adjusting for a net basis is net pension wealth: a measure of the stock of future discounted flows of pension benefits after taxes and social contributions that accounts for taxes and transfers. It can be thought of as the total net benefits that will be received on average from the mandatory retirement-income schemes. *Net pension wealth* is defined as the present value of the flow of pension benefits, taking into account the taxes and Social Security contributions that retirees have to pay on their pensions. It is measured and expressed as a multiple of net annual individual earnings in the specific country. Taxes and contributions paid by pensioners are calculated conditional on the mandatory pension benefit to which individuals are entitled at different earnings levels. The calculations take into account all standard tax allowances, tax relief, and concessions granted either to pension income or to people of pension age. Table 6.4 presents variation in net pension wealth across G6 countries and OECD average as well as different earnings levels.

Higher individual replacement rates and the increased tax allowance for many pensioners mean that net pension wealth relative to individual net earnings tends to be higher for low earners than for average earners, at least as the estimations here abstract from differences in life expectancy across income levels. For men with individual earnings equal to half of average earnings, net pension wealth is 12.4 times their net earnings on average, compared

Table 6.4   Net pension wealth by earnings.

| | Individual earnings, multiple of mean | | | | | |
	0.5	1.0	1.5	0.5	1.0	1.5
	Men			Women		
France	13.0	13.5	12.6	14.9	15.3	14.4
Germany	11.2	10.4	10.3	12.4	11.5	11.4
Italy	14.4	14.4	14.8	16.3	16.3	16.8
Japan	8.8	7.0	6.4	10.3	8.3	7.5
UK	9.7	5.4	3.8	10.8	6.0	4.3
US	10.4	8.4	7.2	11.0	8.9	7.6
OECD	12.4	10.6	9.9	13.8	11.7	10.9

SOURCE: OECD[7].

with 10.6 times for average wage workers. Similarly, for women with low earnings, net pension wealth of 13.8 compares with 11.7 times individual earnings for average earners. For higher earners, net pension wealth is on average 9.9 for men and 10.9 for women, only slightly lower than that for average earners, with Luxembourg again highest and the UK lowest.

The OECD pension modelling team notes that in countries where the duration of retirement is shorter and pension benefits are DB, such as Estonia and Hungary, the individual pension wealth is smaller. The effect is the opposite in Switzerland and some Nordic countries (in DB systems), where life expectancies are high. Similarly, since women's life expectancy is longer than men's, pension wealth for women is higher in all countries that use unisex mortality tables or have DB systems.

The gender pension gap is quite significant in many countries, as shown in Figure 6.1; and given that women live longer than men, this gap is likely to worsen in a future of low growth prospects.

In addition to the gender inequality of pensions, old-age poverty is an important policy priority that concerns richer advanced countries and reflects the uncertainty of allocating income and savings over the indefinite increasing retirement period. This is an indirect

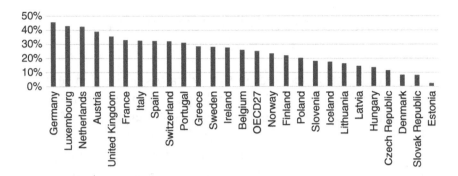

Figure 6.1   Gender pension gap: 2015 or latest.
SOURCE: OECD[7].

indicator of how well older segments of the population are doing relative to the average. Old-age provision of retirement income has been one of the main objectives of Social Security and public pension schemes since the times of Bismarckian Germany. Despite the existence of old-age income security and pension funds in many advanced countries, as Figure 6.2 shows, old-age poverty rates are a prominent blot on their achievements and natural objectives.

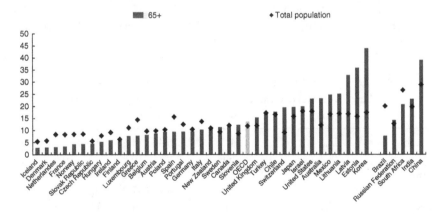

Figure 6.2   Poverty rates among older age groups and the total population.
SOURCE: OECD[7].

6.3   Evaluating Age-Related Pension Expenditures Across Countries

The previous section focused on the indicators of pension replacement rates and pension wealth from the perspective of average wage earners in different countries. We also presented data on effective retirement ages relative to normal, the pension gender gap, and old-age poverty. But there is the other side: the cost of pension provision and pension expenditures as a share of a country's GDP. These public expenditures are a huge drag on public finances, especially during periods of low growth. Table 6.5 shows how expensive the welfare state is in terms of pensions. We had previously discussed this in Chapter 3 when we focused on fiscal policy and sustainability.

In a world of ageing and lower projected economic growth, these levels of public pension spending are too high for even the richest of countries, and they also do not include other age-related expenditures such as health and long-term care. As argued in Chapter 4, the public pension promises or commitments of governments create not just a sense of entitlement for the population but also, in aggregate, enormous fiscal sustainability strains. In The "Age of Responsibility"[8], we advocated that savings rates at individual and household levels need to increase to 15% to support and alleviate the

Table 6.5   Cash expenditures on public pensions.

	Level (% of total government spending)		Level (% of GDP)				
	2000	2015	1990	2000	2005	2010	2015
France	22.2	24.4	10.4	11.4	12.0	13.2	13.9
Germany	24.2	23.1	9.5	10.8	11.1	10.6	10.1
Italy	28.9	32.2	11.4	13.5	13.7	15.4	16.2
Japan		23.9	4.7	7.0	8.1	9.6	9.4
UK	13.4	14.8	4.5	4.8	5.0	6.3	6.2
US	16.7	18.7	5.8	5.6	5.7	6.6	7.1
OECD	16.3	18.4	6.3	6.6	6.8	7.7	8.0

SOURCE: OECD Social Expenditures Database (SOCX); OECD Main Economic Indicators Database.

fiscal sustainability strains. This basically boils down to the issue that long-term public pension promises are largely unsustainable[9].

The EU, which includes some of the oldest countries in the world, has, along with the OECD, devoted considerable policy attention to ageing and its manifestations in terms of labour participation, retirement age, health, and fiscal sustainability. The Ageing Report of the European Commission (EC) and the companion Fiscal Sustainability Reports have concentrated the attention of European policy makers on the societal, economic, and financial aspects of the critical issues of ageing from a holistic perspective. Detailed discussions of ageing's implications from a fiscal sustainability perspective were presented in Chapter 3.

The EC Ageing Report 2020 (published in 2021) uses a set of standard common assumptions, although separate budgetary projections were carried out for four government expenditure items: pensions, healthcare, long-term care, and education. The Member States ran the projections for pensions using their own national model(s), reflecting current pension legislation and allowing the projections to capture country-specific conditions due to different pension legislation but still ensuring consistency. The projections for healthcare, long-term care, and education were run by the EC services (Directorate-General for Economic and Financial Affairs [DG ECFIN]) based on a common projection model for each expenditure item, taking into account country-specific settings where appropriate. The results of these separate projections were aggregated to provide an overall projection of age-related public expenditures. Table 6.6 presents results of the projection exercise for pension expenditures, accounting for policy changes already in place or in legislation.

The importance of pensions in the EU's budget is underscored by the fact that nearly 12% of GDP is projected to be spent on public pensions. The fiscal burden could increase with the possibility of low growth and ageing in the absence of health improvements at the individual, family, and national level. It is important to assess the trajectory of pensions expenditure increases for countries on an individual basis between 2019 to 2045 and then on to 2070.

Table 6.6   Public pensions as share of GDP: 2019–2070.

Country	2019	2045	2070	Change 2019–2070
Belgium	12.2	15.1	15.2	3.0
Germany	10.3	12.1	12.4	2.1
Ireland	4.6	7.2	7.6	3.0
Greece	15.7	13.7	11.9	–3.8
Spain	12.3	13.2	10.3	–2.1
France	14.8	14.6	12.6	–2.2
Italy	15.4	17.3	13.6	–1.8
Netherlands	6.8	9.0	9.1	2.3
Austria	13.3	14.9	14.3	1.0
Finland	13.0	12.6	14.4	1.3
Sweden	7.6	7.0	7.5	–0.1
Norway	11.0	12.6	13.6	2.6
Euro Area	12.1	13.3	12.1	0.1
European Union	11.6	12.7	11.7	0.1

SOURCE: *EU Ageing Report 2020.*

6.4   Pensions and Pension Systems: The Experts

Peter Drucker is acknowledged by leading pension experts across Canada, Netherlands, Japan, the US, and the UK as the "guru" of pensions for his foresight and insights in his pioneering book *The Unseen Revolution* nearly five decades ago. A management guru who was a visionary in the fields of pensions and demographics, he warned the world as follows in his 1976 book[10]: "Indeed the demographic change may well be a more important event than those revolutions to which historians are wont to pay exclusive attention: the Bourgeois or Communist revolution, or even the "Industrial Revolution" in technology. After all, it may have more direct and faster impact than any of these on individual and family". He argued that workers are the true capitalists and owners of the means of production—owning, controlling, and directing the country's capital fund through their pension funds. He stated that the largest employee pension funds control the top 1000 US industrial companies and pension funds control 50 of the largest non-industrial companies in the sectors of banking, insurance, retail, communications, and transportation. This is what he called the *unseen revolution*. He argued that if socialism is defined as control of the means of production by workers, then the US is a truly socialist country, more than Castro's Cuba or Allende's Chile. He predicted that by the end of the twentieth century, pension funds would own two-thirds of the equity capital and perhaps 40% of the debt capital of the US economy.

Elaborating on his original ideas from 1976, in a 1995 follow-up book edited by him titled *The Pension Fund Revolution*[11], he highlighted the growing role of institutional investors (especially pension funds) that had become the controlling owners of America's large companies—the country's only capitalists. He maintained that General Motors led the charge by establishing the first modern pension fund in 1952.

Drucker argued that through pension funds, ownership of the means of production had become socialised without becoming nationalised. This idea was not accepted by the mainstream of managers and investors in America in the 1970s, and even the ageing of America was not taken seriously. In *The Pension Fund Revolution*, Drucker predicted that a significant healthcare issue would be longevity, with pensions and Social Security being central to the American economy and society. He foresaw and advocated an extension of the retirement age. He believed that American politics would increasingly be dominated by middle-class issues and the values of elderly people.

The importance of pension systems and policies received policy prominence thanks to the efforts of the researchers and policy experts at the World Bank who have guided and shaped pension policy across many countries, including poor developing ones, since the 1980s. This was brought together in an influential policy research report, *Averting the Old Age Crisis*[12]. The contribution of the World Bank pension group catalysing pensions and ageing-related policy prescriptions has been critical. In the report, the authors highlighted the role of governments in averting the old-age crisis by designing pension systems and making crucial policy choices.

In the introduction, the report set the scene by highlighting the rapid pace of ageing across developing countries and the inadequacy of old-age security systems worldwide, accompanied by weakening informal community and family-based arrangements. They highlighted that income security is a global problem with different manifestations across different countries and regions. They also emphasised that more than half of the world's old rely on family or extended family for food, shelter, and care. With industrialisation and urbanisation, family sizes have become smaller, and people withdraw from productive work, live alone, and rely on non-family sources of income. As populations of countries age, governments have a role to play to alleviate individual shortcomings of myopia, inadequate savings, information gaps, insurance market failures, and long-term poverty. The key policy issues for alternative income-security systems include (i) whether they are voluntary or compulsory, and at what level; (ii) the role of savings vs. redistribution; (iii) whether the risk of unexpected outcomes should be borne by pensioners or others; (iv) whether systems are fully funded or pay as you go; and (v) whether they should be managed centrally.

Evaluation of governments' policy choices in constructing, developing and maintaining old-age security systems should help the old by (i) facilitating people transforming income over their life cycles; (ii) redistributing additional income to the old who are lifetime poor without perverse unintended intergenerational redistributions; and (iii) providing old-age insurance against risks. The financing and management of these objectives can be done via three arrangements. (a) Public pay-as-you-go (PAYG) systems are mandatory for covered workers in all countries and universal in advanced countries, with wide prevalence in middle-income countries. The role of governments is to mandate, finance, manage, and insure public pensions. These are mainly delivered as defined benefits not tied to contributions financed out of payroll taxes and some supplemental government revenue. (b) Occupational, privately managed pension plans are offered by employers to attract and retain workers. Often facilitated by tax concessions and regulated by governments, these have been DB and partially funded in the past. The growing trend is for defined contributions (contributions are specified, and benefits depend on contributions plus invested returns) and occupational plans that are better funded. (c) Personal saving and annuity plans are fully funded, and workers/plan participants bear the investment risks as benefits are not defined in advance.

To serve the three functions of saving, redistribution, and insurance, the authors (World Bank and global pension experts) argued that a single public pillar is not adequate. They laid the foundation for a multi-pillar pension system wherein they recommended separating the saving function from the redistribution function and placing them under different financing and managerial arrangements in two pillars—one public and tax-financed, the other privately managed and fully funded—supplemented by a voluntary pillar for those who want more. They argued that a multi-pillar system helps make transparent decisions, diversify risks, increase long-term savings, and insulate the system from inefficiency and inequity. They acknowledged that *the right mix of pillars is not the same at all times and places—it depends on a country's objectives, history, and current circumstances*—with an emphasis on redistribution vs. savings, financial markets, taxing, and regulatory capacity. The pension reforms and pace will vary across countries.

After a decade of advice and engagement, and noting the reform experiences across more than 70 countries, the World Bank pensions group modified the original three-pillar pension system to a five-pillar pension system, which is the currently recommended standard. Holzman and Hinz[13] summarised the experiences in a much-referred-to "guide to pension system reform", providing an international perspective to pension systems and their reforms. The World Bank had been involved in pension reform in more than 80 countries and provided financial support for reform to more than 60 countries, and that has significantly expanded the knowledge and insights of the staff and stimulated further evaluation and refinement of the policies.

The original three-pillar structure—(i) a mandated, unfunded, and publicly managed DB system; (ii) a mandated, funded, and privately managed DC scheme; and (iii) voluntary retirement savings—has been extended to include two additional pillars: (iv) a basic (zero) pillar to deal more explicitly with the poverty objective; and (v) a nonfinancial pillar to include the broader context of social policy, such as family support, access to healthcare, and housing.

The World Bank policy evolution was based on five characteristic changes to its perspective through (i) a better understanding of reform needs and measures including assessment of reform need, understanding the limits and consequences of mandated pension systems participation—particularly for low-income groups with more immediate and substantial needs than pensions—and reassessing the importance of prefunding for dealing with population ageing; (ii) the extension of the multi-pillar model to encompass as many as five pillars and experience with low-income countries the need for a basic or zero (or non-contributory) pillar; (iii) appreciating the diversity of effective approaches, including the number of pillars, the appropriate balance among the various pillars, and how each pillar is formulated in response to particular circumstances or needs; (iv) a better understanding of the extent to which the inherited pension system, as well as a country's economic, institutional, financial, and political environment, dictate the options available for reform; and (v) a strong interest and support of country-led innovations in pension design and implementation, including (a) the notional DC system as a promising approach to reforming or implementing an unfunded first pillar, (b) the clearinghouse to reduce transaction costs for funded and privately managed pillars, (c) the transformation of severance payments into combined unemployment and retirement-benefit savings accounts, and (d) public prefunding under an improved governance structure as introduced in several high-income countries.

Table 6.7 presents an abridged view of the World Bank's multi-pillar system. The five pillars are detailed in terms of characteristics, participation, and funding.

Holzmann et al.[14] created a pension reform primer to illustrate and explain the World Bank's pension reform framework and lay down the criteria for evaluating pension systems. The authors

Table 6.7 Summary of the five-pillar pension system.

Pillar no.	Characteristic	Participation	Funding
0	Basic or social pension; at least social assistance	Universal or residual	Budget or general revenues
1	Public pension plan, publicly managed (defined benefit or notion defined contribution)	Mandated	Contributions with some financial reserves
2	Occupational or personal pension plans (fully funded defined benefit or fully funded defined contribution)	Mandated	Financial assets
3	Occupational or personal pension plans (partially or fully funded defined benefit or funded defined contribution)	Voluntary	Financial assets
4	Access to informal support (family), other formal social programs (healthcare), and other individual financial and nonfinancial assets (homeownership)	Voluntary	Financial assets / non-financial assets

SOURCE: World Bank[13,14].

emphasised the primary and secondary criteria for the evaluation of pension reforms. The primary evaluation criteria reflect the system's ability to maintain adequacy, affordability, sustainability, equity, predictability, and robustness. The secondary evaluation criteria are the system's capacity to minimise labour market distortions, contribute to savings mobilisation and to financial market development. They underscored that it is essential that over time, pension systems contribute to growth and output to support the promised benefits.

Thirty years after Peter Drucker's warning regarding the importance and significance of pension funds controlling investments and finance, an influential group of central bankers and policy makers convened in Geneva as part of the 2006 Centre for Economic Policy

Research and International Center for Monetary and Banking Studies (CEPR-ICMB) annual conference to assess the role of pension funds[15]. The central bankers addressed pension funds as the new giants that, alongside insurance companies, control large shares of equity and bond markets in the developed world. However, they acknowledged the role of pension funds as financial intermediaries to help individuals save for old age and protect the value of pensions. Through efficient risk-sharing across time and pension fund participants, pension funds can support innovation and growth.

The report highlighted the importance of the following essential dimensions for assessing pensions: financial literacy, delegation of financial life-cycle planning to pension funds, asset-liability risk matching, the role of governments and other institutions in risk management, optimal risk sharing across participants, and labour market and human capital policies to aid flexible working. The report advocated reforms of public PAYG plans, highlighted the transaction efficiency and financial literacy advantages of collective DC plans, welcomed mark to market accounting, and called for harmonised improved regulation. The authors agreed that liability-driven investing (LDI) cannot eliminate all risks of DB plans as it creates financial stability issues, with more efficient and transparent intergenerational risk sharing benefiting both growth and stability. The authors argued for the development of hybrid collective pension schemes in which participants can transform DC claims into DB claims as they become older and rely on pension wealth for consumption.

Franco Modigliani has been considered one of the leading experts in pensions, building on his insights into how individuals earn, consume, save, and allocate resources over their lives. Building on his research showing the limitations of PAYG and DB pensions, his 2004 book *Rethinking Pension Reform*, written along with A. Muralidhar[16], has lessons that apply to the world today. They assessed the global state of pension systems relative to their objectives in Latin America, the US, and Spain. They discussed the costs of system design and factors affecting costs, suggesting that financial innovation can help mitigate the risks of pension funds.

Their analysis of pension reform choices and impact on retirement income provision led them to advocate the future of pension systems as hybrids that do better than either DB or DC schemes. This is a critical lesson that other pension experts and others have also been highlighting recently.

The growth of hybrid pension plans and their design has posed challenges to accounting standards boards that have stressed the need to investigate further how accounting standards and legislations may be adapted to account for hybrid pension plans[17,18].

In addition to US pension expert(s) contributions, Theo Kocken and Keith Ambachtsheer made pioneering contributions based on the Dutch and Canadian pension experiences. Their advice and impact have helped guide the debates, discussions, and implementation of pension reforms in their own countries and beyond. The Dutch pension debate has been well initiated and supported by conferences arranged by their central bank and regulators covering fiscal sustainability of pensions, design of systems with prefunding, pension governance and literacy, and the role of risk-based supervision[19].

The pension contract is like a long-term contract that has been researched in contracting theory and mechanism design. Kocken's *Curious Contracts*[19] highlight the issues that Drucker and I have raised regarding the efficiency, design, and enforceability of such contracts. I believe these contracts were designed when few of them were required, as people didn't live that long and faced the uncertainties underlying implementation that we are noticing presently. The uncertainties of longer-term health, life expectancy, cost of living, and the macro environment are the primary reasons these contracts cannot be complete: we cannot write down all possible future outcomes in a contract. As the World Bank report highlighted, this creates the natural bond with the insurance element of pensions.

Kocken[19] highlighted the absence of clear agreements between all the stakeholders in a pension contract, the use of derivatives in risk management, the applicability of embedded options, and their use in redesigning the pension system. The reform of the Dutch pension system over the last few years has seen many of the nuances highlighted in the book play out in greater detail. He highlighted the unsustainability of DB pension systems similar to Muralidhar and Modigliani, as well as my own views from a macro-sustainability perspective. He assessed the role of parent corporate guarantees in the corporate pension world and the role of incentives to achieve the best possible outcomes. The design of the optimal pension contract is a variant of the problem of incentive-compatible mechanism design in applied microeconomics and industrial organisation.

Muralidhar[20] also highlighted investment tools and techniques to measure, monitor, and manage risks of pension funds in his book, which elaborated on how to make decisions about asset allocation, manager selection, and manager retention. He blended practical and theoretical insights in asset allocation, risk management, performance evaluation, and implementation, arguing for integrating asset-liability management (ALM), allowing for the use of derivatives, and appreciating the benefits of leverage.

Keith Ambachtsheer has contributed over the last three decades by providing an integrative and holistic view of pension fund management. He and D. Ezra posed a significant challenge to the pension industry[21], highlighting the lack of a universal paradigm that brings together governance, finance, and investments of pensions to maximise pension fund stakeholder value. They showed the way to achieve excellence through governance, investment, and funding policy for the fiduciaries. In his book *The Pension Fund Revolution*[22], Ambachtsheer highlighted the lack of integrative thinking and business progress in delivering performance for the stakeholders. He critiqued the existing systems and advocated how to create TOPS (The Optimal Pension System).

In a call to arms to the pension industry, Ambachtsheer[23] emphatically made a case for why a pension revolution is needed, decrying both DB and DC pension plans as possible solutions, and proposing that hybrid pension plans may provide better governance and risk-adjusted performance than either of the traditional alternatives. He stated, "workplace pension arrangements around the world are sick and in need of strong medicine. Pension coverage and adequacy are too low, and pension uncertainty too high. The prescription of some pension experts is to resurrect the traditional defined-benefit (DB) plan. Others say broad defined-contribution (DC) plan coverage is the cure. This article argues that we have to move from an 'either-or' to an 'and-and' mindset if we want to seriously improve global workplace pension coverage, adequacy, and certainty". He stressed that redesign of the pension system is not the complete solution as the delivery mechanism of pensions needs to be reformed to meet the scale, expertise, and "in the interests of" requirements for pension participants.

Barr and Diamond[24] provided principles for pension reform rooted in economic theory: pension systems have multiple objectives, the analysis should consider the pension system as a whole, the analysis should be framed in a second-best context, different systems share risks differently, and systems have different effects by generation and by gender. Drawing on theory for policy reforms, the authors conclude that (i) there is no single best pension design, (ii) earlier retirement does little to reduce unemployment, (iii) unsustainable pension promises need to be addressed directly, (iv) a move from PAYG toward funding in a mandatory system may or may not be welfare-improving, and (v) implementation matters—policy design that exceeds a country's capacity to implement it is bad policy design.

Barr and Diamond suggested different pension policy reform options for countries that are at different stages of development. They summarised their views as lessons to pension policy makers and researchers as follows: (i) pension finance problems have roots in the longer term; (ii) pension systems have multiple purposes, diverse institutions, diverse histories, diverse politics, and various constraints—there is no single best system; (iii) options widen as capacity constraints relax, but there are benefits to keeping choices simple even in the most advanced economies; and (iv) pension reform advice requires an understanding of the underlying principles of pensions. There is room for disagreement about choosing sensible strategies, but there is broad agreement on some aspects of bad policies. They state that in responding to long-run trends, any finance improvement of a pension system must involve one or more of (i) higher contribution rates, (ii) lower benefits, (iii) later retirement at the same benefit, and (iv) increased saving.

Ambachtsheer's latest book, *The Future of Pension Management*[25], lays down a further roadmap for how pension funds should better integrate design, governance, and investment, acknowledging that the pension landscape has evolved away from pure DB or DC plans to hybrid versions such as *defined ambition* and *target benefit*. Pension coverage is also increasing through auto-enrolment, and pension governance tries to balance representation vs. being strategic.

Global retirement and investment expert Zvi Bodie, with Michael Clowes[26], highlighted how investors can build safe portfolios and be worry-free rather than wrongly assume that stocks diversify all types of risks in the long run. The average investor and household has to contend with longer periods of lifetime uncertainty and therefore safeguard their accumulated assets while aiming to grow the income derived from them. This book provided insights into using treasury inflation-protected securities (TIPS) and bonds in portfolios. The authors challenged myths underlying the conventional wisdom of investing and provided a practical six-step guide to worry-free investing.

How much do people really understand about retirement and investments? As previously highlighted by regulators and supervisors like the De Nederlandsche Bank (DNB), European Insurance and Occupational Pension Association (EIOPA), and the OECD, Mitchell[27] stresses that financial literacy is a particularly crucial element of lifelong learning that is critical to lifetime financial planning. Mitchell and Lusardi[28] devised three questions for the University of Michigan's long-running Health and Retirement Study of US people over 50. The two researchers were stunned to discover that older people had remarkably low levels of financial knowledge. Lauded as comprehensive yet concise, their "Big Three" questions have been used in numerous other surveys and more than 20 countries, painting a picture of low financial literacy among the young, the old, women, and low-income groups worldwide. Mitchell and Lusardi also looked at the broader implications of financial knowledge and found that financial literacy can explain between 30 and 40% of wealth inequality. That study also included the surprising finding that Social Security benefits may actually discourage accumulating financial knowledge and thereby contribute to wealth inequality.

Subsequent research has found that financial literacy matters enormously for financial decision-making. Those who are financially literate are more likely to plan and save for retirement, make better investments, and experience less financial stress. Mitchell[27] cites the fact that one study found that the most financially knowledgeable employees in a business received retirement plan returns 130 basis points, or 1.3 percentage points, higher each year, compared with the average worker.

A critical project combining health, retirement, and living conditions from the perspective of an individual in Europe was led by retirement expert Axel Borsch Supan and his colleagues based on the Survey of Health, Ageing and Retirement in Europe (SHARE)[29]. Their book explored 28,000 life histories of individuals in Europe as part of SHARE and addressed policy questions regarding how the welfare state affects people's incomes, housing, families, retirement, volunteering, and health.

David Blake of the Pension Institute published two books[30] detailing the economics and finance underlying pensions from individual savings and retirement decisions, lifetime asset allocation, corporate decisions and pension system choices, asset choices within pension investments, corporate pension finance, aspects of DB pension plans, and the financial aspects of DC plans during the accumulation and decumulation phases of the life cycle.

Holzmann[31] assessed the state of pension reform across countries globally in the context of the updated prescriptions provided by the World Bank in 2008. He highlighted that pension systems are in flux, and their reforms are driven by shifting objectives, moving reform needs, and changing macro environments. He mentioned that this has led to innovations including (i) the introduction or strengthening of basic protections for the vulnerable elderly, (ii) the move toward funded and unfunded mandated DC schemes, and (iii) increased nudging by governments to encourage benefit coverage and "top-ups" under voluntary and funded provisions. He emphasised that the fiscal conditions after the global financial crisis and the fiscal implications of the expected further ageing of populations limit governments' capacity and willingness to take care of the whole retirement income task. Therefore, providers of funded provisions will need to work hard to deliver what is promised to keep their share in the retirement income market.

The growth of pension research centres such as the Center for Retirement Research (CRR) in Boston, the Network for Studies on Pensions, Aging and Retirement (Netspar) in Tilburg (the Netherlands), the Center for Research on Pensions and Welfare Policies (CeRP) in Torino (Italy), the Pension Research Council in Wharton, the Munich Center for the Economics of Aging (MEA), and the Pensions Institute in London are few of the prominent leading research institutes that are facilitating knowledge, research, and expertise sharing across the world. Ageing and retirement are issues affecting all countries and, directly or indirectly, all people across all countries and all generations.

Muralidhar[16], who had suggested that hybrid pension plans will evolve due to the lack of adequate retirement income under DC pension plans, detailed an innovative solution to the DC retirement crisis in his *50 States of Gray*[32]. He focused on the US 401K system with DC features which exhibit growth on an aggregate basis. He described specific bond structures to enhance retirement income security and some innovations to DC schemes that provide increased flexibility.

As we mentioned at the outset of this book, demographics is about consumer and worker characteristics that are reflected in their actions and behaviour. In theory and applied work, both microeconomics and macroeconomics have advanced over the last three decades to accept that complete rational behaviour and full rationality are assumptions in models and theory but not validated by data and experiments. The trend toward DC pension plans where plan participants make decisions regarding their pensions is a field where behavioural assumptions about household and individual savings behaviour could be tested. The flexibility and portability underlying DC pension plans require wise choices by the plan participants. The pioneering paper laying the foundations for nudges and policy interventions to encourage better behaviour was "Save More Tomorrow" by Thaler and Benartzi[33].

In the field of savings and retirement, a significant review paper by Bernartzi and Thaler[34] summarised the behavioural research foundations for policy interventions to influence behaviour. They argue that standard life-cycle theories have three embedded assumptions of behaviour: an explicit assumption that savers accumulate and then decumulate assets to maximise some lifetime utility function, and two implicit assumptions regarding household behaviour: (i) they have the cognitive ability to solve the necessary optimisation problem, and (ii) they have sufficient willpower to execute this optimal plan. The authors stated that the implicit assumptions are invalidated by real-world data.

Saving for retirement is a difficult problem, and most plan participants are not trained to make the relevant investment decisions and therefore are likely to be passive. They are inertial in joining new advantageous plans by rarely changing and sticking to naïve diversification strategies. These participants need help through effective yet low-cost approaches: small changes (nudges) in plan design, sensible default options, and opportunities to increase savings rates and rebalance portfolios automatically. These design features help less sophisticated investors while maintaining flexibility for more sophisticated types.

Another research report by Beshears et al.[35] drew on evidence from US pension plans, highlighting the importance of default options in incentivising the right behaviour and nudging the plan participants out of inertia and other heuristic biases. They presented strong evidence suggesting that defaults impact savings outcomes at every step along the way by considering evidence from the US, Chile, Sweden. They presented data showing how defaults influence retirement savings outcomes at all stages of the savings life cycle, including savings plan participation, savings rates, asset allocation, and post-retirement savings distributions. This then paved the way for the role of public policy in using defaults, such as auto-enrolment as in the recent past for UK pensions.

David Blake[36] summarises the use of nudges and other policy tools in affecting retirement savings. His paper validates the advocacy in Redington's "The Age of Responsibility", a combined report by industry participants and policy makers on why aggregate societal responsibility requires the UK to save more. Blake argues that individuals are not rational life-cycle financial planners as they face behavioural barriers and have behavioural biases that prevent them from behaving optimally over their lifetimes. Lessons from behavioural economics can help overcome these barriers. He shows how nudges can encourage greater savings to ensure better living standards in retirement and how to draw down accumulated pension savings to maximise retirement spending without running out of money.

6.5   Pensions, Asset Allocation, Investments, and Capital Markets

In the area of pensions for institutions, actuaries and investment consultants act as trusted gatekeepers and advisors for decision-making. This section draws heavily on two significant reports produced by Willis Towers Watson and Mercer. In addition, it is supplemented by reports from the OECD and EIOPA, two institutions that are involved with pensions.

Willis Towers Watson conducted a global study on major pension markets[37]. We present here the findings over 20 years based on the latest and past issues of the study by their Thinking Ahead Institute.

Table 6.8 illustrates that the universal trend over the last two decades in the seven largest pension markets is that the category "Others", which captures alternative asset classes like real estate, commodities, private equity, and hedge funds, has grown significantly, whilst the share of equities has decreased universally. The only country that has more than a small allocation of cash is Canada. While equity indices have performed very well over the last year, institutional pension investors have been cautious due to three periods of market crises for very different reasons: the dot .com boom and then bust, the global financial crisis and Great Recession, and the COVID pandemic.

It is worth referring to the reputed reference source of global asset returns by Dimson, Marsh, and Staunton in the Credit Suisse *Investment Returns Yearbook* 2021[38]. The relative performance of equities, bonds, and other assets might provide some insights in addition to the rising uncertainty of longevity that influences the liabilities. In a historical context, the section on world returns (constructed by the authors based on 23 markets) reports:

- Over the period 1900–2021, real equity returns were 5.3% p.a., real bond returns were 2.1% p.a., and real US T-bill returns were 0.8% p.a.
- World real equity returns over the first two decades of this century have been −0.6% and 3.7% p.a., respectively. World real bond returns over the first two decades of this century have been 6.2% and 5.2% p.a., respectively.
- The long-term equity risk premium relative to bonds over 1900–2020 was 3.1% p.a. Over 2010–2020, the equity risk premium was 3.3%. However, the equity risk premium over 2000–2010 was −6.4% p.a. and over 2000–2020 was −1.4% p.a.

Understanding longer-term asset returns and their volatilities in the equity context requires a longer-term view of equity and financial market returns over longer periods and business cycles.

Peter Oppenheimer[39] analyses cycles in markets, providing an understanding of factors that drive financial market returns. He provides an understanding of the characteristics and triggers of different markets to best forecast future performance and make profitable investment decisions in a risk-managed fashion.

The need to create pension portfolios that match liabilities have governed pension asset allocation. The need to meet liabilities has

Table 6.8   Pension asset allocation trends: 2001–2020.

	2001 (% in asset class)				2021 (% in asset class)			
	Equities	Bonds	Cash	Others	Equities	Bonds	Cash	Others
Australia	62	19	5	14	48	14	15	24
Canada	62	26	2	10	38	29	1	32
Japan	52	46	0	2	26	59	3	12
Netherlands	44	44	11	1	36	54	0	10
Switzerland	36	35	20	9	31	34	5	31
UK	67	18	5	10	26	65	2	8
US	65	28	2	5	47	21	1	30

SOURCE: Thinking Ahead Institute[37].

defined strategic asset allocation (SAA) and asset liability management (ALM) in the pension and insurance industries. Both assets and liabilities ought to be managed in a consolidated fashion, and I believe that not understanding this led to considerable hype in the pension industry about LDI. Many leading experts in the industry believe that ALM and LDI are similar, with assets being given precedence in one approach and liabilities in the other. I believe this should be a part of a jointly determined, transparent, holistic process. Cardinale, Navone and Pioch[40] illustrate the power of dynamic asset allocation based on long-term predictability of equity and bond returns.

The objective of pension plans is to match the liabilities that are coming due in the future. As argued, there are uncertainties about liabilities and assets; many of the underlying macro factors influence both assets and liabilities, such as inflation and interest rates. The importance of strategic asset allocation on practical portfolios was first highlighted by Brinson et al.[41] as being the far more important decision than the choice of specific bonds or equities within the asset class.

Campbell and Viceira[42] provided a conceptual framework for all long-term investors to allocate strategically across asset classes by benefiting from the empirical distributions of past asset returns and their correlations, along with how to construct future variance-covariance matrices across asset classes to generate strategic portfolio weights. They have extended their work to alternate asset classes, including TIPS and real estate.

Hoevenars et al.[43] applied strategic asset allocation techniques using a variant of the Campbell-Viceira framework to conduct SAA to meet liabilities in a dynamic framework accounting for evolving variance-covariance dynamics over time and across asset classes. They found horizon effects in time diversification, risk diversification, inflation hedge, and real interest rate qualities. They showed that alternative assets classes add value for long-term investors. Differences in strategic portfolios for asset-only and asset-liability investors are due to differences in the global minimum variance and liability hedge portfolio.

They illustrated that the benefits of long-term investing are more extensive when there are liabilities. The authors studied the problem of an investor with risky liabilities that are subject to inflation and interest rate risk, who invests in stocks, government bonds, corporate bonds, T-bills, listed real estate, commodities, and hedge funds. Liabilities are a predetermined component in the institutional investor's portfolio. Since liabilities are subject to real interest rate risk and inflation risk, assets that hedge against long-term liabilities risk are valuable for an institutional investor. The hedging demand for alternative asset classes like credits, commodities, hedge funds, and real estate will depend on the covariance between assets and liabilities at different horizons.

Understanding and forecasting long-term volatility are essential for strategic asset allocation. Volatility is a key input for strategic asset allocation, yet most studies have focused on short-term volatility properties. A recent paper by Cardinale, Naik, and Sharma[44] focuses instead on calibrating long-run volatility assumptions using insights from the history of global equity and bond markets since 1934. The authors use a large sample to test the predictive power of different long-horizon volatility models, finding that the best approach to forecasting long-horizon volatility is to use a long historical window and capture both long-term mean reversion and short-term volatility clustering properties. The results support the authors' model specification for lower forecasting errors rather than a naïve model based on the simple extrapolation of historical volatility.

The use of optimisation models and techniques for pensions has been pioneered by corporate consultants ORTEC in the Netherlands using vector autoregression systems. The application of new ALM techniques to pensions and insurance is detailed in the *Asset and Liability Management Handbook*[45] and *Asset and Liability Management Tools* by Scherer[46]. Nobel laureate W. Sharpe and L.G. Tint[47] proposed a practical approach away from asset-only focus or full surplus optimisation by presenting a new approach for liabilities.

Another feature of the largest pension systems is the split between DB and DC. We earlier mentioned leading experts like Modigliani, Ambachtsheer, and others in favour of developing hybrid pension plans that have benefits dominating both DB and DC schemes. Table 6.9 shows that DC schemes are not yet universally dominant, with the Netherlands, Japan, the UK, and Canada still having the major share of pensions allocated to DB.

The growing importance of pension funds was anticipated by Peter Drucker and acknowledged by the Geneva conference of central banks. One way to assess the importance of the size of the largest pension markets is to assess them relative to the size of the country's GDP. Table 6.10 presents the relative pension market assets to GDP for certain selected countries.

Aside from the size of the pension market, the pension system type and asset allocation, other characteristics define pension systems. Mercer, the pension and HR consultant, has compiled a

Table 6.9   DB-DC asset split: 2001–2020.

	2001		2020	
	DC (%)	DB (%)	DC (%)	DB (%)
Australia	83	17	86	14
Canada	3	97	39	61
Japan	0	100	5	95
Netherlands	2	98	6	94
UK	8	92	19	81
US	52	48	64	36

SOURCE: Thinking Ahead Institute[37].

system to assess efficiency and effectiveness by ranking and scoring global pension systems. The latest version of the Global Pension index 2020 produced by Mercer[48] was in collaboration with the CFA Institute and the Monash Business School.

The report acknowledges that the comparison of pension systems is complex and cites the OECD's 2019 report[7], stating "Retirement Income regimes are often diverse and involve several different programmes". The Global Pension Index 2020 is based on aggregating three different sub-indices scoring the adequacy of the system (40% weight), sustainability of the system (35% weight), and integrity of the system (25% weight). The study scores and ranks 39 retirement

Table 6.10   Pension market size: 2020.

	Total assets	Total assets/GDP
	USD billions	Percent
Australia	2333	174.8%
Canada	3080	192.5%
Japan	3613	73.6%
Netherlands	1900	214.4%
Switzerland	1163	164.3%
UK	3564	135.1%
US	32567	156.5%

SOURCE: Thinking Ahead Institute[37].

income systems and also includes newcomers Israel and Belgium. The best overall systems scoring higher than 80 are the Netherlands and Denmark, ranked as A-grade systems. In contrast, the UK, the US, and France are ranked as C+ systems. Very surprisingly, Japan gets a D alongside China, Russia, Mexico, and India; this shows the difficulty of aggregate scores for systems as coverage ratios, age, labour markets, GDP per capita, health, and longevity differ across these countries. Australia, Canada, Chile, Israel, Singapore, Switzerland, Sweden, Norway, and Germany are graded as B.

6.6   Pensions and Corporate Finance/Equity Prices

An interesting question to ask is, does the pension plan affect the valuation and returns of a parent company? This was the focus of an academic study by three leading academics, Jin, Merton, and Bodie[49], who studied whether systematic equity risk of US risks measured by beta from the capital asset pricing model (CAPM) reflects risks of their pension plans. Despite opaque and archaic pension accounting rules, the empirical findings support the hypothesis that equity risk reflects the risk of the firm's pension plan and is consistent with the informational efficiency of capital markets. The authors suggested adjusting deleveraged betas for risk of pension assets and liabilities in computing the cost of capital for capital budgeting.

Another academic finance research paper by Franzoni and Marin[50] investigated links between pension plan funding and stock market efficiency, finding that the market significantly overvalues firms with severely underfunded pension plans. The underfunded pension companies earn lower stock returns than their healthier counterparts for at least five years since underfunding first appears. The authors found that the low returns are not explained by risk, price momentum, earnings momentum, or accruals. They found evidence that investors do not anticipate the impact of pension liability on future earnings and are surprised when the negative implications of underfunding materialise. The authors reported that underfunded firms earn lower returns and have poor operating performance, although they are value companies.

Empirical research by Cardinale[51] studied whether pension information derived from accounting disclosures is priced in corporate bond spreads. Using corporate bond data from US companies for the 2001–2004 period, he found that unfunded pension liabilities are incorporated in credit spreads, and the sensitivity of market spreads to deficits is greater than the sensitivity to ordinary long-term debt. Additionally, the relationship was not a linear monotonic function, and the sensitivity of bond spreads to deficits is substantially higher for high-yield than for investment-grade bonds.

But do pensions affect capital structure? Another study by Shivdasani and Stefanescu[52] found that firms incorporate the magnitude of their pension assets and liabilities into their capital structure decisions by examining the capital structure implications of DB corporate pension plans. The magnitude of the liabilities arising from these pension plans is substantial. They showed that leverage ratios for firms with pension plans are about 35% higher when pension assets and liabilities are incorporated into the capital structure. They estimated that tax shields from pension contributions are about a third of those from interest payments.

6.7   The Future of Retirement and Conclusions

Retirement planning is a complex issue that overlaps health and longevity. It is complex not only for individuals but also for institutions and countries—holistic, integrated thinking with conditional tinkering or tweaking to adapt for unplanned consequences is essential. This planning may be better framed within exercises contingent on scenario planning rather than non-transparent complex stochastic projection plans. In many reports, discussions, and presentations over a decade, I have recommended that policy to deal with longevity and pension challenges be holistic and incorporate commensurate reforms in labour, education, retirement, taxes, health, and technology.

In a radical challenge to the current state of retirement planning, we[53] advocated changes to mindset, tools, and asset allocation in order to exploit advances in financial econometrics, numerical techniques, optimisation, and behavioural finance. Pensions thinking needs to evolve with the conditions of the macroeconomy, monetary policy that influences short-term and long-term rates differently than in the past, liquidity, regulatory issues, and the complexity of objectives and needs. Long-term planning and dynamic optimisation techniques are needed rather than simple period mean-variance optimisation, with asset return distributions not catering to the standard normal ones. Incorporating changing liabilities and richer investment opportunity sets that include alternative asset classes and rely on risk management with derivatives is essential to gain the most from savings accumulated for retirement. Lessons from behavioural finance can be used at the level of both individuals and the state or industry to improve pensions and investment outcomes.

There have been pension reforms in developing countries in Latin America, Asia, and Africa that are different due to systemic conditions varying across countries, as highlighted by the Mercer Global Pension Index. Ageing rates and changes are different across countries and regions, necessitating different reforms. A universal conclusion across all countries is the need for households and countries to save more, as mentioned in "The Age of Responsibility"[8]. The IMF also advocated this in a staff discussion note[54] that investigates impending demographic shifts and pension system design impacts future national saving (public and private), which is the primary source of financing. Even currently in Europe, many business leaders have appealed for an increase in business investments as in the US, especially in technology and new areas of biotech.

The findings suggest that public pension reforms in emerging markets and advanced economies could stimulate higher private savings and reduce longer-term fiscal strains if calibrated carefully. The authors suggest that developed countries with developed financial systems should complement the public pension system with a funded defined contribution scheme to encourage private savings; this may require shifting from a pay-as-you-go system to a funded system. They recommend that financial and labour market reforms be considered part of a pension reform package focusing more on gender inequality reduction and encouraging older worker participation.

Finally, financial literacy, financial education, skills upgrading, and focus on governance, transparency, and costs are critical in garnering operating efficiencies and reduce potential risks. The focus has changed from asset allocation to people's behaviour, systems, groups, and committee decision-making. This was what Keith Ambachtsheer focused on in his discussion of the optimal pension system[22] and what Dutch pension experts[55] also addressed in an insightful book on creating excellent pension institutions. Rather than blaming trustees of long-term institutions for failures, the authors help guide trustees toward best practice in enhancing their understanding of risk concepts, return expectations, investment tools, and benchmarks. The goal is to enhance board excellence and provide strong pension fund performance.

This is similar to *In Search of Excellence*[56], which provided insights into the excellence of corporate behaviour nearly four decades ago.

A good epitaph to this chapter combines the "unseen revolution" challenge posed by Drucker with Aldous Huxley's *Brave New World* and the recommendations and advocacy in "The Age of Responsibility". The world requires coordinated, holistic, responsive, dynamic, brave policy reform with brave, active decision-making by individuals and households to arrive at a collective state of retirement well-being for the future.

This chapter traced through the history of pensions and the development of pension systems citing the approaches by World Bank, OECD and others. It highlighted issues in pensions asset allocation, ALM, governance, Fiduciary aspects etc. Retirement challenges need to receive greater individual, household, corporate and government attention to ensure adequate post-retirement living standards.

Chapter 7
Quality of Life, Gender, Governance and Sustainability

I n this chapter, we take a holistic approach away from the economics, finance, and investment perspective, instead focusing on the overall well-being of individuals, households, corporations, and countries. This chapter focuses on broader indicators relevant to the state of institutions and the overall state of a country or society within which individuals and households consume and work. The people characteristics that we focus on are influenced by the environment, institutions, and the society in which individuals live.

The indicators summarise ways to evaluate well-being beyond mere economic indicators like GDP and GDP per capita, focusing on inequality, quality of life, happiness, corruption, sustainability, etc. After all, nominal income and wealth indicators do not always reflect workers' happiness, quality of life, or work-life balance. The focus on macro-sustainability indicators was captured by the Sustainable Development Goals (SDGs, which evolved from earlier Millennium Development Goals, MDGs) developed by the UN. In a new sense of social and environmental focus on not just the public sector but also the private sector, the 17 SDGs have received tremendously increased attention. In Rio de Janeiro, Brazil (June 2012). the UN Member States decided to launch a process to develop a set of SDGs to build on the MDGs and establish the UN High-Level Political Forum on Sustainable Development. I have been following these indicators since the late 1980s, and it is heart-warming to see sustainability and development intermesh as a global focal point with SDGs.

In 2015, the United Nations Member States adopted the 2030 Agenda for Sustainable Development that created a shared future blueprint for peace and prosperity for people and the planet. At its core are the 17 SDGs, which are an urgent global partnership call for action: (i) no poverty, (ii) zero hunger, (iii) good health and well-being, (iv) quality education, (v) gender equality, (vi) clean water and sanitation, (vii) affordable and clean energy, (viii) decent work and economic growth, (ix) industry, innovation, and infrastructure, (x) reduced inequality, (xi) sustainable cities and communities, (xii) responsible consumption and production, (xiii) climate action, (xiv) life below water, (xv) life on land, (xvi) peace, justice, and strong institutions, and (xvii) partnerships to achieve the goal. The member countries recognised that ending poverty and other deprivations must go hand-in-hand with strategies that improve health and education, reduce inequality, spur economic growth, and tackle climate change while preserving our oceans and forests. As per the latest count on the UN website, the SDG program has 169 targets, has conducted 3078 events, and has produced 1303 publications and 5448 actions.

7.1 Utility Theory, Social Welfare, and Happiness

The founding fathers of economics—Adam Smith, Alfred Marshall, and Paul Samuelson—and many others developed the concept of *utility*, borrowing from philosophers like Jeremy Bentham and John Stuart Mills. Modern microeconomic theory is often couched in terms of consumers and households maximising utility and also in terms of individual choices regarding labour and leisure. Nobel laureate George Stigler[1] provided a detailed two-part study on the history of utility theory as it is one of the fundamental frameworks for applied economic analysis and understanding the theory of consumer and worker behaviour. His objective was to outline the steps in the development of utility theory as it contributes to the understanding of modern economics. The first part covered the seventeenth and eighteenth centuries starting with Adam Smith and going on to Slutsky, who developed ways of constructing and depicting utility functions. Smith distinguished between *value in use* and *value in exchange*, stating that things that have the most significant value in use may have little or no value in exchange, and things that are highly valued in exchange frequently have little value in use. There have been many critics of that statement, but the article summarises the contributions of Bentham, Marshall, Walras, Ricardo, and Slutsky in shaping utility theory and its links to demand theory, price determination, and equilibrium.

The contributions of Kenneth Arrow, Gerard Debreu, and Paul Samuelson derived the rigour behind utility functions in helping measure and order utility choices for individuals and in aggregate to help understand preferences, equilibria, and welfare. Variants of utility theory such as marginal utility, expected utility theory[2], cardinal utility, and ordinal theory have made it one of the most critical constructs for understanding consumers and workers. John von Neumann and Oskar Morgenstern[3] showed that the expected utility hypothesis could be derived from a set of apparently appealing axioms on preference. The standard microeconomics textbooks at both the undergraduate and graduate levels spend a significant share of initial chapters developing and explaining utility theory.

Another field of economics that assesses the impact of individual decisions on collective well-being or welfare is *welfare economics*, and its extension to aggregative government decision-making on behalf of its citizens is covered in *public economics*. Welfare economics also laid the foundations for an analytical framework called *cost-benefit analysis* that is widely used in public economics to evaluate public choices and decision-making. Economic efficiency and income distributions are often analysed using *Pareto analysis*, a subfield that focuses on understanding *Pareto efficiency* (a situation where no individual or preference criterion can be better off without making at least one individual or preference criterion worse off or without any loss thereof; the concept is named after Vilfredo Pareto [1848–1923]).

GDP (gross domestic product) and GNP (gross national product) are not good or comprehensive measures of economic well-being and have been criticised for their focus on measuring market-based or -valued economic activity and other limitations by Pilling[4] and Kapoor and Debroy[5].

Pilling cites Kuznets, as the founder of GDP, not subscribing to the fact that GDP measures well-being. He states, "gross domestic product has been the global elite's go-to number. Fast growth, as measured by GDP, has been considered a mark of success in its own right, rather than as a means to an end, no matter how the fruits of that growth are invested or shared". His critique can be summed up by his example showing the limitation of global GDP, which treats Kim Jong-un's nuclear warheads just like hospital beds or apple pie. He says GDP is better at evaluating the quantity of services rather than the quality of services, does not account for internet or distribution of output, and measures only market activity; and he blames it for suggesting that bigger is better.

Kapoor and Debroy[5] use examples from India to argue that GDP was not designed to assess welfare or the well-being of citizens but instead was designed to measure production capacity and economic growth. Yet policymakers and economists often treat GDP as an all-encompassing unit to signify a nation's development. They suggest that it's time to acknowledge the limitations of GDP and expand our view of development to include welfare. They contend that using GDP and economic gain to measure development ignores the negative effects of economic growth on society, such as climate change and income inequality. As policy advisors to the Indian leadership, they refer to a new indicator, the *Ease of Living Index*, which measures quality of life, economic ability, and sustainability. They stress that if economic well-being is an economy's primary goal, economic growth should be only part of the toolkit to guide the economy.

The difference between economic growth and economic development is a well-known distinction that has been the focus of many research papers and policy initiatives in development economics focusing on non-advanced economies, which have a large sector that is informal and non-market-valued. These distinctions are important when we want to indulge in international comparisons, as prices, valuations, and costs of living differ. To facilitate international comparisons, the concepts of purchasing power parity (PPP) and cost of living adjustments (COLA) were developed. A popular practical index to facilitate price comparability across countries is the *Big Mac index*, based on the price of a McDonald's Big Mac in different countries.

Economic indicators such as GDP were never designed to be comprehensive measures of prosperity and well-being. We need adequate indicators to address global challenges in the twenty-first century, such as climate change, poverty, resource depletion, health, and quality of life. In 2007, the EC, European Parliament, Club of Rome, OECD, and WWF hosted the high-level conference Beyond GDP. The objectives were to clarify which indices are most appropriate to measure progress and how these can best be integrated into the decision-making process and taken up by public debate.

The OECD's research in *Beyond GDP*[6] shows that over-reliance on GDP as a measure of economic progress misled policymakers who did not see the 2008 crisis coming and did not adequately assess its economic and social consequences. They argue that we need to develop dashboards of what matters: who is benefitting from growth, whether that growth is environmentally sustainable, how people feel about their lives, and what factors contribute to an individual's or a country's success. The report argues that different metrics, including better measures of people's economic insecurity, could have shown that the consequences of the recession were much deeper than GDP statistics indicated, and governments might have responded more strongly to mitigate the negative impacts of the crisis.

Richard Layard advised the UK government on the concept of happiness and has focused on happiness research for more than 20 years. In his latest book, *Can We Be Happier?*[7], he argues that the goal for society must be the greatest possible all-around happiness and shows how we can all become effective creators of happiness, both as citizens and in our organisations.

David Blanchflower[8] presented a review of happiness economics, charting its progress, links to health, and usefulness in propagating this field for its comprehensive view of human well-being. He concluded that a growing body of literature has emerged on the economics of happiness and mental well-being. It is now fashionable to try to understand the pursuit of happiness, and there are growing databases that measure happiness. Blanchflower summarised the following based on a review of the literature on happiness and its determinants: happiness tends to be greater among women, people with lots of friends, the young and the old, married and cohabiting people, the highly educated, the healthy, those with high income, the self-employed, people with low blood pressure, those who have sex at least once a week with the same partner, right-wing voters, the religious, members of non-church organisations, volunteers, those who exercise, and those who live in Western countries. Happy people are less likely to commit suicide.

The latest World Happiness Report 2021[9] focuses on COVID's impact on happiness and is the ninth annual report of the series. The first eight were created in line with the Bhutan government's initial initiative to call world experts to research happiness in 2011. The Bhutanese resolution passed by the UN General Assembly in June 2011 invited national governments to give more importance to happiness and well-being in determining how to achieve and measure social and economic development. A Thimphu meeting, chaired by Prime Minister Jigme Y. Thinley and Jeffrey D. Sachs, was called to plan for a UN high-level meeting on "Well-Being and Happiness: Defining a New Economic Paradigm" at the UN on April 2, 2012.

The first World Happiness Report was prepared to support that meeting and review evidence from the emerging science of happiness. It was based in the Earth Institute at Columbia University, with the Centre for Economic Performance's research support at the London School of Economics & Political Science (LSE) and the Canadian Institute for Advanced Research.

The Happiness Index is dominated by small, homogenous countries from Northern Europe, Australia, New Zealand, and Israel. Larger countries make the top 25 but are not at the top of the rankings. Although 2020 was dominated by COVID, we have abstracted some of the core findings from the World Happiness Report 2021:

- There has been surprising resilience in how people rate their lives overall. The Gallup World Poll data are confirmed for Europe by separate Eurobarometer surveys and several national surveys. The change from 2017 to 2019 to 2020 varied considerably among countries, but not enough to alter the rankings significantly. The same countries remain at the top.
- Emotions changed more than life satisfaction during the first year of COVID-19, worsening more during the lockdown and

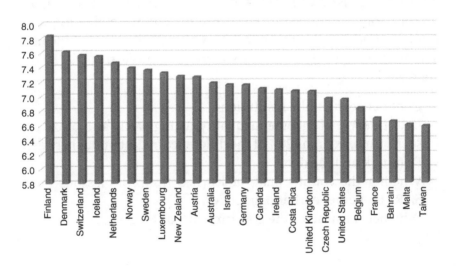

Figure 7.1 World Happiness Index 2021 score.
SOURCE: Sustainable Development Solutions Network[9].

recovering faster, as illustrated by large samples of UK data. For the world as a whole, based on the annual data from the Gallup World Poll, there was no overall change in positive affect, but there was a roughly 10% increase in the number of people who said they were worried or sad the previous day.

- Trust and the ability to count on others are major supports to life evaluations, especially in the face of crises. To feel that your lost wallet would be returned if found by a police officer, a neighbour, or a stranger is estimated to be more important for happiness than income, unemployment, and significant health risks.

Trust is even more important in explaining the vast international differences in COVID-19 death rates, which were substantially higher in the Americas and Europe than in East Asia, Australasia, and Africa. Almost half of these differences were due to differences in the age structure of populations (COVID-19 is much more deadly for the old), whether the country is an island, and how exposed each country was, early in the pandemic, to large numbers of infections in nearby countries. Whatever the initial circumstances, the most effective strategy for controlling COVID-19 was to drive community transmission to zero and keep it there. Countries adopting this strategy had death rates close to zero, were able to avoid deadly second waves, and ended the year with less loss of income and lower death rates. The factors supporting successful COVID-19 strategies include:

- Confidence in public institutions.
- Lower degree of income inequality, acting partly as a proxy for social trust, explains 20% of the difference in death rates between Denmark and Mexico.
- Whether the country had, or learned from, the lessons from SARS and other earlier pandemics.
- Whether the head of the government was a woman.

7.2   Quality of Life: Human Development Index (HDI)

In addition to the World Happiness Index, which is based more on psychology—emotions and feelings—an alternate index featuring criteria for economic development is the Human Development Index (HDI), created and produced by the United Nations Development Programme. This is another widely followed global index. The HDI was created to emphasise that people and their capabilities should be the ultimate criteria for assessing the development of a country, rather than economic growth alone. We discussed earlier the difference between development and growth in the context of the limitations of GDP as a measure of well-being and development. The HDI scores are part of the Human Development Report (HDR)[10], which has evolved to reflect changing social, human, and planetary concerns worldwide.

The HDI can help evaluate policy choices by examining why two countries with similar income per capita levels (gross national income [GNI] per capita) can have different development levels. The HDI is a summary measure aggregating achievement along three dimensions—health, education, and standard of living—by computing a composite geometric mean of scores along the three dimensions.

The health dimension is assessed by life expectancy at birth, the education dimension may mean school years for adults over age 25 and expected school years for children starting school, and the standard of living is based on gross national income per capita. The HDI uses the logarithm of income to reflect the diminishing importance of income with increases in GNI. It is important to note that the HDI reflects only part of human development, not covering inequality, poverty, gender, human security, and empowerment, which are covered by other indices. HDR 2020 presents Table 7.1 with sub-indices to help understand the construction of the HDI based on the dimensions underlying the index. The table lists the

Table 7.1 Human Development Index ranks: 2019.

Country	Rank out of 189 countries	HDI score (2020)	Life expectancy at birth, years (SDG 3)	Expected years of schooling (SDG 4.3)	Mean years of schooling (SDG 4.6)	Gross national income per capita, PPP $, (SDG 8.5)	GNI rank - HDI rank
Norway	1	0.957	82.4	18.1	12.9	66,494	7
Ireland	2	0.955	82.3	18.7	12.7	68,371	4
Switzerland	2	0.955	83.8	16.3	13.4	69,394	3
Hong Kong, China (SAR)	4	0.949	84.9	16.9	12.3	62,985	7
Iceland	4	0.949	83.0	19.1	12.8	54,682	14
Germany	6	0.947	81.3	17.0	14.2	55,314	11
Sweden	7	0.945	82.8	19.5	12.5	54,508	12
Australia	8	0.944	83.4	22.0	12.7	48,085	15
Netherlands	8	0.944	82.3	18.5	12.4	57,707	6
Denmark	10	0.940	80.9	18.9	12.6	58,662	2
Finland	11	0.938	81.9	19.4	12.8	48,511	11
Singapore	11	0.938	83.6	16.4	11.6	88,155	-8
United Kingdom	13	0.932	81.3	17.5	13.2	46,071	13
Belgium	14	0.931	81.6	19.8	12.1	52,085	6
New Zealand	14	0.931	82.3	18.8	12.8	40,799	18
Canada	16	0.929	82.4	16.2	13.4	48,527	5
United States	17	0.926	78.9	16.3	13.4	63,826	-7
Austria	18	0.922	81.5	16.1	12.5	56,197	-3
Israel	19	0.919	83.0	16.2	13.0	40,187	14
Japan	19	0.919	84.6	15.2	12.9	42,932	9

SOURCE: UN *Human Development Report 2020*.

leading 20 countries in terms of HDI ranks and sub-index scores for life expectancy, education tenure, and standard of living. The last column presents the difference between GNI and HDI ranks; a positive score indicates that the country's GNI rank is below the HDI rank, and a negative score indicates that its GNI rank is higher than its HDI rank.

The US glaringly stands out as the only country with a life expectancy below 80, which leads it to get a low HDI score and rank despite the very high GNI per capita. This raises issues about income distribution and allocation of resources to public health. The US and Austria are the two countries with a negative difference indicating high GNI per capita but low values on education and life expectancy combined. The opposite end of the spectrum includes countries like New Zealand, Australia, and Iceland, which are highly ranked on HDI relative to GDP. It is worth noting that the HDI index is computed based on specific indicators that map into the SDGs.

The HDI index score and rank are an incomplete summary of the state of development as they do not factor in inequality, poverty, gender, human security, empowerment, etc. As highlighted in my policy research and in Chapter 3, gender equality is a significant policy that needs attention to deal with growth, equity, and sustainability issues. The following sections highlight gender and corruption as critical issues to deliver efficient and equitable outcomes for current and future generations.

7.3   Gender and Governance

We focus on gender first and apologise at the outset for not being able to comprehensively cover all of the excellent research on the topic by the multilateral institutions: IMF, World Bank, UN, Asian Development Bank (ADB), Inter-American Development Bank (IADB), etc. Gender equality is imperative as women live longer than men in most countries and, in advanced and middle-income countries, the higher education ratios for women are higher than those of men. Utilising the human capital of women over their life-times is perhaps one of the most critical global imperatives in addition to focusing on healthy life expectancy. Our previous research[11] showed the potential for *four golden dividends from investing in gender equality: higher growth, lower debt, lower inequality, and better sustainability.* This was based on using state-of-the-art econometrics and extending earlier research done by the IMF, which showed that the benefits of closing the gender gap[12] were underestimated.

The UN's Human Development Report constructs a Gender Inequality Index (GII) for each country, as shown in Table 7.2, thereby laying down markers of how much progress needs to be made by individual countries to give women their just due of equality on every front and in every walk of life. The GII helps classify countries by their score and rank. Despite progress to reduce gender inequality, it remains high even in countries with high HDI scores. Women and girls face discrimination in health, education, financial access, and political representation, inhibiting the full development of their human skills and talents.

The GII represents gender inequalities along three dimensions of human development: reproductive health (measured by maternal mortality ratio and adolescent birth rates), empowerment (proportion of males and females in parliamentary seats and proportion of adult females with secondary education), and economic status (labour force participation rates for males and females older than 15). *It measures the human development costs of gender inequality, with higher GII values indicating more significant loss to human development.*

Collated research from different research teams at the IMF[13] argues that women make up a little over half of the world's population, but their contribution to measured economic activity and growth is far below its potential. The challenges of growth, job creation, and inclusion are closely intertwined. The research volume provides policy prescriptions and case studies from IMF member countries and looks at the gender gap from an economic point of view.

Table 7.2   Gender Inequality Index.

HDI rank	Country	Value	Rank
		2019	2019
HDI rank	**Very high human development**		
1	Norway	0.045	6
2	Ireland	0.093	23
2	Switzerland	0.025	1
6	Germany	0.084	20
7	Sweden	0.039	3
8	Netherlands	0.043	4
10	Denmark	0.038	2
11	Finland	0.047	7
11	Singapore	0.065	12
13	United Kingdom	0.118	31
16	Canada	0.080	19
17	United States	0.204	46
19	Japan	0.094	24
26	France	0.049	8
29	Italy	0.069	14
High human development			
74	Mexico	0.322	71
84	Brazil	0.408	95
85	China	0.168	39
Medium human development			
131	India	0.488	123
150	Zimbabwe	0.527	129
151	Syrian Arab Republic	0.482	122
154	Pakistan	0.538	135
155	Papua New Guinea	0.725	161
Low human development			
157	Mauritania	0.634	151
159	Uganda	0.535	131
160	Rwanda	0.402	92

SOURCE: UN *Human Development Report 2020.*

Because human capital is central to the World Bank Group's efforts to end extreme poverty by 2030, the World Bank has developed a new measure focusing on human capital, as it is one of the most important indicators of individual and collective development. This initiative is part of a global effort to accelerate more and better investments in people for greater equity and economic growth. With the ongoing pandemic, they emphasise that it is imperative that countries should invest in human capital (HC) and raise the incomes of the bottom 40% of people in each country. The vision of the Human Capital Project (HCP)[14] is a world in which all children reach their full potential—growing up well-nourished and ready to learn, attaining real learning in the classroom, and entering the job market as healthy, skilled, productive adults.

The Human Capital Index (HCI)[14] database provides data at the country level for each of the components of the HCI as well as for the overall index, disaggregated by gender. The index measures the amount of human capital that a child born today can expect to attain by age 18, given the risks of poor health and poor education that prevail in the country where the child lives. It is designed to highlight how improvements in current health and education outcomes shape the productivity of the next generation of workers, assuming that children born today face over the next 18 years the educational opportunities and health risks that children in this age range currently face. This is consistent with Angus Deaton's vision of well-being in *The Great Escape*[15].

A McKinsey Global Institute report[16] estimated that gender equity advances could contribute $12 trillion to the global economy. An IMF staff discussion note[17] argues the case for closing the gender gap for opportunities in finance. The report argues that women are underrepresented at all levels of the global financial system and that greater inclusion of women as users would benefit from addressing gender inequality. Narrowing the gender gap would foster greater stability in the banking system and enhance economic growth. It could also contribute to more effective monetary and fiscal policy.

The analysis by the authors suggests that the presence of women and a higher share of women on bank boards appears associated with greater financial resilience and that a higher share of women on boards of banking-supervision agencies is associated with greater bank stability. This evidence strengthens the case for closing the gender gaps in leadership positions in finance.

7.4   Corruption and Transparency

We argue that even in advanced countries, institutions and their governance matter as well as delivery. This is the cornerstone of designing efficiency in pension institutions, as we discussed in Chapter 6. The ethics and integrity of business and government generally distinguish efficient, educated, and legally grounded systems for delivering the best macro-environment within which people consume and work.

The existence of corruption, dictatorships, nepotism, cronyism, personal networks, mafia, etc. are inimical and adverse to the progress of developing countries. Non-transparent and often non-democratic institutions can thwart the easy progress and equitable distribution of opportunities in both poor and rich countries. This can also extend to discrimination across gender, race, caste, education, religion, region, etc.

The need for morality in an open capitalist system where the Invisible Hand operates was also highlighted in Adam Smith's *The Theory of Moral Sentiments*[18] (the precursor to his epic *The Wealth of Nations*), which provided the philosophical, psychological, and methodological backdrop to his other treatises on economics. Ethics and justice are key in public economics for distributing or allocating public resources across different groups or even across different generations.

In the days of social media and the internet, much more is known about institutions, individuals, clubs, groups, and guilds, but what is key for decision-making is a set of rules or guiding principles. The role of law and order is most apparent in low-income dictatorships and feudal regimes like those that existed in the past and still exist in the present. These are also responsible for crises, crashes, bubbles, and manias, as highlighted in Charles Kindleberger's classic

Manias, Panics, and Crashes[19]. The links between politics, philosophy, and economics were known for centuries and underlie the thinking and debate that formed the basis for the prestigious Politics, Philosophy and Economics (PPE) degree at Oxford University.

John Maynard Keynes referred to *animal spirits* as related to behaviours and tendencies as well as instincts that influence and determine human behaviour. In a broader interpretation, this includes trust and can be measured as consumer confidence, an indicator that resides in a macro-environment where individuals consume and work.

In an inquiry and review into why institutions and the macro-system failed during the global financial crisis (GFC), Nobel laureates George Akerlof and Robert Shiller, in their challenging book *Animal Spirits*[20], made a case for the role of government in restoring confidence amongst consumers, investors, and workers. They highlighted the role of psychology and values such as confidence and trust. These values of individuals and society are best seen within the context of justice. They made a case for a more robust macroeconomy with an active role for government by detailing the pervasive effects of animal spirits in contemporary economic life: such as confidence, fear, bad faith, corruption, a concern for fairness, and the stories we tell ourselves about our economic fortunes. Confidence and fairness are essential for both macroeconomics and individuals. They talked about the role of the confidence multiplier and fairness, highlighting that loss of confidence affects consumption and credit provision. They criticised economics for often ignoring the role of fairness in reputed economic journals and mainstream economic discussions. They argued that explanations that include fairness can better explain involuntary unemployment and the relation between inflation and aggregate output.

Transparency International creates an annual Corruption Perceptions Index (CPI, distinct from the Consumer Price Index). It details country-wide scores on corruption to highlight the gains to transparency and efficient rule of justice (law and order) for the ordinary citizen in a world of responsibility in challenging changing times where the behaviours of institutions, countries, families, and individuals are rapidly changing by historical standards. The

CPI results present country-specific scores for the index ranging from 0 to 100, where zero is highly corrupt and 100 is very clean. The index is based on perceived levels of public sector corruption according to experts and businesspeople. Highlights from the most recent CPI follow[21]:

- More than two-thirds of the countries scored less than 50 on their 2020 CPI scores.
- The top countries on the CPI are Denmark and New Zealand, with scores of 88, followed by Finland, Singapore, Sweden, and Switzerland, with scores of 85.
- The bottom countries are South Sudan and Somalia, with scores of 12, followed by Syria (14), Yemen (15), and Venezuela (15).
- The existence of corruption undermined a quick and equitable response to COVID-19 and other crises, thus highlighting the importance of transparency and anti-corruption during emergencies.

The overall recommendations of Transparency International in their latest report, having followed the impact of COVID in 2020, is that countries ought to (i) strengthen oversight institutions, (ii) ensure open and transparent contracting, (iii) defend democracy and promote civic space, including independent media for accountability, and (iv) publish relevant data and guarantee access to relevant data in a timely fashion. Transparency International also publish the Global Corruption Barometer (GCB), https://www.transparency.org/en/gcb, which supplements the CPI by surveying ordinary citizens worldwide. Since its introduction in 2003, the world's largest public survey on corruption has collected valuable data about the experiences and perceptions of tens of thousands of people.

Nobel laureate Amartya Sen[22] highlighted that welfare economics could be enriched by paying more explicit attention to ethics and that modern ethical studies can also benefit from closer contact with economics. Predictive and descriptive economics can be helped by making room for welfare-economic considerations in the explanation of behaviour.

7.5   Sustainability and Climate Change

The UN's 17 SDGs encompass an extensive range of economic, social, human, and environmental development goals for the world. Two of the biggest concerns over the last two decades that have garnered attention, concern, calls to action, and actions are sustainability and climate change. These concerns transcend generations, governments, countries, and regions and have implications for the entire planet.

The Intergovernmental Panel on Climate Change (IPCC) is the UN body charged with assessing the science of climate change. The IPCC was created to provide policymakers and governments with scientific assessments on climate change, including its future implications and potential risks. They advise on ways to adapt to climate change and mitigate its effects. The IPCC was awarded the Nobel Peace Prize in 2007 jointly with Vice President Al Gore for its collective contributions to build up and disseminate greater knowledge about human-caused climate change and lay the foundations for measures to counteract such change. The IPCC has 195 member countries and presents assessment reports by other agencies of the UN, such as the UN Environmental Programme (UNEP) and the World Meteorological Organization (WMO). IPCC reports are neutral and policy-relevant but not policy prescriptive. The Paris One Summit in 2017 established the Network for Greening the Financial System (NGFS): a group of central banks and financial supervisors voluntarily contribute to developing environmental and climate risk management in the financial sector and share best practices to facilitate the transition to a sustainable economy.

There are many providers of sustainability indices and metrics: MSCI, Dow Jones STOXX, and the S&P, to name just a few. The definitions, interpretations, and scope vary across these providers, with new institutions also entering this vastly growing field of commercial, policy, and societal concerns. Our focus is more on the broader SDGs of the UN. The question then is how to rate countries with an overall SDG-based score. *Sustainable Development Report*

2021[23] presents the SDG index and dashboards for all UN member states, outlines the short-term impacts of COVID-19 on the SDGs, and describes how the SDGs can frame recovery. It was prepared by teams of independent experts at the Sustainable Development Solutions Network (SDSN) and Bertelsmann Stiftung. Led by Jeffrey Sachs of the Earth Institute at Columbia University, the latest Sustainable Development Report (SDR) shows a reversal in progress since 2015 for the first time.

SDR 2021, published in June 2021, calls for a decade of action to urgently make progress on the SDGs. The authors state that the pandemic has created a sustainable development crisis. To restore much-needed SDG progress, developing countries need greater fiscal commitments and space through global tax reform and expanded financing by the multilateral development banks. Table 7.3 lists the combined SDG index 2021 scores[24].

How can we also measure countries' climate effects and policies, given that all generations and countries are concerned with and affected by climate change, directly and indirectly, to different degrees? The Climate Change Performance Index (CCPI)[25] is an index covering 57 countries and the EU since 2005. It stresses that to reduce the magnitude of the climate crisis's impacts, we must limit global warming to 1.5° C as per the Paris Agreement.

Table 7.3   SDG index scores (select countries).

Country code	Country	2021 SDG index score	2021 SDG index rank
BRA	Brazil	71.3	61
CAN	Canada	79.2	21
CHN	China	72.1	57
DEU	Germany	82.5	4
FRA	France	81.7	8
IND	India	60.1	120
ITA	Italy	78.8	26
JPN	Japan	79.8	18
USA	United States	76.0	32
GBR	United Kingdom	80.0	17

SOURCE: Sachs et al.[24].

Decisive actions will help reduce greenhouse gas emissions, which are responsible for climate change, and the CCPI plays a leading role in helping with the Paris Agreement's implementation. The CCPI analyses countries' climate protection performance to help create transparency in climate policy, compare climate protection efforts, and evaluate progress. Results are compiled with the aid of 400 national experts evaluating their countries' most recent national and international climate policies.

The CCPI's country rankings are based on each country's overall score. This is calculated from the individual scores in four categories: (i) greenhouse gas emissions (40% weight), (ii) renewable energy (20%), (iii) energy use (20%), and (iv) climate policy (20%). The categories include 14 indicators. The findings state that (a) no country performs well enough in all index categories to achieve an overall Very High rating in the index. Therefore, once again, the first three ranks of the overall ranking remain empty. (b) Of the G20 countries, this year, only the EU as a whole, along with the UK and India, rank among High performers, while six G20 countries rank under Very Low performers. (c) Hungary and Slovenia supersede Poland as the worst performing in the EU. Seven EU countries (excluding the UK) and the EU are High performers this year. The EU gains six places. Ranks 6 through 10 are occupied by Sweden, the UK, Denmark, Morocco, Norway, Chile, and India. Canada and the US are ranked 58th and 61st· respectively.

7.6   Politics and Geopolitics

As discussed earlier, demographics is intimately connected with both politics and geopolitics. The need to control larger populations and areas has been part of the grand design and aspiration of empires and leaders with ambitions to control larger numbers of people.

The World Bank provides data on world governance indicators that created scores for countries on six indicators of governance over 1995–2019: (i) voice and accountability, (ii) political stability and absence of violence, (iii) government effectiveness, (iv) regulatory quality, (v) rule of law, and (vi) control of corruption. These aggregate indicators combine the views of many enterprises, citizens, and expert survey respondents in industrial and developing countries. They are based on over 30 individual data sources produced by various survey institutes, think tanks, non-governmental organisations, international organisations, and private sector firms.

Demographics' links with geopolitics were first articulated by Sam Huntington in a *Foreign Affairs* article titled "The Clash of Civilizations" and later expanded to a book of the same name[26], where he defines civilisation, the culture of civilisation, conflicts generated by Western universalism, the militancy of cultures, and Chinese rise of power. He argues that clashes of civilisation are the greatest threat to world peace and an international order based on civilisations is the surest safeguard against war. He foresaw 9/11 and its aftermath in Chapter 5 of his book, where he explained Asian assertiveness based on economic growth and Muslim resurgence based on demographics. He included a provocative chart on the demographic challenge of Islam, Russia, and the West. He charted the rise of Asia versus the West and drew attention to the Muslim youth bulge and related issues, predicting the dynamics seen during the Arab spring in the early 2010s. In previous research building on this idea, we suggested that high youth unemployment[27] is a threat to economic growth and political stability, not just in Arab economies but also in poorer Asian and African economies.

A recent EC report[28] outlines the impact of demographic change via migration on the twin green and digital transitions. The focus on green and digital cities will have implications for large, crowded cities. Climate change and biodiversity loss are expected to significantly influence migration patterns because environmental changes, e.g. desertification, ocean acidification, and coastal erosion, directly impact people's livelihoods and their capacity to survive. The same report also highlighted the geopolitics of demographics from the perspective of the EU. The authors point out that Europe's share of the world population is decreasing, its population is older on average, and Europe's share of global GDP is shrinking—therefore, a complementary strategic partnership with Africa will be necessary. The report advocates that upholding the rules-based global order and its institutions (UN or the World Trade Organization) and playing a more active role in international structures will be all the more critical.

In *Foreign Affairs*[29], Eberstadt argued that demographics will shape geopolitics. He stated that "few factors influence the long-term competition between great powers as much as changes in the size, capabilities, and characteristics of national populations." He mentioned that for a century after 1850, the US had the largest skilled workforce and educated population, which led to military and economic pre-eminence. These favourable demographic fundamentals have been more important than geography or resources. He believes that China and Russia are currently facing their own demographic challenges; and therefore, relative to them, the US is in a strong position thanks to its large and highly educated population, relatively high fertility rates, and welcoming immigration policies, which have also empowered its geopolitics.

7.7   Conclusion

This chapter has outlined the links between demographics and several qualitative yet important strategic indicators and phenomena: happiness, human development, geopolitics, political stability, climate change, and sustainability. It is important to take a holistic approach to understand how demographics impact these, as the economic impact may lead to only a partial appreciation of their impact. A broader, interdisciplinary appreciation of demographics is what Peter Drucker was alluding to, if we are not to miss the point. A focus on qualitative indicators that capture overall wellbeing of all the citizens of a country, region or world is a must if we are to be successful in creating a Brave New Sustainable World.

Chapter 8
Summary and Conclusions

As Peter Drucker had said and written about, the demographic revolution and the pension revolution were largely unseen and not interpreted broadly and completely. One of the main reasons is the preference for mainstream research and inquiry of economics and markets to be very structured and almost siloed within subdisciplines. After the global financial crisis (GFC), a critical review and re-examination of economics led George Akerlof and Robert Shiller to highlight why macroeconomic models and frameworks had failed to anticipate the crisis; they concluded that psychology affects economies and markets but had been overlooked and ignored.

Narrow manifestations of research beliefs and methods often dominate and guide our knowledge and analysis, until the likes of Drucker, Shiller, and Akerlof challenge the orthodoxy of mainstream research and ideas. This book is the fruition of ideas that led me to use my interdisciplinary proclivity for reading across areas to give a broader interpretation of demographics—focusing on characteristics beyond population numbers and age, and subscribing to a more versatile and holistic approach to many economic issues.

There is a renewed emphasis on how economists, central banks, and researchers communicate and narrate their findings to the broader community[1-3]. News and communications of economic events affect people in terms of their behaviour as consumers and workers, savers and investors, decision-makers, policy makers, etc. The transmission of information and news in the digital age has added another layer to the complexity of the value of usable information and the veracity of information. Information and knowledge influence individuals, institutions, households, corporations, and nations—but the characteristics of people as consumers and workers influence their receptivity and use of information. This book is about not considering demographics as synonymous or identical with age or demographics as long-term only.

Demographics is about people, and people are at the core of all of economics and finance. The psychology of people, their backgrounds, and their experiences all shape how they consume and how they work. The use of technology, their human capital, and their access to resources, physical and non-physical, also interface with their characteristics to influence GDP, GDP per capita, asset prices, capital flows, and people flows. People's decisions are unlike those of a robot or a computer, and they are influenced by their demographics. For example, consider the fact that 10 years ago, no one could foresee the rapid adoption and use of smartphones, and social media and platforms to the extent that they are now hugely prevalent worldwide. Ten years in the future, it is hard to forecast whether my choice will be an iPhone version 25, a Samsung Galaxy 18, or some other version; those choices then will still impact how I consume and how I work.

Demographics should not be considered a linear age extrapolation exercise where all that matters is my age 10 years from now; my development and growth over the next 10 years are unlikely to be similar to or extrapolatable based on my last 10 years, as the macro, social, and technological environments change over time. The point I am making is that naïve extrapolation and lazy interpretation suggesting that 10 years in the future I will be very similar to someone 10 years older than me today is fraught with myopia and incorrectness. Human characteristics are essential, and they evolve dynamically with the environment they are exposed to in the past and the present.

The principal summary points that need to be taken away from this book are as follows:

- Demographics is not about age alone. Demographics is not only long-term in terms of impact and implications. Demographics is about people characteristics—people as consumers and workers. Their characteristics evolve and are not static and preformed at birth. The conventional unidimensional interpretation viewing demographics as being identical to one's age is flawed. Two individuals of the same age or two countries with the same median age are still vastly different in terms of individual characteristics or aggregate characteristics. People characteristics are a complex composite of their past background, genetics, experiences, psychology, gender, ethnicity, and culture and not just age alone.
- Demographics interpreted as consumer and worker characteristics have short-term, medium-term and long-term effects on macro variables and asset prices. Demographics influence the balance sheets and income statements of individuals, households, firms and countries.
- Demographics definitionally are intimately related to heterogeneity. Broad groupings of countries and regions based on their geography or median age often lead to false conclusions. By way of example, the EU comprises vastly different countries in terms of their age, culture, history, institutions, conventions, and norms. The extant heterogeneity within the EU makes common policy formulation and interpretation very challenging, and the EC has recently accepted the impact of EU demographics on the geopolitics and role of the EU in the world.
- Classification of the world as older advanced countries and younger emerging (developing) countries is likely to mask significant differences in advanced or emerging countries. *Heterogeneity* is a pervasive adjective aligned with demographics. Looking at the data carefully is a must to avoid certain myths

and hypes that been propagated. The UN Population Division has done an excellent and shareworthy job of presenting and making available detailed data and frameworks to facilitate understanding of population characteristics through comparisons across people and over time.

- Macroeconomics and many other fields of economics are intimately linked and influenced by demographics, which is about consumer and worker characteristics. These characteristics influence the economics of individuals, households, and countries. Demographics influences and determines the aggregate economic activity of nations captured by gross domestic product (GDP) or gross national income through worker characteristics that combine with resources and technology. Chapter 3 details the connections and impact of demographics on inflation, living standards, current account, and fiscal and monetary policy.

- Repeated individual and household decisions about consumption and savings lead to the aggregate stock of savings that is in modern times invested in assets so that they grow and can be used later over the entire retirement cycle. The life cycle hypothesis, permanent income hypothesis, and other theories have been tested over time to provide economic insights validated by data about how individuals and households consume, save, and invest. The preferences of individuals and households or firms are reflected in their consumption, savings, work, leisure, investment, and risk.

Chapter 4 details the influence of demographics on equity and bond prices. We discuss the findings of demographic effects on house prices and commodity prices. Demographics affects interest rates, the most fundamental of them r* (the natural rate of interest), as acknowledged by pioneering Fed modellers, as well as equity premia. Asset prices are affected by the preferences of individuals; and with advances in behavioural economics as well as behavioural finance, newer ways of modelling and understanding preferences at a point in time and over time (intertemporally) have emerged.

Chapter 4 has implications for all types of investors—retail as well as institutional—since even at the institutional level, decision-makers are human beings whose psychology matters. The decision-making of individuals is not entirely rational, as borne out by results of experiments and data. Explaining many asset pricing puzzles requires a better understanding of complex human preferences and markets that may not be completely modelled based on the sophistication of existing mathematical frameworks and models. Demographics and psychology underlie individual humans' behaviour and evolve over their lifetimes.

- Recent times, particularly the last two years, have underscored the importance of resilient and robust public health systems, which have been caught short by the sudden outbreak of the COVID pandemic. Chapter 5 details the changing death (mortality), health and also longevity dynamics. It contains discussion regarding the level of public expenditures currently, and the strains likely in a low-growth world from increased demands on public health. This chapter links public health and the well-known yet underappreciated factor of longevity, which has created a revolution that many countries and individuals have overlooked. The interplay of longevity with public health investments is essential for developing pensions and insurance in both the private and public sectors.

- Chapter 6 focuses on developments in the pension and retirement sector over the last few decades. Increased aggregate uncertainty about longer retirement periods has posed a challenge to individuals, institutions, and investors. Challenges exist in the areas of savings, investments, asset allocation, governance, risk preferences, and attitudes toward climate, environment, equality, and justice. We detail the investment trends in the largest pension markets that total tens of trillions of dollars and have systemic effects globally. We present rankings of pension systems and lessons for pension system design and reform. With pension reforms in advanced countries and system designs in emerging countries underway, we highlight needed changes in mindset, asset allocation, and tools. The tools developed for investments and asset allocations in the 1960s, 1970s, 1980s, and even 1990s are not totally appropriate for longer-term decisions that entail much greater uncertainty.

- In addition to quantitative macroeconomic measures of aggregate activity, individuals and countries need to be assessed along other dimensions (detailed in Chapter 7) such as happiness, human development, political stability, gender equality, climate change, and sustainability. In the modern world and the generations of Millennials and post-Millennials (Generation Y and Generation Z), the focus of society and the human world should be on holistic well-being rather than just wealth and income. The UN, EC, IMF, World Bank, ILO, WHO, and other multilateral banks have pivoted and centred attention on other measures of well-being, and this is a welcome measure. Finally, history teaches that the ambition of leaders of nation-states to lead larger numbers of people and more extensive landed territory has influenced empires, wars, and political alliances. The influence of demographics on politics and geopolitics continues from the emergence of a multi-polar world since the fall of the Berlin Wall to the recent US-China tussle for world dominance in all areas.

A better and more complete understanding of demographics and its myriad facets should enable humanity to enter and be happy, prosperous, and successful in a "Brave New World"[4]. The futuristic world that Aldous Huxley partly envisioned, with its many demographic challenges, may play out in part but collectively society will need to brave those future challenges. I emphasize in closing that the braveness should come from all of us collectively—individuals, households, corporates, countries, and regional alliances if we are to control or own our future.

Notes

Preface

1. Peter Drucker pioneered management thinking in many different unorthodox directions and is considered the guru of all pension gurus by many experts, including Keith Ambachtsheer.
2. Aldous Huxley's *Brave New World* (1926) posed many challenges rooted in the basics of demographics.

Chapter 1: Introduction

1. Drucker, P.F. (2000). *Management Challenges for the Twenty-first Century*. Harper Business.
2. Kash, R. (2002). *The New Law of Demand and Supply*. Currency.
3. Life tables produced by actuaries using historical data giving conditional probabilities of an individual aged 35 years today living to be 45 years old, 10 years later.
4. Wolf, M. (2005). *Why Globalization Works*. Yale University Press.

5. Kahnemann, D. and Tversky, A. (1974). Judgement under uncertainty: heuristics and biases. *Science* 185 (4157): 1124–1131.

6. Thaler, R. (1974). *Quasi Rational Economics*. Russell Sage Foundation.

7. Thaler, R. (2015). *Misbehaving: The Making of Behavioral Economics*. Penguin.

8. Reid, J. (2018). The history (and future) of inflation. Deutsche Bank Research.

9. This is my adaptation of Aldous Huxley's *Brave New World*. We should aim for a Better New World in consistence with the climate change and environmental, social, and governance (ESG) challenges that all of us face.

10. Akerlof, G. and Shiller, R.J. (2009). *Animal Spirits*. Princeton University Press. The title's extension is telling on this point: *Animal Spirits: How Human Psychology Drives the Economy, and Why It Matters for Global Capitalism*.

11. Penn, M.J. (2007). *MicroTrends: The Small Forces Behind Today's Big Changes*. Penguin, UK. And Penn, M.J. (2019). *MicroTrends Squared*. Simon and Schuster. Mark Penn, a political strategist and pollster, documented how these small micro-trends were emerging as major forces to change the world.

12. Peterson, P. (1999). *Gray Dawn*. Crown.

13. Peterson, P. (1996). *Will America Grow Up Before It Grows Old?* Random House.

14. Keating, G., Hokenson, R.J. and Roy, A. (2000). The demographic manifesto: new jobs, new people. Credit Suisse Research.

15. Kotlikoff, L.J. and Burns, S. (2004). *The Coming Generational Storm*. MIT Press. The book delves into the potential fiscal issues.

16. Heller, P. (2003). *Who Will Pay? Coping with Ageing Societies, Climate Change, and Other Long-Term Fiscal Challenges*. International Monetary Fund.

Chapter 2: Core Data: Past, Present, and Future

1. Malthus, T. (1798). *An Essay on the Principle of Population*. J. Johnson.

2. World Population Prospects. (2019). United Nations Population Division. https://population.un.org/wpp.

3. Huntington, S.P. (1996). *The Clash of Civilizations and the Remaking of World Order*. Simon and Schuster. This was an expanded version of his much-discussed and controversial *Foreign Affairs* (Summer 1993) article with the same title.

4. Cipolla, C.M. (1962). *The Economic History of World Population*. Penguin Books.

5. Livi-Bacci, M. (2017). *A Concise History of World Population*. Wiley Blackwell.

6. Kremer, M.J. (1993). Population growth and technological change: one million B.C. to 1900. *Quarterly Journal of Economics* 108 (3): 681–716.

7. Maddison, A. (2006). *The World Economy, Volume 1: A Millennial Perspective* and *Volume 2: Historical Statistics*. OECD Development Centre.

8. Fogel, R.W. (2004). *The Escape from Hunger and Premature Death 1700-2100: Europe, America and the Third World*. Cambridge University Press.

9. Fogel, R.W. (1993). Economic growth, population theory, and physiology: the bearing of long-term processes on the making of economic policy. Nobel Prize Lecture for Economic Sciences.

10. Roy, A. and Punhani, S. (2010). From the demographic lens: US is definitely not Japan and neither is Germany. Credit Suisse Demographics Research.

11. Keating, G., Hokenson, R.J., and Roy, A. (2000). The demographic manifesto: new jobs, new people. Credit Suisse Research.

12. Roy, A. and Le, A. (2019). Why gender equality matters? Better for growth, debt, inequality & sustainability. State Street Global Advisors Research.

13. Roy, A. and Le, A. (2018). Asia at a crossroads—demographics, economics & investment. State Street Global Advisors.

14. Attanasio, O., Sagiri, K., and Violante, G.L. (2006). Quantifying the effects of the demographic transition in developing economies. *The B.E. Journal of Macroeconomics* 6 (1): 1–44.

15. Galor, O. (2011). The demographic transition: causes and consequences. NBER working paper 17057.

16. Collier, P. (2015). *Exodus*. Oxford University Press.

17. Huntington, S. (2005). *Who Are We?* Simon & Schuster. In this book, Sam Huntington discusses the provocative issue of how America's national identity is evolving and under threat.

18. Castles, S. and Miller, M. (1998). *The Age of Migration*. Macmillan Press. This book provides a confluence of views from a sociological, political, and economic perspective of recent migratory trends and expansively includes immigration within the Asia-Pacific region.

19. Roy, A., Boussie, A., and Yuan, M. (2015). A perspective on migration: past to present. Credit Suisse Demographics Research.

20. OECD (2020). *International Migration Outlook* 2020. OECD Publishing.

21. World Urbanization Prospects. (2018). UN Population Division.

22. Towers Watson/Cass Business School. (2005). Uncertain future of longevity. Public Lectures on Longevity.

23. Carnes, B.A. and Olshansky, S.J. (2007). A realist view of ageing, mortality and future longevity. *Population and Development Review* 33: 367–381.

24. Fogel, R.W. (2000). The extension of life in developed countries and its implications for social policy in the twenty-first century. *Population and Development Review* 26: 291–317.

25. Pew Research Center. (2015). The whys and hows of generation research. https://www.pewresearch.org/politics/2015/09/03/the-whys-and-hows-of-generations-research.

26. King E., Finkelstein, L., Thomas, C., and Corrington, A. (2019). Generational differences at work are small. Thinking they're big affects our behavior. *Harvard Business Review*. https://hbr.org/2019/08/generational-differences-at-work-are-small-thinking-theyre-big-affects-our-behavior.

Chapter 3: Demographics and Macroeconomics

1. Musso, A. and Westermann, T. (2005). Assessing potential growth in the Euro area. European Central Bank occasional paper no. 22.

2. Roy, A. and Punhani, S. (2000). A demographic perspective of GDP growth. Credit Suisse Demographics Research.

3. Ito, T. (2015). Japanization: is it endemic or Epidemic? NBER working paper 21954.

4. Bloom, D.E., Canning, D., and Sevilla, J. (2001). Economic growth and the demographic transition. NBER working paper W8685.

5. Bloom, D.E., Canning, D., and Sevilla, J. (2003). *The Demographic Dividend: A New Perspective on the Economic Consequences of Population Change*. Rand.

6. Olshansky, J. (1997). *The Demography of Aging.* In: Geriatric Medicine (ed. C.K. Cassel et al.). Springer.

7. Lee, R. and Mason A. (2006). What is the demographic dividend? *IMF Finance & Development* 43 (3).

8. Mason, A., Lee, R., Abrigo, M., and Lee, S. (2017). Support ratios and demographic dividends: estimates for the world. UN Population Division technical paper.

9. Mason, A. (2005). Demographic transition and demographic dividends in developed and developing countries. https://www.un.org/en/development/desa/population/events/pdf/expert/9/mason.pdf.

10. Galor, O. (2011). The demographic transition: causes and implication. NBER working paper 17057.

11. Dekle, R. (2000). Demographic destiny, per-capita consumption and the Japanese saving-investment balance. *Oxford Review of Economic Policy* l16 (2): 46–60.

12. Reid, J., Nicol, C., Burns, N., and Mahtani, S. (2018). The history (and future of) inflation. Deutsche Bank Research.

13. Deaton, A. (1992). *Understanding Consumption.* Clarendon Press.

14. Roy, A., Punhani, S., and Shi, L. (2011). Longer lives, changing life cycles: exploring consumer and worker implications. Credit Suisse Demographics Research.

15. Bullard, J., Carriga, G., and Waller, C.J. (2012). Demographics, redistribution and optimal inflation. *St Louis Fed Review* 94 (6): 419–440.

16. Liu, Y. and Westelius, N. (2016). The impact of demographics on productivity and inflation in Japan. IMF working paper 16/237.

17. Bielecki, M., Brzoza-Brzezina, M., and Kolasa, M. (2018). Demographics, monetary policy and the zero lower bound, Narodowy Bank Polski working paper no. 284.

18. Goodhart, C.A.E. and Pradhan, M. (2020). *The Great Demographic Reversal: Ageing Societies, Waning Inequality, and an Inflation Revival.* Palgrave Macmillan.

19. Keating, G., Hokenson, R.J., and Roy, A. (2000). The demographic manifesto: new jobs, new people. Credit Suisse Research.

20. Roy, A., Boussie, A., and Yuan, M. (2015). Demographic focus—changing global consumers. Credit Suisse Demographics Research.

21. Penn, M. and Zalesne, E.K. (2007). *MicroTrends.* Twelve-Hachette Book Group.

22. Penn, M. and Fineman, M. (2018). *MicroTrends Squared*. Simon & Schuster.

23. Bryan, M. and Venkatu G. (2001). The demographics of inflation opinion surveys. Federal Reserve Bank of Cleveland Economic Commentary.

24. Juselius, M. and Takáts, E. (2015). Can demography affect inflation and monetary policy? BIS working paper 485.

25. Mojon, B. and Ragot, X. (2019). Can ageing explain lower inflation? BIS working paper 776.

26. Keating, G., Hokenson, R., and Roy, A. (2001). Demographics, productivity & technology. Credit Suisse Demographics Research.

27. Roy, A. and Punhani, S.(2010). European demographics at the core—consumers & workers. Credit Suisse Demographics Research.

28. Acemoglu, D. and Restrepo, P. (2018). Demographics & automation. NBER working paper 24421.

29. Segal, M. (2018). How automation is changing work. *Nature* briefing. https://www.nature.com/articles/d41586-018-07501-y

30. Brynholffson, E. and McAffee, A. (2014). *The Second Machine Age*. Norton.

31. Haskel, J.E. and Westlake, S. (2017). *Capitalism without Capital*. Princeton University Press.

32. Haskel, J.E. (2020). Monetary policy in the intangible economy. Bank of England speech, University of Nottingham, 11 Feb.

33. Nedelkoska, L. and Quintini, G. (2018). Automation, skills-use & training. OECD social, employment, and migration working paper 202.

34. Heller, P.S. (2003). *Who Will Pay? Coping with Aging Societies, Climate Change, and Other Long-term Fiscal Challenges*. IMF.

35. Burnside, C., ed. (2005). Fiscal sustainability in theory and practice. The World Bank.

36. European Commission. (2018). Ageing report: economic & budgetary projections for the 28 EU member states (2016–2070).

37. European Commission. (2019). EU Fiscal Sustainability Report 2018.

38. Roy, A. and Punhani, S. (2010). A demographic perspective of fiscal sustainability: "not just the immediate-term matters". Credit Suisse Demographics Research.

39. Roy, A., Boussie, A., and Yuan, M. (2015). EU's evolving demographics & pensions needs attention. Credit Suisse Demographics Research.

40. Kotlikoff, L.J. and Burns, S.F. (2004). *The Coming Generational Storm*. MIT Press.

41. Nishimura, K.G. (2011). Population ageing, macroeconomic crisis and policy challenges. Bank of Japan speech at 75th Anniversary Conference of Keynes' General Theory, University of Cambridge, June 19–21.

42. Imohoroglu, S., Kitao, S., and Yamada, T. (2019). Fiscal sustainability in Japan: what to tackle. VoxEU/CEPR, 07 June.

43. Encin, K. and von Thadden, L. (2010). Interest rate effects of demographic changes in a new Keynesian life cycle framework. ECB working paper.

44. Miles, D. (2001). Should monetary policy be different in a greyer world? In: *Ageing, Financial Markets and Monetary Policy* (ed. A. Auerbach and H. Herrmann). Springer Verlag.

45. Mester, L. (2017). Demographics and their implications for the economy and policy. Cleveland Fed Speech, Cato Institute's 35th Annual Monetary Conference: The Future of Monetary Policy, Washington, DC.

46. Berg, K., Curtis, C.C., Lugauer, S., and Mark, N.C. (2019). Demographics and monetary policy shocks. NBER working paper 25970.

47. Leahy, J.V. and Thapar, A. (2019). Demographic effects on the impact of monetary policy. NBER working paper 25970.

48. Imam, P. (2014). Shock from graying: is the demographic shift weakening monetary policy effectiveness? *International Journal of Finance & Economics* 20 (2).

49. Roy, A. (2015). Why has recent macro policy not been that effective? A demographic view. Credit Suisse Demographics Research.

50. Favero, C., Gozluklu, A.E., and Yang, H. (2015). Demographics and the behaviour of interest rates. WBS Finance Group research paper 172.

51. Roy, A., Punhani, S., and Hsieh, A. (2013). Rising youth unemployment: a threat to growth and stability. Credit Suisse Demographics Research.

52. Bernanke, B. (2005). The Global Savings glut and the US current account deficit, Federal Reserve Board speech, Sandridge Lecture, Virginia Association of Economics, Richmond, Virginia, 10 March.

53. Poole, W. (2005). A perspective on the graying population and current account balances. Global Economic Conference, Florida.

54. Brooks, R. (2003). Population ageing and global capital flows in a parallel universe. IMF staff paper.

55. Borsch-Supan, A. (2006). Demographic change, saving and asset prices: theory and evidence. Reserve Bank of Australia Conference.

56. Higgins, M. (1998). Demography, national savings, and international capital flows. *International Economic Review* 39 (2): 343–69.

57. Roy, A., Price, A., Prendergast, J., and Alvisi, U. (2007). Demographics, capital flows and exchange rates. Credit Suisse Demographics Research.

Chapter 4: Demographics and Asset Prices

1. Modigliani, F. and Brumberg, R. (1954). Utility analysis and the consumption function: an interpretation of cross-section data. In: *Post Keynesian Economics* (ed. K.K. Kurihara). Rutgers University Press.

2. Ando, A. and Modigliani, F. (1963). The "life cycle" hypothesis of saving: aggregate implications and tests. *American Economic Review* 53 (1): 55–84.

3. Friedman, M. (1957). *A Theory of the Consumption Function*. Princeton University Press.

4. Samuelson, P.A. (1958). An exact consumption-loan model of interest with or without the social contrivance of money. *Journal of Political Economy* 66 (6).

5. Deaton, A. (2005). Franco Modigliani and the life cycle theory of consumption. Convegno Internazionale Franco Modgliani.

6. Meghir, C. (2002). A retrospective on Friedman's theory of permanent income, Institute for Fiscal Studies working paper 04/01.

7. Lee, R.D. (2019). Samuelson's contributions to population theory and overlapping generations in economics. IZA working paper.

8. Samuelson, P.A. (1976). The optimum growth rate for population: agreement and evaluations. *International Economic Review* 17 (2).

9. Dixit, A.K. (2012). Paul Samuelson's legacy. *Annual Review of Economics* 4: 1–31.

10. Poterba, J. (2001). Demographics and asset returns. *Review of Economics and Statistics* 83 (4): 565–584.

11. Abel, A. (2001). Will bequests attenuate the predicted meltdown in stock prices when Baby Boomers retire? *Review of Economics and Statistics* 83 (4): 589–595.

12. Bakshi, G. and Chen, Z. (1994). Baby Boom, population ageing and capital markets. *Journal of Business* 67 (2): 165–202.

13. Sheshinski, E. and Tanzi, V. (1989). An explanation of the behavior of personal savings in the US over recent years. NBER working paper 3040.

14. Poterba, J., Schleifer, A., Shiller, R.J., and Samwick, A. (1995). Stock ownership patterns, stock market fluctuations and consumption. Brookings paper on economic activity 95 (2): 295–372.

15. Bergantino, S.M. (1998). Life cycle investment behavior, demographics, and asset prices. PhD dissertation, MIT.

16. Poterba, J. (2004). Impact of population ageing on financial markets. NBER working paper 10851.

17. Brooks, R. (1998). Asset market and saving effects of demographic transitions. Ph.D. dissertation, Yale University Department of Economics.

18. Roy, A., Punhani, S., and Shi, L. (2012). How demographics affect asset prices. Credit Suisse Demographics Research.

19. Goyal, A. (2004). Demographics, stock market flows and stock returns. *Journal of Financial and Quantitative Analysis* 39 (1).

20. Geanokpolos, J., Magill, M., and Quinzi, M. (2004). Demography and the long-run predictability of the stock market. Brookings papers on economic activity.

21. Roy, A., Boussie, A., and Yuan, M. (2015). Changing global consumers. Credit Suisse Demographics Research.

22. Liu, Z. and Spiegel, M.M. (2011). Boomer retirement: headwinds for US equity markets? *FRBSF Economic Letter* (August 22).

23. Favero, C., Gozluklu, A., and Tamoni, A. (2011). Demographic trends, the dividend-price ratio and the predictability of long-run stock market returns. *Journal of Finance and Quantitative Analysis* 46 (5): 1493–1520.

24. Siegel, J. (2005). *The Future for Investors: Why the Tried and the True Triumph Over the Bold and the New*. Crown Business.

25. Brooks, R. (2000). What will happen to financial markets when Baby Boomers retire? IMF working paper 0118.

26. US Government Accountability Office. (2006). Retirement of Baby Boomers is unlikely to precipitate dramatic decline in market returns, but broader risks threaten retirement security. Report 06-718.

27. Lim, K.M. and Weil, D.N. (2003). The Baby Boom and the stock market boom. *Scandinavian Journal of Economics* 105 (3): 359–378.

28. Roy, A., Punhani, S., and Hsieh, A. (2014). Exploring how demographics affects sovereign spreads. Credit Suisse Demographics Research.

29. Favero, C., Gozluku, A., and Yang, H. (2016). Demographics and the behavior of interest rates. *IMF Economic Review* 64 (6): 732–776.

30. Gozluklu, A. and Morin, A. (2020). Stocks vs. bond yields and demographic fluctuations. *Journal of Banking and Finance* 109 (C).

31. Carvalho, C., Ferrero, A., and Nechio, F. (2016). Demographics and real interest rates: inspecting the mechanism. *European Economic Review* 88 (C): 208–226.

32. Gagnon, E., Johanssen, B.K., and Lopez-Salido, D. (2021). Understanding the new normal: the role of demographics. *IMF Economic Review* 69 (2): 357–390.

33. Holston, K., Laubach, T., and Williams, J. (2017). Measuring the natural rate of interest: international trends and determinants. *Journal of International Economics* 108 (Supplement): S59–S75.

34. Ho, P. (2020). Estimating the effects of demographics on real interest rates: a robust Bayesian perspective. Federal Reserve of Richmond working paper.

35. Anderson, D., Bonnar, S., Oberoi, J., and Pittea, A. (2020). The connection between population structure and bond yields. Stage 3 final report, Society of Actuaries, Canadian Institute of Actuaries, and Institute & Faculty of Actuaries.

36. Dimson, E., Marsh, P., and Staunton, M. (2002). *Triumph of the Optimists: 101 Years of Global Investment Returns*. Princeton University Press.

37. Kocherlakota, N.R. (1996). The equity premium: it's still a puzzle. *Journal of Economic Literature* 34 (1): 42–71.

38. Ang, A. and Maddaloni, A. (2005). Do demographic changes affect risk premiums? Evidence from international data. *Journal of Business* 78 (1): 341–380.

39. Kopecky, J. and Taylor, A.M. (2020). The murder-suicide of the rentier: population aging and the risk premium. NBER working paper 26943.

40. Jagannathan, R. and Kocherlakota, N. (1996). Why should older people invest less in stocks than younger people? Federal Reserve Bank of Minneapolis. Quarterly Review.

41. Ameriks, J. and Zeldes, S. (2004). How do household portfolio shares vary with age? Columbia University Business School working paper.

42. Parker, K. and Fry, R. (2020). More than half of U.S. households have some investment in the stock market. Pew Research Center. https://www.pewresearch.org/fact-tank/2020/03/25/more-than-half-of-u-s-households-have-some-investment-in-the-stock-market.

43. Dellavigna, S. and Pollet, J. (2007). Demographics and industry returns. *American Economic Review* 97 (5): 1667–1702.

44. Roy, A. and Price, A. (2007). Global demographic change and sector implications. Credit Suisse Research.

45. Penn, M. and Zalesne, E.K. (2007). *MicroTrends*. Twelve-Hachette Book Group.

46. Penn, M. and Fineman, M. (2018). *MicroTrends Squared*. Simon & Schuster.

47. World Urbanization Prospects. (2018). UN Population Division.

48. Mankiw, N.G. and Weil, D. (1989). The Baby Boom, the baby bust and the housing market. *Regional Science & Urban Economics* 19 (2): 235–258.

49. Engelhardt, G.V. and Poterba, J. (1991). House prices and demographic change: Canadian evidence. *Regional Science and Urban Economics* 21 (4): 539–546.

50. Green, R. and Hendershott, P. (1996). Age, housing demand, and real house prices, *Regional Science and Urban Economics* 26 (5): 465–480.

51. Credit Suisse Research. (2000). The baby bulge and asset markets. *US Economics Digest*.

52. Takats, E. (2012). Ageing and house prices. *Journal of Housing Economics* 21 (2): 131–141.

53. Congressional Budget Office. (2008). The outlook for housing starts, 2009 to 2012.

54. Miles, D. (2012). Demographics: house prices and mortgage design. Bank of England External MPC Unit discussion paper 35.

55. Gevorgyan, K. (2019). Do demographic changes affect house prices? *Journal of Demographic Economics* 85 (4): 305–320.

56. Swaminathan, M.S. (1998). Population, science and sustainable food security. *Current Science* 74 (3).

57. Deaton, A. and Laroque, G. (1990). The behaviour of commodity prices. NBER working paper 3438.

58. Goldhub. (2021). Gold demand trends Q1 2021. https://www.gold.org/goldhub/research/gold-demand-trends/gold-demand-trends-q1-2021.

Chapter 5: Health and Longevity

1. We will argue, based on research by experts (including our own research), that longevity and mortality risks have policy and investment implications globally for governments, insurers, reinsurers, and pension plans as well as the pharma/biotech industry.

2. Fogel, R.W. (2000). The extension of life in developed countries and its implications for social policy in the twenty-first century. *Population & Development Review 26* (Supplement: Population and Economic Change in East Asia): 291–317.

3. Fogel, R.W. (1997). *Economic and Social Structure for an Ageing Population,* Philosophical Transactions: Biological Sciences 352 (1363: 1905–1917).

4. Roy, A. (2010). A demographic perspective of fiscal sustainability: not just the immediate-term matters. Credit Suisse Research.

5. Deaton, A.W. (2015). *The Great Escape: Health, Wealth, and the Origins of Inequality.* Princeton University Press.

6. Roy, A., Punhani, S., and Shi, L. (2012). How increasing longevity affects us all? Market, economic & social implications. Credit Suisse Global Demographics & Pensions Research.

7. Roy, A., Punhani, S., and Shi, L. (2011). Longer Lives, Changing Life Cycles: Exploring Consumer and Worker Implications, Credit Suisse Global Demographics & Pensions Research.

8. Global Health Security Index. (2019). https://www.ghsindex .org/wp-content/uploads/2020/04/2019-Global-Health- Security-Index.pdf.

9. Murray, C.J.L. and Lopez, A.D. (eds). (1996). The global burden of disease: a comprehensive assessment of mortality and disability from diseases, injuries, and risk factors in 1990 and projected to 2020: summary. World Health Organization. https://apps.who.int/iris/handle/ 10665/41864.

10. Murray, C.J.L., Aravkin, A.Y., Zheng, P. et al. (2020). Global burden of 87 risk factors in 204 countries and territories, 1990–2019: a systematic analysis for the Global Burden of Disease Study 2019. *The Lancet* (396): 1223–1249. https://www.thelancet.com/journals/lancet/ article/PIIS0140-6736(20)30752-2/fulltext.

11. The epidemiological quantification of all disease impact on DALYs was first highlighted by the earlier versions of the GBD. Murray, C.J.L., Barber, R.M., Foreman, K.J. et al. (2015). Global, regional, and national disability-adjusted life years (DALYs) for 306 diseases and injuries and healthy life expectancy (HALE) for 188 countries, 1990–2013: quantifying the epidemiological transition. *The Lancet* (386):2145–2191.http://www.healthdata.org/research-article/ global-regional-national-dalys-306-diseases-injuries- hale-188-countries-2013.

12. The World Bank. (2017). Tracking universal health coverage: 2017 global monitoring report. https://www.worldbank.org/en/topic/ universalhealthcoverage/publication/tracking-universal- health-coverage-2017-global-monitoring-report.

13. Fogel, R.W. (1998). Can we afford longevity? Capital Ideas, GSB Chicago.

14. GBD 2017 and HALE Collaborators. (2018). Global, regional, and national disability-adjusted countries and territories, 1990-2017: a systematic analysis for the Global Burden of Disease Study 2017. *The Lancet* 392 (10159): 1859–1922.

15. Edwards, M. (2020). What is the difference between mortality and Longevity? IFoA Longevity Bulletin.

16. van Raalte, A.A., Klüsener, S., Oksuzyan, A., and Grigoriev, P. (2020). Declining regional disparities in mortality in the context of persisting large inequalities in economic conditions: the case of Germany. *International Journal of Epidemiology* 49 (2): 486–496.

17. Keating, G., Hokenson, R.J., and Roy, A. (2000). The demographic manifesto: new jobs, new people. Credit Suisse Research. And the OECD publication series "Live Longer, Work Longer".

18. Dudel, C. and Myrskyla, M. (2018). How long do older Americans work? N-IUSSP. https://www.niussp.org/education-work-economy/long-older-americans-work.

19. Dudel, C. and Myrskylä, M. (2017). Working life expectancy at age 50 in the US and the impact of the Great Recession. *Demography* 54 (6): 2101–212.

20. Vaupel, J.W. and Olshansky, J.R. (2005). The uncertain future of longevity. Watson Wyatt/Cass Business School Public Lectures on Longevity.

21. Kontis, V., Bennett, J.E., Mathers, C.D. et al. (2017). Future life expectancy in 35 industrialised countries: projections with a Bayesian model ensemble, *The Lancet* 389 (10076): 1323–1335.

22. Roy, A. (2012). Innovative approaches to managing longevity risk in Asia; lessons from the West. ADBI working paper 352.

23. Booth, H. and Tickle, L. (2008). Mortality modelling and forecasting: a review of methods. *Annals of Actuarial Science* 3: 3–43.

24. Antolin, P. (2007). Longevity risk and private pensions. OECD Working Papers on Insurance and Private Pensions 3. OECD Publishing.

25. Barrieu, P. et al. (2010). Understanding, modeling & managing longevity risk: key issues & main challenges. *Scandinavian Actuarial Journal* (1): 1–29.

26. Shkolnikov, V.M., Jdanov, D.A., Andreev, E.M., and Vaupel, J.W. (2011). Steep increase in best-practice cohort life expectancy. *Population and Development Review* (September): 419–434.

27. Roy, A. et al. (2011). Macro fiscal sustainability to micro economic conditions of the old in the oldest five countries. Credit Suisse Global Demographics Research.

28. Vaupel, J.W., Villavicencio, F., and Bergeron-Boucher, M.P. (2021). Demographic perspectives on the rise of longevity. *Proc Natl Acad Sci USA* 118 (9).

29. Djeundje, V.B., Haberman, S., Bajekal, M., and Lu, J. (2020). An analysis of mortality trends in developed countries, focusing on the recent slowdown in mortality improvements. Longevity Science Panel working paper. `https://www.longevitypanel.co.uk`.

30. Dong, Y., Huang, F., Yu, H., and Haberman, S. (2020). Multipopulation mortality forecasting using tensor decomposition. *Scandinavian Actuarial Journal* (8): 754–775.

31. Zuo, W., Jiang, S., Guo, Z. et al. (2018). Advancing front of old-age human survival. *Proc Natl Acad Sci USA* 115 (44): 11209–11214.

32. Shang, H.L. and Haberman, S. (2020). Retiree mortality forecasting: a partial age-range or a full age-range model? *Risks* 8 (3): 69.

33. Sheshinski, E. (2008). *The Economic Theory of Annuities*. Princeton University Press.

34. Insurance Information Institute. (2021). *2021 Insurance Fact Book*. `https://www.iii.org/publications/2021-insurance-fact-book`.

35. Brown, J. R., Mitchell, O.S., Poterba, J.M., and Warshawsky, M.J. (2001). *The Role of Annuity Markets in Financing Retirement*. MIT Press.

36. Cannon, E. and Tonks, I. (2008). *Annuity Markets*. Oxford University Press.

37. Rusconi R. (2019). National annuity markets: features and implications. OECD Working Papers on Insurance and Private Pensions.

Chapter 6: Pensions and Retirement

1. For details on US Social Security, this section draws on the history section of the US Social Security Administration website: `https://www.ssa.gov/history/briefhistory3.html`.

2. This subsection draws on Georgetown University Law Center, (2010), "A timeline of the evolution of retirement in the United States", Workplace Flexibility 2010, `https://scholarship.law.georgetown.edu/legal/50`.

3. Clark, G.L., Munnell, A.H., and Orszag, J.M. (eds.) (2006). *The Oxford Handbook of Pensions and Retirement Income*. Oxford University Press.

4. Pensions Archive Trust. (n.d.). The history of pensions. `https://www.pensionsarchive.org.uk/historyofpensions`.

5. Bozio, A., Crawford, R., and Tetlow, G. (2010). The history of state pensions 1948–2010. IFS briefing note BN 105.

6. The Pensions Commission. (2005). A new pensions settlement for the twenty-first century.

7. This section draws heavily from the OECD's *Pensions at a Glance: OECD and G20 Indicators* (2019), a biannual publication that presents detailed data and models enabling cross-country comparability and policy lessons to be drawn.

8. Redington. (2012). The Age of Responsibility. First Byte. `https://redington.co.uk/wp-content/uploads/2021/09/Age-of-Responsibility.pdf`.

9. Roy, A. et al. (2010). A demographic perspective of fiscal sustainability: not just the immediate term matters. (2013). European demographics & fiscal sustainability. (2015). EU's evolving demographics and pensions need attention. Credit Suisse Global Demographics and Pension Research.

10. Drucker, P.F. (1976). *The Unseen Revolution: How Pension Fund Socialism Came to America*. Harper & Row.

11. Drucker, P.F. (ed.) (1995). *The Pension Fund Revolution*. Routledge.

12. World Bank. (1994). *Averting the Old-Age Crisis*. Oxford University Press.

13. Holzmann, R. and Hinz, R. (2005). Old age income support in the 21st century. World Bank.

14. Holzmann, R., Hinz, R.H., and Dorfman, P. (2008). Pension systems and reform: conceptual framework. Social protection discussion paper. World Bank.

15. Boeri, T., Bovenberg, L., Coeure, B., and Roberts, A. (2006). Dealing with the new giants: rethinking the role of pension funds. Geneva reports on the world economy. CEPR-ICMB.

16. Muralidhar, A. and Modigliani, F. (2004). *Rethinking Pension Reform*. Cambridge University Press.

17. IASB. (2019). Overview—Research findings on hybrid pension plans. `https://www.iasplus.com/en/news/2019/03/overview-research-findings-on-hybrid-pension-plans`.

18. Broeders, D., Eijffinger, S., and Houben, A. (2008). *Frontiers in Pension Finance*. Edward Elgar.

19. Kocken, T. (2006). *Curious Contracts: Pension Fund Redesign for the Future*. The Netherlands: Tutein Nolthenius.

20. Muralidhar, A. (2002). *Innovations in Pension Fund Management*. Stanford Economics & Finance.

21. Ambachtsheer, K. and Ezra, D. (1998). *Pension Fund Excellence*. Wiley.

22. Ambachtsheer, K. (2008). *The Pension Fund Revolution*. Wiley.

23. Ambachtsheer, K. (2008). Why we need a pension revolution. *Canadian Public Policy* 34 (special supplement on private pensions and income security in old age: an uncertain future): 7–14.

24. Barr, N. and Diamond, P. (2008). Reforming pensions. MIT working paper.

25. Ambachtsheer, K. (2016). *The Future of Pension Management*. Wiley Finance.

26. Bodie, Z. and Clowes, M. (2003). *Worry-Free* Investing. Financial Times-Prentice Hall.

27. Walker, P.J. (2020). Retirement behaviorist. *Finance &Development* 57 (1): 42–45.

28. Lusardi, A. and Mitchell, O. (2013). The economic importance of financial literacy: theory and evidence. *Journal of Economic Literature* 52 (1): 5–44

29. Borsch-Supan, A., Brandt, M., Hank, K., and Schroder, M. (2011). *The Individual and the Welfare State: Life Histories in Europe*. Springer.

30. Blake, D. (2006). *Pension Economics* and *Pension Finance*. Pensions Institute, Wiley.

31. Holzmann, R. (2012). Global pension systems and their reform: worldwide drivers, trends, and challenges. IZA DP no 6800.

32. Muralidhar, A. (2018). *50 States of Gray*. Investments & Wealth Institute.

33. Thaler, R.H. and Benartzi, S. (2004). Save more tomorrow: using behavioral economics to increase employee savings. *Journal of Political Economy* 112 (5): S164–S187.

34. Benartzi, S. and Thaler, R.H. (2007). Heuristics and biases in retirement saving behaviour. *Journal of Economic Perspectives* 21 (3): 81–104.

35. Beshears, J., Choi, J.J., Laibson, D., and Madrian, B.C. (2008). The importance of default options for retirement saving outcomes: evidence from the United States. In: *Lessons from Pension Reform in the Americas* (ed. S.J. Kay and T. Sinha), 59–87. Oxford University Press.

36. Blake, D. (2020). Nudges and networks: how to use behavioural economics to improve the life cycle savings-consumption balance. Pensions Institute, Cass Business School.

37. Thinking Ahead Institute. (2021). *Global Pension Assets Study*. Willis Towers Watson.

38. Dimson, E., Marsh, P., and Staunton, M. (2021). *Investment Returns Yearbook*. Credit Suisse.

39. Oppenheimer, P. (2020). *The Long Good Buy*. Wiley Finance.

40. Cardinale, M., Navone, M., and Pioch, A. (2014). The power of dynamic asset allocation. *Journal of Portfolio Management* 40 (3): 47–60.

41. Brinson, G.P., Hood, L.R., and Beebower, G.L. (1986). Determinants of portfolio performance. *Financial Analysts Journal* 42 (4): 39–48.

42. Campbell, J.Y. and Viceira, L. (2002) *Strategic Asset Allocation*. Oxford University Press. (Also in *Oxford Handbook of Retirement and Pensions*, 2006.)

43. Hoevenaars, R., Molenaar, R.D.J., Schotman, P.C., and Steenkamp, T.B.M. (2008). Strategic asset allocation with liabilities. *Journal of Economic Dynamics and Control* 32 (9): 2939–2970.

44. Cardinale, M., Naik, N.Y., and Sharma, V. (2021). Forecasting long horizon volatility for strategic asset allocation. *Journal of Portfolio Management* 47 (4): 83–98.

45. Mitra, K. and Schwaiger, K. (eds.) (2011). *Asset and Liability Management Handbook*. Palgrave Macmillan.

46. Scherer, B. (ed.) (2003). *Asset and Liability Management Tools: A Handbook for Best Practice*. Risk Books.

47. Sharpe, W.F. and Tint, L.G. (1990). Liabilities—a new approach. *Journal of Portfolio Management* 16 (2): 5–10.

48. Mercer. (2020). CFA Institute Global Pension Index 2020. https://www.cfainstitute.org/en/research/survey-reports/2020-mercer-cfa-institute-global-pension-index.

49. Jin, L., Merton, R.C., and Bodie, Z. (2006). Do a firm's equity returns reflect the risk of its pension plan? *Journal of Financial Economics* 81 (1): 1–26.

50. Franzoni, F. and Marin, J. (2006). Pension plan funding and stock market efficiency. *Journal of Finance* 61 (2): 921–956.

51. Cardinale, M. (2007). Corporate pension funding and credit spreads. *Financial Analysts Journal* 63 (5): 82–101.

52. Shivdasani, A. and Stefanescu, I. (2010). How do pensions affect capital structure decisions? *Review of Financial Studies* 23 (3): 1287–1323.

53. Roy, A. and Le, A. (2019). Retirement planning requires changes in mindsets, tools and asset allocation. SSG Demographics and Pensions.

54. Amaglobelli, D., Chai, H., Dabla-Norris, E. et al. (2019). The future of saving: the role of pension system design in an aging world. IMF staff discussion note 01.

55. Koedijk, K., Slager, A., and Van Dam, J. (2019). *Achieving Investment Excellence: a Practical Guide for Trustees of Pension Funds, Endowments and Foundations*. Wiley.

56. Peters, T. and Waterman, R. (1982). *In Search of Excellence*. Harper & Row.

Chapter 7: Quality of Life, Gender, Governance, Politics, and Sustainability

1. Stigler, G. (1959). The development of utility theory I and II. *Journal of Political Economy* 58 (4): 307–327 and 58 (5): 373–396.

2. Bernoulli, D. (1738). Specimen theoriae novae de mensura sortie. Commentarii Academiae Scientarium Imperialis Petropolitanae. This laid the foundations of expected utility theory as one of the precepts of decision-making under uncertainty.

3. Von Neumann, J. and Morgenstern, O. (1947). *Theory of games and economic behavior* (2nd rev. ed.). Princeton University Press.

4. Pilling, D. (2018). 5 ways GDP gets it totally wrong as a measure of our success. World Economic Forum, Future of Economic Progress. https://www.weforum.org/agenda/2018/01/gdp-frog-matchbox-david-pilling-growth-delusion.

5. Kapoor, A. and Debroy, B. (2019). GDP is not a measure of human well-being. *Harvard Business Review*. https://hbr.org/2019/10/gdp-is-not-a-measure-of-human-well-being.

6. OECD. (2018). *Beyond GDP: Measuring What Counts for Economic and Social Performance*. OECD Publishing.

7. Layard, R. (2020). *Can We Be Happier? Ethics and Evidence*. Penguin.

8. Blanchflower, D. (2008). Happiness economics. *NBER Reporter* (2).

9. Sustainable Development Solutions Network. (2021). World happiness report 2021. https://worldhappiness.report/ed/2021.

10. United Nations Development Programme. (2020). Human development report.

11. Roy, A. and Le, A. (2019). Gender equality better for growth, debt, inequality and sustainability. SSGA Global Macro Research.

12. Dobla-Norris, E. and Kochchar, K. (2019). Closing the gender gap. Finance and Development, IMF.

13. Kochchar, K., Jain-Chandra, S., and Newiak, M. (2017). Women, work and economic growth: levelling the playing field. IMF.

14. World Bank. (2021). Human Capital Project. https://www.worldbank .org/en/publication/human-capital.

15. Deaton, A. (2015). *The Great Escape: Health, Wealth, and the Origins of Inequality.* Princeton University Press.

16. McKinsey. (2020). Ten things to know about gender inequality. https:// www.mckinsey.com/featured-insights/diversity-and-inclusion/ten-things-to-know-about-gender-equality#.

17. Sahay, R. and Cihak, M. (2018). Women in finance: a case for closing gaps. IMF staff discussion reports.

18. Smith, A. (1759). *The Theory of Moral Sentiments.* London: Liberty Fund.

19. Kindleberger, C.P. (2005). *Manias, Panics, and Crashes*, 5e. Wiley Investment Classics.

20. Akerlof, G.A. and Shiller, R.J. (2010). *Animal Spirits: How Human Psychology Drives the Economy and Why It Matters for Global Capitalism.* Princeton University Press.

21. Transparency International. (2021). CPI 2020: Global highlights. https://www.transparency.org/en/news/cpi-2020-global-highlights.

22. Sen, A. (1987). *On Ethics and Economics.* Cambridge University Press.

23. Sachs, J., Kroll, C., Lafortune, G. et al. (2021). *The Decade of Action for the Sustainable Development Goals: Sustainable Development Report 2021.* Cambridge University Press.

24. Sachs, J. et al. (2021). Sustainable Development Report 2021. https:// www.sdgindex.org.

25. Burck, J., Hagen, U., Höhne N. et al. (2020). Climate Change Performance Index 2021. https://ccpi.org/download/the-climate-change-performance-index-2021.

26. Huntington, S.P. (1996). *The Clash of Civilizations and the Remaking of the World Order.* Simon and Schuster.

27. Roy, A., Punhani, S., and Hsieh, A. (2013). High youth unemployment: a threat to growth and political stability. Credit Suisse Demographics Research.

28. European Commission. (2020). Report on the impact of demographic change.
29. Eberstadt, N. (2019). With Great Demographics Comes Great Power: Why population will drive geopolitics. *Foreign Affairs* (July/August).

Chapter 8: Summary and Conclusions

1. McCloskey, D. (1983). *The Rhetoric of Economics*. University of Wisconsin Press.
2. Shiller, R.J. (2019). *Narrative Economics*. Princeton University Press.
3. Shin, H., Cechchetti, S., Schoenholz, K., and Steinsson, J. (2019). Federal Reserve communications. Fed Listens Chicago Conference.
4. Huxley, A. (1932). *A Brave New World*. Longman Literature.

Index

283